MUSIC AT THE MIDDLE LEVEL

BUILDING STRONG PROGRAMS

Edited by June Hinckley

MUSIC EDUCATORS NATIONAL CONFERENCE

Music Educators National Conference
1806 Robert Fulton Drive
Reston, VA 22091-4348

Printed in the United States of America.

ISBN 1-56545-043-4

CONTENTS

INTRODUCTION

June Hinckley
Fine Arts and Instructional Specialist
Florida Department of Education

The concept of the middle school has been around for about thirty years, but to many music educators, it is a relatively new idea. Why? Though 70 percent of all middle-level institutions are now organized as middle schools, in 1970 that figure was 46 percent, according to the National Middle School Association. Middle schools spread slowly across the country and had some false starts. The early middle schools varied widely in philosophy and instructional practices and in many cases the change from junior high to middle school was more cosmetic than foundational. Currently there are more than twelve thousand middle-level schools operating in the United States, and as the middle school philosophy has become more widely accepted, they are becoming increasingly similar in the way they look and operate.

Though the original intention of the middle school was to provide a learning environment that took advantage of the developmental changes in students ages nine through thirteen, in many communities middle schools were instituted to achieve racial desegregation. In others, demographics took a hand: the loss of students at the high school level and the increase of students in elementary schools due to the baby boom of the 1970s made it financially prudent for schools to shift one grade out of elementary schools and add it to the junior high school—thus creating middle schools. For a long while, the most observable difference in schools where districts implemented a middle school program was the change in grade configuration.

Middle schools had originally been intended to better meet the needs of the student that is in between—in between childhood and adolescence, a period some educators call *transescence*. These students, who are neither adults nor children, experience rapid physical growth but emotionally may seem to be falling apart. The approval of friends is often more important than that of parents or teachers. They embrace every new fad, but not for very long. They are all discovering the opposite sex but are at diverse stages of physical development; some have childlike bodies while others are more mature and well developed. They want to be like all their friends but cry out to be treated fairly, according to their own individual needs. The teacher they like most of all is one who is "nice" but sets limits.

The need for providing a school environment more in tune with the needs of the young adolescent had been discussed since the early 1900s. Junior high schools were intended to meet this need, but they quickly began to look like little high schools for younger students. They failed many students because they focused more on academic preparation for high school than on the developmental and emotional needs of students.

During the 1960s, a time of social upheaval, the issue of making schools for students in the middle more developmentally appropriate was again raised. In the first middle schools, a few new ideas such as short-term exploratory courses and the change in grade configuration influenced music programs only slightly. The worst musical effects of these changes were the loss of maturing ninth-grade male voices in choral programs, the loss of mature players in instrumental programs, and the unwanted inclusion of short-term, exploratory, unified arts courses or the "wheel" in teaching schedules. Some teachers complained about teaching "babies" and about the time spent teaching unified arts, but that was about all.

In the mid-1980s, when more emphasis was placed on innovative scheduling practices for middle-level schools, we started to realize that the shift to the middle school philosophy meant change for music teachers. Suddenly, we had educational leaders suggesting that middle schools meant a variety of imposing novelties—block scheduling, team teaching, exploratory courses, multigrade grouping, thematic instruction, and integrated curricula.

"Wait a minute," said the music teachers. "What about band, chorus, and orchestra?" Grouping students into academic grade-level teams (which emphasize strong peer-group identification) affected the schedules within which we could teach our large ensemble groups. Scheduling the "academic courses"—most often considered to be math, science, social studies, and language arts—during blocks of instructional time that were several hours long meant that we could not always have students from different grade levels in our ensembles. Teachers were organized into instructional leadership teams, but these teams seldom included those who taught electives, so music teachers did not usually participate. The call for interdisciplinary instruction even influenced the material we were expected to teach. Special advisement programs took up instructional time. Finally, emphasizing instruction that focused on the learning process (thinking, problem solving, creating) over the final product (performance) suddenly meant that music programs could not operate as they always had.

These changes have been traumatic for some teachers, who hoped music educators would band together and fight the idea of middle schools. Clearly such effort would be wasted. By now the middle school train is out of the station and well down the track. We cannot nor should we try to stop it. It is viewed by many other educators and the public as developmentally sound, socially appropriate, and academically successful. The idea of middle schools has taken hold in American education.

Music educators can see this philosophical shift as a part of the demise of music in our schools, or they can grasp it as an opportunity to reach more students than ever before. This book starts with the view that music programs that succeed in the 1990s will embrace the middle school philosophy and use it to their advantage.

The purpose of this collection is to provide teachers with solutions to both parts of the middle school instructional puzzle—why and how to successfully teach students in middle school. For the "why," there are essays that summarize the research and theoretical literature, written by respected leaders in music education and experts in middle-level instruction and administration. For the "how," this book offers ideas and practices that other middle school teachers have found to be successful. The authors are teachers who have discovered ways to make music a vital and successful part of the middle school where they work. Their ideas have withstood the test of the classroom, while the theory and research articles provide the philosophical support and basis for effective middle-level instruction. All the authors are currently teaching or have had extensive experience with middle school students.

The topics were chosen by surveying music supervisors in school districts with middle schools to determine what information teachers need most. As a conclusion, Jeff Kimpton offers an overview of middle-level music education in the United States. He is director of education for the Yamaha Corporation and was a member of MENC's 1991 Future Directions Task Force on Middle Schools.

Many music teachers are discovering success within middle schools that they had never achieved in more traditional settings. They love the opportunity to be more creative, to work and plan with other teachers, and to place more emphasis on caring more about individual student needs than the end-of-the-year performance. Such teachers have not lessened their efforts to build aesthetic awareness or to awaken musical sensitivity within the students they teach. They attend to how well the youngsters sing and play, and they foster excellence in performance—but they never do so at the expense of a child's self-image. They believe that all young people want to make music.

I hope this book will provide teachers who are seeking assistance the help they need to adapt to the new vision of middle-level instruction.

ISSUES AND IDEAS

THE ADOLESCENT LEARNER

NURTURING THE YOUNG ADOLESCENT
High Stakes for the School and Social Environment

Timothy Gerber

Transition. Competence. Identity. These three concepts are at the heart of adolescence. They are influenced powerfully by gender and race, by socioeconomic status, and by family circumstance. As developmental tasks, they are intensely personal, yet they apply to everyone. All adolescents must endure the long *transition* from childhood to adulthood, emerging with the confidence that they can contribute to society. All adolescents must acquire real *competence* in the "big four" domains–intellectual, physical, social, emotional–if they are to gain the mature self-sufficiency that will sustain their purposes in life. And all must develop a strong sense of themselves as unique and responsible individuals. Ultimately, their *identities* will be shaped by consistent affiliations with individuals and groups and by the positive messages they receive.

The schools for young adolescents, for students approximately eleven to fourteen years old, should play a central role in supporting these developmental tasks. In fact, the concepts of transition, competence, and identity should serve as basic themes for the mission of middle grade schools. But to what extent do these schools genuinely assist their widely diverse populations in making transitions? Beyond routine training of low-order cognitive skills, what levels of competence do such schools actually cultivate? And given normal teaching loads, how realistic is it for middle grade teachers to be concerned with individual quests for identity?

Timothy Gerber is professor of music education in the School of Music, Division of Music Education, at The Ohio State University in Columbus, Ohio.

The Middle Grades as the Last Best Chance

The facts about the efficacy of middle-level schools vary with the landscape. Some envied pockets of innovation and excellence, usually located in well-heeled suburbs or other identifiable communities, provide ideal settings where young adolescents thrive. Other schools, often on the mean streets of big cities, are plagued by overcrowding, student and teacher absenteeism, armed adolescents, and nonexistent homework. Between these extremes are literally thousands of average, middle grade schools with all varieties of grade and curriculum organization. They appear to be reasonably productive and happy places in which everyone survives the travails of peer pressure. Here, each youngster gradually becomes a bit more intellectually competent, and parents discover that puberty doesn't necessarily invite academic trouble. Although few faculty have been prepared specifically to teach young adolescents at these particular grade levels, teachers in average middle schools usually do their jobs very professionally, reaching most of the kids most of the time.

A closer and uncompromising look at these average schools reveals, however, that many fall short by leaving behind at least some of their young people. Most schools normally favor the best students, challenging those who are motivated and who attend regularly. They typically tolerate the mediocre kids, providing remediation and encouragement when warranted. But tragically, they write off the rest, those who are already far behind and who appear not to care. These often troubled—and troubling—youngsters come primarily from families that abdicate their child-rearing responsibility to the local school system. These are the students who have never known academic success. They are easily identifiable because soon after the move from the elementary building to the middle grade school, they frequently get grouped with other like-minded kids of generally lower ability and negligible motivation.

If middle grade schools are truly committed to their societal and democratic obligations, there is wide consensus that they must do a better job of serving the basic educational needs of *all* young adolescents, especially those who risk facing a grim adulthood. According to *Turning Points* (1989), the ground-breaking report published by the Carnegie Council on Adolescent Development, a "fundamental transformation of the education of young adolescents is urgently required" in the United States (p. 36). Experts in many disciplines believe that the very future of our nation depends on this pivotal period in schooling (Eccles & Midgley, 1988; Epstein & Petersen, 1991; Johnston & Markle, 1986; NASSP, 1985; Sprinthall, 1985).

The problem that will accompany the new millennium is that cumulatively, all those good, average schools produce a huge population of forgotten and often alienated young people who never were helped to accomplish essential developmental tasks. Collectively, these kids represent the next generation of Americans who will live lost lifestyles that often include a combination of ignorance, illness, poverty, crime, drugs, and dead-end jobs. Good schools could make an enormous difference in changing these prospects. Indeed, for countless young adolescents, the middle grade years are the turning point that "represents their last best chance to avoid a diminished future" (Carnegie Council, 1989, p. 8).

The Carnegie Council (1989) estimates that "by age 15, millions of American youth are at risk of reaching adulthood unable to meet adequately the requirements of the workplace, the commitments of relationships in families and with peers, and the responsibilities of participation in a multicultural society and of citizenship in a democracy" (p. 21). Nearly seven million of these, a fourth of the population in the United States aged ten to seventeen, are considered to be "extremely vulnerable to the negative consequences of multiple high-risk behaviors such as school failure, substance abuse, and early unprotected intercourse" (Carnegie Council, 1989, p. 27). According to recent news reports, medical and insurance experts cannot accurately estimate the staggering societal costs of AIDS and substance abuse alone. Indeed, few in the research community paint rosy pictures for the burgeoning population of "have-nots" in our society, all of whom once were—and are—students in our middle schools.

The Adolescent Experience

Personal experience reminds us that adolescence stands out as a fascinating period of remarkable physiological and psychological growth. This is the time in the lifespan when people first realize that change is a constant. One of the greatest upheavals is the transition from the security of an elementary school to the often frightening unknowns of a middle grade building. Another transformation is the growth in intellectual ability, characterized by a growing capacity for thinking at the abstract rather than the concrete level (Inhelder and Piaget, 1958). And at roughly the same time as the school change and the advance of new mental capability, children hit puberty—or vice versa.

Accompanied by the engrossing magnificence of sexual awakening, adolescence begins with puberty and ends whenever young people maturely accept the basic financial and societal responsibilities of independent adulthood. For most Americans, it starts around age eleven or twelve and is often postponed well into one's twenties (Garbarino, 1985). According to one research physician, advances in nutrition, hygiene, and disease control have contributed to the drop in the average age of menarche from sixteen to twelve over the past 150 years. A parallel drop to an earlier onset of puberty applies to boys as well. However, the tendency to extend the period of social dependence and maturation into the traditionally early adult years is a relatively recent phenomenon (Nightingale, 1988).

The everyday juxtaposition of puberty with teacher

and parental expectations, fragile relationships, and messages from the media frequently leads to unpredictable behavior. Young adolescents can switch from sweet to sullen in seconds. They can be friendly one day and distant the next. They can go from being naïve nerds to party animals in the same week. They seek attention for being weird or unique, but then quickly conform to bathe in the security of peer approval. They wallow in egocentric excess–only to snap suddenly out of it. This is normal. As Larson and Csikszentmihalyi (1984) point out, the "shifting from black to white and from hot to cold is what adolescence is all about" (p. xii).

The peer group–or one's perception of it–is partially responsible for shifts in behavior, especially among younger adolescents. Psychologist David Elkind (1967) claims that adolescents carry in their minds an "imaginary audience" with whom they communicate about all sorts of important things, most notably about appearance and behavior. In Elkind's view, the imaginary audience contributes to the extremely self-conscious behavior that characterizes this age group. Adolescents anticipate–and receive–highly critical judgments from their own phantom audiences. Of course, one's real-life audience can be cold and cruel, but it is far less critical than the imaginary audience: most young people are so preoccupied imagining what others are thinking that they don't have time to criticize anyone else.

The truth is that adolescents can be tormented terribly by what others actually say, or worse, by what they *think* others will say. This makes it all the more crucial for teachers and parents to realize how powerful words can be in reinforcing or destroying an adolescent's self-confidence. A sincere, well-placed remark can almost miraculously fortify a tenuous self-esteem.

Young adolescents have no real escape routes from their developmental purgatory. Although they are aware that they are neither children nor adults, they are still expected to act responsibly and grown-up most of the time. They begrudgingly discover that one of their first chores is "learning to allocate attention to various activities in a manner acceptable to adults" (Larson and Csikszentmihalyi, 1984, p. 4). With ripening levels of natural curiosity, they are confronted with tough and tempting choices but have little experience in making informed decisions or envisioning the consequences. The mixed messages from Madison Avenue don't help. In back-to-back commercials, Nike slickly encourages kids to "just do it" while the White House admonishes them to "just say no." During these wonder years adolescents are largely unappreciated, playing no meaningful roles in society other than that of consumers and baby-sitters. Perhaps this explains why few people, if given Aladdin's lamp, would sincerely ask to be thirteen again.

Recent Research on Adolescence

An important new wave of research published since 1989 has identified several essential features of adolescence that can help us improve school environments for middle grade students. After waiting in the wings for years, the problems of schooling during early adolescence have recently received more attention than ever before. One promising trend is the realization among scholars and school-reform leaders that early adolescence may be a more important period in human development than was previously believed (Petersen & Epstein, 1991). According to *Turning Points,* middle grade schools, irrespective of grade organization, "are potentially society's most powerful force to recapture millions of youth adrift" (1989, p. 32).

In addition to the work of the Carnegie Council on Adolescent Development, *At the Threshold: The Developing Adolescent,* an anthology of research reports edited by Feldman and Elliott (1990), and *The Encyclopedia of Adolescence* (Lerner et al., 1991) offer fresh data and helpful perspectives on how better to nurture the young adolescent. These data reaffirm, for example, that adult guidance is crucial. Early adolescence signals the start of the search for independence and autonomy. As this quest begins, parents and teachers should acknowledge the natural need for adolescents to make some decisions for themselves and provide just enough counsel to keep them out of harm's way. Serious conflict is *not* inevitable. In fact, most serious domestic conflicts stem from parenting styles that are either too permissive or too strict. These extreme parenting practices can be signs of deeper family problems (Steinberg, 1990).

While peer affiliations certainly become more important during adolescence, peer group influences do not present the strong opposition to parental authority that once was thought. As an adolescent, the values of one's peer group are likely to reflect rather than reject the values and opinions of one's parents (Brown, 1990). Young adolescents may have argumentative mood swings at home, but they usually do not practice wholesale repudiation of their parents; they are far more dependent on them than the experts had realized. Likewise parental influence actually has a strong impact on adolescent behavior outside the home, providing an important guide to the appropriateness of behavior while in social settings with both peers and other adults.

Adult support and modeling are vital during the very early adolescent years because this is the time when identity begins to take shape. Adult advocacy establishes expectations and sets the stage for further behavior. But since an overwhelming majority of today's adolescents come from homes where every adult works, most teenagers have more unsupervised time on their own than in any previous generation.

Although they hate to admit it, they need greater access to adults. In particular, they need to develop close and caring relationships with adults outside the family if they are to become independent from their parents. If they do not get quality time at home, and if the schools are unable or unwilling to provide it, then who will be the role models for these kids? Who will provide the guidance and reinforcement they so desperately need?

Another important finding is the confirmation of the highly malleable nature of early adolescence. These are the years when young people develop patterns of behavior that will last well into adulthood. In particular, early adolescence is the time when the tendency toward drug and alcohol use is most likely to become ingrained, leading consequentially to long-term substance abuse as older adolescents and adults. Clearly, if young people are to be counseled and steered away from harmful health practices, this is the time to do it—before and during the moments when they first get involved (Millstein and Litt, 1990; Carnegie Council, 1989).

The statistics on unhealthy habits are staggering at best, but they should come as no surprise to veteran middle school teachers. For example, 56 percent of a large sample of recent high school graduates reported that they first began to consume alcohol sometime during the sixth through the ninth grades. More than 51 percent had first tried cigarettes during this time, and 28 percent had first experimented with illicit drugs during these middle grade years. Many accidents, the leading cause of death among youngsters ten to fourteen, involve substance abuse, especially when linked to older adolescents who were driving while intoxicated.

As increasing numbers of middle grade students are becoming sexually active, it is estimated that one-fourth of these adolescents will contract a sexually transmitted disease before high school graduation (Carnegie Council, 1989, pp. 22–25). The number of births to adolescent mothers continues to rise. In 1988, for example, 322,406 babies (a number roughly equivalent to the population of Omaha) were born to unmarried teenagers in the United States (Childrens' Defense Fund, 1991). Of these infants, 9,907 were delivered by girls age 14 and under; in 1989 the number of births to adolescents in that age group grew to 10,612 (U.S. Public Health Service, 1990; 1991).

Even watching television is none too healthy. Everyone knows that adolescents watch too much TV, but cutting down on tube time could have positive results. One study found that adolescents who reported light television viewing rates were more outgoing, intelligent, imaginative, and physically fit than were those who reported heavy TV watching (Tucker, 1987).

In another relevant study, Larson and Richards (1991) looked at potential causes of boredom in a large sample of fifth- through ninth-grade students from working- and middle-class suburbs of Chicago. Defining boredom primarily as a function of understimulation ("when there is nothing to do" in the words of adolescents) or of forced effort ("when you don't like what you're doing"), the researchers found no significant differences among the five different middle grade levels. However, they did discover that boredom was not confined exclusively to school. While boredom is highest in school (32 percent of reported time samples), a substantial rate of boredom (23 percent) was reported outside of school. The researchers observed that boredom cuts across all areas of adolescents' lives, and even includes activities they choose to do, like listening to music. In addition, students who report great levels of boredom in school are also highly bored outside of school, indicating that "the origins of boredom may have less to do with school and more to do with the individual" (p. 435).

Rates of school boredom were greatest for all students in teacher-directed classroom activities (lectures) and in student presentations (oral reports). High ability students were bored more often in school than at home; this points out the lack of stimulating challenges for these students in the classroom. The researchers also found that "boredom is higher in classes with more abstract content (social studies, science, foreign language) as opposed to classes that deal with skill development (shop, music, gym)" (Larson and Richards, 1991, p. 439). They recommend that all middle grade teachers use the more social, hands-on, high-involvement techniques employed by music, art, and shop teachers. (Music teachers, however, are not immune to boredom inducement: imagine, at age thirteen, sitting through a week of a teacher's lectures on the symphony or a string of fellow students' reports on great composers.)

The High Stakes of Intellectual Growth

With the approach of a new century, the stakes have been raised for middle grade schools to develop healthy, thoughtful, and productive citizens. The stakes are higher now because unlike all previous generations, young adolescents at the close of the twentieth century will need to be intellectually prepared for a dynamic, global economy. They will need to think critically and creatively in order to get good jobs and subsequently deliver high quality services and products that are competitive in international markets. But tomorrow's new occupations will require more than mere literacy; they will demand problem solving, collaboration, and craftsmanship in professional, technical, clerical, sales, and managerial fields.

Within the next decade or so, today's adolescents will inherit the responsibility to support themselves and their families—as well as their schools, community agencies, the growing elderly population, and the social institutions of this nation. They will need to secure rewarding occupations if they are to make a living, but they must acquire a solid and well-rounded education if they are to make a rewarding living. They must learn to cope and keep up with the fiber-optic pace of the information age. They must respond resourcefully to change. They must live together harmoniously in the global village. And regardless of lifestyle, they will be required to solve tough problems on all fronts. They will need big hearts and disciplined minds in the future: They must have good middle schools now.

One of the most pressing concerns in middle-level education today revolves around what the Carnegie Council calls "intellectual underdevelopment," a crisis of gross and pervasive deficiencies in young adolescents' higher order thinking skills. It is accompanied by the revelation that American eighth-graders have fallen far behind eighth-graders in other industrialized nations in mathematics and science proficiency. It is highlighted by the fact that sometime before they reach age thirteen, nearly a third of all American boys have been kept back a year in school, thus placing them at least one year below their expected grade levels (U.S. Census Bureau, 1988). It is punctuated by an embarrassing high school dropout rate of nearly 30 percent nationally, the seeds of which are sewn in the middle grades and reaped disproportionately by Black and Hispanic youth.

Research conducted over the past two decades reveals varied but consistent examples of arrested intellectual growth beginning in the middle grades. For instance, Renner and Stafford (1976) concluded that just 20 percent of a randomly sampled group of three hundred middle grade students functioned at the Piagetian level of formal operations. They also claimed that "73 percent of today's tenth-graders are not capable of formal-operational thought" (p. 97). Looking at trends over a thirteen-year period, the National Assessment of Educational Progress (1985) reported that only a meager 11 percent of eighth-grade students could qualify as adept readers. Another National Assessment measure (1986) concluded that most eighth-graders could not think with sufficient clarity and analytic ability to write a persuasive essay.

Plenty of people claim to be alarmed by this state of affairs, but what explains it? Is there just too much for one to know? Have we put too much faith in the work of Piaget? Do the schools expect too little? Is TV rotting adolescents' brains? Have America's teachers been poorly prepared by out-of-touch university personnel? Do adolescents simply fail to see the value of learning to think? Even at the college level, evidence of the weak foundation built in the middle grades leaps out. Through a test of five hundred *college* students in eleven states, O'Neill (1990) found that 62 percent did not recognize what NAACP refers to, 33 percent did not know what a Nazi is, and nearly half could not identify the author of *King Lear*.

Part of the problem with intellectual underdevelopment can be traced to what adolescents have come to believe about themselves. Linn and Songer (1991) claim that "students construct views of themselves as learners, influenced importantly by their social context, and these views determine the enthusiasm with which they attack the process of understanding" (p. 412). We need to acknowledge that during early adolescence, one's self-concept can actually shape cognitive growth and govern intellectual achievement (Purkey & Novak, 1984; Beane & Lipka, 1986). Moreover, middle grade schools themselves often prescribe students' self-concepts, sending messages through grouping or school climate that are injurious and totally unwarranted. For example, assigning students to classes based on achievement or reading level is a widespread practice, but tracking of this sort conspicuously labels and distinguishes the fast learners from the slow learners. This practice tells students who they are and what they are likely to become, publicly confirming their relative academic status and value in the eyes of the school. It also promotes racial prejudice and reinforces stereotypes among young adolescents because poor and minority students often make up the bulk of lower academic tracks. This hardly motivates enthusiasm for learning.

Improving the School Environment

One thing that middle grade schools can do to improve their educational endeavors is to make the school climate more hospitable to the young adolescent. As Eccles et al. (1991) claim, "the nature of middle-grades school environment affects the motivation, school attachment, and academic performance of early adolescents" (p. 532). In particular, school administrators should make it a point to sensitize their faculties to the delicate and difficult nature of making the transition from an elementary school. For many youngsters, the move to a middle grade school is traumatic because they have known only one building, one faculty, and one set of school friends for their entire lives as students. Just remembering to bring everything to the new middle school, which bus to take, how to find and open your locker, where and when your next class is, what rules apply to different teachers, where the restrooms are, and how to get a lunch can bring on a tearful anxiety attack of crisis proportions.

Middle grade professionals can benefit by learning more about the transition process. For example, after looking at hundreds of adolescents in four types of grade configurations, Eccles et al. (1991) concluded that student outcomes did not differ when comparing a 6–8 middle school structure with a 7–9 junior high structure. Despite differences in philosophy, they observed that "more often than not, middle schools look like, and operate very similarly to, traditional junior high schools" (p. 526). Clearly, the key is not the grade organization, but the way students are treated by their teachers. Toepfer (1988) concurs by writing that "curriculum and program, not grades, make a school. The effectiveness of middle-level schools depends upon the degree to which they respond to the developmental needs and characteristics of students at that age" (p. 110). School transitions may always be difficult irrespective of grade level or whether puberty has arrived, but individual teachers can soften the switch.

Everyone knows that elementary and middle grade schools are very different places, but now we have evidence that middle school teachers should be more like their elementary counterparts. Eccles et al. (1991) claim that seventh-grade teachers view both their students and themselves in less positive ways than do sixth-grade teachers. The researchers followed several large groups of young adolescents as they moved from elementary to junior high schools in twelve different midwestern school districts. They surveyed the groups' sixth-grade teachers one year and then posed the identical questions to their respective seventh-grade teachers one year later. Compared to the various sixth-grade personnel, the seventh-grade teachers believed these same students were less trustworthy and needed more discipline and control. The seventh-grade teachers also "felt significantly less efficacious than did sixth-grade teachers in their ability to influence the learning of all of their students" (p. 535). Similarly, in the opinions of both students and observers, the seventh-grade teachers were perceived to be not as fair, friendly, or supportive as were the sixth-grade teachers.

Midgley et al. (1988) studied changes in student motivation before and after the transition from elementary to junior high school. They discovered that students valued school subjects according to the perceived degree of teachers' personal supportiveness: when youngsters moved from elementary teachers they believed were high in personal support to middle grade teachers who were low in support, they dropped their high regard for that particular subject. The reverse was also true: when they moved from low support teachers to teachers they felt were highly supportive, they increased the value attached to the subject. Eccles et al. (1991) concluded that declines in school motivation, while not inevitable after the transition to a middle grade school, are "linked to rather specific classroom environmental characteristics, such as the quality of the student-teacher relationship" (pp. 536–537). Clearly, adolescents who are motivated in school feel an affiliation with the classroom, an affiliation that begins with the teacher.

In essence, the individual teacher is the key in early adolescence; transitions to a positive environment and a supportive teacher produce desired results and high motivation. These studies corroborate research in music education and other disciplines that indicates that young adolescents prefer their teachers to be child-centered rather than subject-centered (Gerber, 1989; Veaco & Brandon, 1986). In the eyes of the students, what teachers know about students is more important than what they know about their chosen subject matter. They need teachers who care about them, and they learn more from teachers they like.

Several other related suggestions represent sensible and practical approaches to improving the learning environment for young adolescents. These include (1) making sure students have more personal contact and closer relationships with a consistent set of adults in the school by working in teams that make up small communities for learning; (2) eliminating ability tracking and replacing it with cooperative learning schema and flexible scheduling; (3) emphasizing a core academic program in which adolescents are taught to think critically in subjects that have been integrated across several disciplines; (4) providing opportunities for engaging in supervised service activity in the school and in related school-community partnerships; (5) promoting sobriety, good health, and appropriate fitness both in and out of school; (6) engaging students intellectually through problem-solving activities; and (7) inviting higher levels of student incentive by sharing ownership in classroom decision making (Carnegie Council, 1989; Gerber, 1991; Boswell, 1991).

In view of the high stakes in teaching the young adolescents who will enter adulthood at the dawn of a new century, the most important priority for middle grade schools should be to enfranchise individual faculty to help each and every student develop a sense of individual efficacy and self-worth. The teachers themselves should create uniquely rewarding and successful experiences that will shape each student's purpose and identity. They must take deliberate steps to help adolescents feel that they belong and are wanted in the school community. They must identify those at risk and simultaneously make a commitment to improve the social and academic quality of the middle grade environment for all students. They must match academic opportunities with their students' developmental needs. They must nurture the future.

References

Beane, J. A., & Lipka, R. P. (1986). *Self-concept, self-esteem, and the curriculum.* New York: Teacher's College Press.

Brown, B. B. (1990). Peer groups and peer cultures. In S. S. Feldman and G. R. Elliott (Eds.), *At the threshold: The developing adolescent.* Cambridge, MA: Harvard University Press.

Boswell, J. (1991). Comparison of attitudinal assessments in middle and junior high school general music. *Council of Research in Music Education, 108,* 49-57.

Carnegie Council on Adolescent Development. (1989). *Turning points: Preparing American youth for the 21st century.* New York: Carnegie Corporation of New York.

Childrens' Defense Fund. (1991). *The state of America's children.* Washington, D. C.: Author.

Eccles, J. S., & Midgley, C. (1988). Stage/environment fit: Developmentally appropriate classrooms for early adolescents. In R. E. Ames & C. Ames (Eds.), *Research on motivation in education, vol. 3.* New York: Academic Press.

Eccles, J. S., Lord, S., & Midgley, C. (1991). What are we doing to early adolescents? The impact of educational contexts on early adolescents. *American Journal of Education, 99(4),* 521-42.

Elkind, D. (1967). Egocentrism in adolescence. *Child Development, 38(4),* 1025-34.

Epstein, J. L., & Petersen, A. C. (1991). Discussion and outlook: Research on education and development across the years of adolescence. *American Journal of Education, 99(4),* 643-57.

Feldman, S. S., & Elliott, G. R. (Eds.). (1990). *At the threshold: The developing adolescent.* Cambridge, MA: Harvard University Press.

Garbarino, J. (1985). *Adolescent development: An ecological perspective.* Columbus, Ohio: Charles E. Merrill.

Gerber, T. (1989). Student perceptions of teachers and teaching. *Update, 7(2),* 21-23.

Gerber, T. (1992). Meeting the challenge of middle school teaching. *Music Educators Journal, 78(6),* 37-41.

Inhelder, B., & Piaget, J. (1958). *The growth of logical thinking from childhood to adolescence.* New York: Basic Books.

Johnston, J. H., & Markle, G. C. (1986). *What research says to the middle-level practitioner.* Columbus, OH: National Middle School Association.

Larson, R., & Csikszentmihalyi, M. (1984). *Being adolescent: Conflict and growth in the teenage years.* New York: Basic Books.

Larson, R., & Richards, M. H. (1991). Boredom in the middle school years: Blaming schools versus blaming students. *American Journal of Education, 99(4),* 418-43.

Lerner, R. M., Petersen, A. C., & Brooks-Gunn, J. eds. (1991). *Encyclopedia of adolescence, vols. 1 & 2.* New York: Garland.

Linn, M. C., & Songer, N. B. (1991). Cognitive and conceptual change in adolescence. *American Journal of Education, 99(4),* 379-417.

Midgley, C., Feldlaufer, H., & Eccles, J. S. (1988). Student/teacher relations and attitudes toward mathematics before and after the transition to junior high school. *Child Development, 60,* 375-95.

Millstein, S. G., & Litt, I. F. (1990). Adolescent health. In S. S. Feldman and G. R. Elliott (Eds.), *At the threshold: The developing adolescent.* Cambridge, MA: Harvard University Press.

National Assessment of Educational Progress. (1985). *The reading report card, progress toward excellence in our schools, trends in reading over four national assessments, 1971-84.* Princeton, NJ: Educational Testing Service.

National Assessment of Educational Progress. (1986). *The writing report card, writing achievement in American schools.* Princeton, NJ: Educational Testing Service.

National Association of Secondary School Principals (NASSP). (1985). *An agenda for excellence at the middle level.* Reston, VA: Author.

Nightingale, E. O. (1988). *Adolescent rolelessness in modern society.* Invited address for the American Medical Association, National Congress on Adolescent Health: Charting a Course through Turbulent Times, May 12-14, 1988, Chicago.

O'Neill, J. (1990). *What do you know?* New York: Bantam Books.

Petersen, A. C., & Epstein, J. L. (1991). Development and education across adolescence: An introduction. *American Journal of Education, 99,* 373-78.

Purkey, W. W., & Novak, J. M. (1984). *Inviting school success* (2nd ed.). Belmont, CA: Wadsworth Publishing.

Renner, J. W., & Stafford, D.G. (1976). The operational levels of secondary school students. In J. W. Renner, D. G. Stafford, A. E. Lawson, J. W. McKinnon, F. E. Friot, & D. H. Kellogg, *Research, teaching and learning with the Piaget model.* Norman: University of Oklahoma Press.

Steinberg, L. (1990). Autonomy, conflict, and harmony in the family relationship. In S. S. Feldman and G. R. Elliott (Eds.), *At the threshold: The developing adolescent.* Cambridge, MA: Harvard University Press.

Sprinthall, N. A. (1985). Early adolescent and opportunities for growth in the 1980's: Ships passing in the night, again. *Journal of Early Adolescence, (5)4,* 533-47.

Toepfer, C. F. (1988). "What to know about young adolescents." *Social Education, (5)2,* 110-12.

Tucker, L. A. (1987). Television, teenagers, and health. *Journal of Youth and Adolescence, 16(5),* 415-25.

United States Census Bureau. (1988). *School enrollment–social and economic characteristics of students: October, 1986.* (Current Population Report, Series P-20, No. 429). Washington, D.C.: USGPO.

United States Public Health Service. (1990). *Vital statistics of the United States, 1988, volume 1, natality*. Washington, D.C.: USGPO.

United States Public Health Service. (1991). *Advance report of final natality statistics, 1989: Monthly vital statistics report supplement, volume 40, no. 8, December 12, 1991 supplement*. Washington, D.C.: USGPO.

Veaco, L., & Brandon, C. (1986). The preferred teacher: A content analysis of young adolescents' writings. *Journal of Early Adolescence, 6*, 221–29.

THE MIDDLE SCHOOL LEARNER

Suzanne Shull and Kathleen Vande Berg

Ridgeville Middle School is an urban school in Atlanta, Georgia. Approximately 50 percent of the 750 students are minorities. The school population at Ridgeville is extremely diverse with many talented and gifted students as well as learning-disabled students. All students are mainstreamed for exploratory music classes and performing music.

Teaching middle school music can be exhilarating, exhausting, gratifying, and frustrating. More highs and lows are associated with teaching this age group than with any other. If focused, the middle school child is extremely capable and energetic; if unfocused, he or she can be scattered and unruly. The problem most teachers face at this level is how to present music in a way that is acceptable to the child whose primary interests seem to be interacting with peers and listening to current popular music.

A wealth of information is now available to middle school teachers on all aspects of dealing with the middle school child. Becoming knowledgeable in current learning theories and teaching strategies can make life easier in the classroom on a day to day basis. The ultimate goal is to be able to *teach music,* which is an art, a discipline, a way of expression, and for many a basic human need.

Characteristics that Contradict

The confusion brought on by rapid physical, emotional, and intellectual changes can be baffling to any adult who is trying to help the child through an incredible period of adjustment. "A walking contradiction" is an accurate character description of the middle school student. The teacher who recognizes the existence of contradictions can view the behavior of the young person with perspective and good humor while working within the chaotic framework of the child struggling to become an adult. These are some of the most common contradictions the authors have observed:

Suzanne Shull teaches general and choral music at Ridgeview Middle School. Kathleen Vande Berg teaches general and choral music at White Plains Middle School.

1. Wishes to be independent	1. Very dependent upon a peer group
2. Struggles for freedom	2. Yearns for structure especially from adults
3. Has adult vocabulary and knowledge[1]	3. Uses child-like logic and feelings for making decisions
4. Has a short attention span	4. Can obsess on a subject of interest
5. Anxious to wear adult clothing	5. Embarrassed by growth into adult body
6. Exhibits high energy level	6. Submits to lethargy and depression
7. Displays an air of confidence	7. Feels insecure about self and relationship with peers
8. Denies affection and approval of adults[2]	8. Seeks affection and approval of adults
9. Can seem like an adult in a child's body	9. Can seem like a child in an adult's body

The Classroom, A Safe Learning Environment for Middle Schoolers

The music classroom can provide infinite opportunities for the confused middle schooler to gain a sense of self and accomplishment. Learners of all ages work better if they perceive that they are valued as individuals; however, at this age the need to feel liked and accepted seems to be an overriding factor. Initial indicators that teachers may use to show that they value students as individuals are learning and using names as soon as possible, using a colorful and welcoming decor, and showing an interest in students' activities outside of the music classroom. The bottom line, however, is that the foundation of a caring and safe environment is inherent within the music lesson.

Students feel valued when provided with opportunities to *experience* music by performing, creating, and listening to learn skills and grow in knowledge of the subject. Students feel valued when messages they receive are, "I like your thoughtful answers," "It's OK to make a mistake when you are trying," and "I *care* that you learn this."

Structuring the Environment: Rules for Behavior

While a thoughtfully planned lesson and welcoming environment can often prevent negative and distracting behaviors among most students, some will continue to test the situation. Setting limits on behavior and handling students firmly and consistently will usually get the desired result. Children need to perceive that they are operating in a safe environment, but they also need and *expect* parameters for behavior.

Rules should be applicable to specific observable behaviors, such as: "follow instructions the first time they are given," or "raise your hand if you wish to be called upon to speak." A hierarchy of rewards and consequences may be posted on the wall near the rules. Many middle schoolers respond well to tangible rewards while others need little more than a word of encouragement to participate actively. Keeping track of participation and behavior on a chart in the front of the room can be valuable if done in a manner that rewards rather than punishes.

The Individual Learner: Recognizing Learning Styles

Most of our schools reward children who can sit and listen and read. Most standard testing only tests the child's linguistic and mathematic ability. All learners, adults as well as children, receive and process information in different ways and under different conditions–some depend more on memory while others rely on intuition; some remember what they see, others what they hear; some enjoy working in a dark room while others need light; many simply cannot work on an empty stomach.[3]

Knowing how people learn and teaching to those differences can help the music teacher structure a dynamic class that encompasses activities and approaches that reach various types of learners. Giving consideration to the different styles when planning lessons stretches the teacher beyond a certain comfortable approach and challenges students to expand their ability to learn in different ways. Some examples of how a teacher can be sensitive to different learning styles are making a quiet corner for a student to work alone on guitar when he or she is frustrated with the noise level of large-group practice; giving oral as well as written tests; using charts as well as verbal instruction; and using singing, playing, and listening activities to reinforce a single musical concept.

The Individual Learner: Understanding Temperaments

Understanding differences in the way people perceive themselves, relate to others, process thought, go about work, and organize their lives can help to relieve the frustration of dealing with individual children as part of a group. For instance, knowing that an introvert must have some alone time to think about a problem and that an extrovert must be able to work through an external process helps the teacher to be patient with both personality types. The extroverted child who has made an inappropriate remark may come up with a better way of phrasing a response if asked to "think about what you just said and try again." The introvert who needs a little extra time to think about an idea before putting it into words can be rushed into silence by an impatient response.

Some children are task oriented: "Well, that's done." Some would rather think up tasks to be done, get them underway, and let someone else finish them while they think of more to do. Some children are team players, others make better golfers. Some children need to see the whole plan: "Do I put my name on the front right, front left, do I write with a pencil?" Others will wait, unconcerned, confident that they will find out (or figure out) what to do eventually. Some are planners, goal setters; some live from day to day. Some teachers can be very creative "in the moment" during a classroom experience. Others must plan every detail of what will transpire in the time allotted. Some people will make a careless decision quickly just to have closure. Some people need so little closure that they may hesitate to make a decision until everyone around them has lost all patience. *All types* of people function in the world. One type is not better than another. Learning to work together and accept differences can be a difficult task for adults, and trying to help middle school learners understand and appreciate differences contradicts a basic need of the children to conform to a compatible group. However, middle school teachers *can* help children understand their differences *and* work together if they are knowledgeable of the different types of temperaments.[4]

Teaching Strategy: Critical Thinking

Listening to music is a pastime that occupies many hours and gives pleasure to most of us throughout our lives. Middle school students spend much of their day "wired to the latest tunes" but know surprisingly little about what they are hearing. Simple questions such as, "What style is this chart? What instruments do you hear? How many times do you hear the refrain? Why do you like to listen to this song? What is the mood?" are often greeted with puzzlement. Descriptive adjectives about musical selections are usually limited to "nice," "it has a good beat," or "boring."

Not only are our students listening passively to music, their listening choices are narrowly defined by their subculture. They fear loss of peer approval if they should make an independent decision to listen to or "like" music other than the hits currently touted by their classmates. In this climate, it is axiomatic that the students express their displeasure with the teacher's listening choices.

Traditional music-listening methods (e.g., a synopsis of the composer's life, an examination of musical form, and the playing of thematic material on the keyboard) only serve to reinforce a resistant and passive attitude toward listening. Call charts that focus a student's energies to the worksheet so that the "correct, teacher-required" response may be written not only turn the focus away from listening to the music, but require little of the student's creativity and critical thinking abilities.

The emotional and physical energy of the middle school learner can be put to productive use in listening lessons. When encouraged, the student will show a remarkable ability to analyze, synthesize, create, and hypothesize—all critical thinking skills that will enhance a lifetime with music. These critical thinking skills nurtured in a safe, secure environment where all contributions to the discussion are accepted as worthy, will allow students to develop the vocabulary needed to voice their music learning beyond the usual "pretty," "dumb," "boring," or "got a good beat."

Accessing the critical thinking ability of the student requires constructing a problem to solve that is perplexing or challenging to the learner.[5] The following activities require the student to create, analyze, synthesize, and hypothesize:

1. Problem: When the composition employs repetition, what happens musically so that the listener is not bored?

2. Problem: Which of these architectural styles (as shown in pictures displayed by the teacher) best represents how the music sounds? Why? (e.g., play an example of plainsong and ask the students to select the picture of the building that best exemplifies how the music sounds.)

3. Problem: Compare three recordings of the same song. Discuss which recording best conveys the spirit of the composition. Defend your choice by using a descriptive vocabulary of both musical and nonmusical terms.

Teaching Strategy: Cooperative Learning

"I would like to be able to fly if everyone else did; otherwise it would be rather conspicuous." This remark, attributed to a twelve year old, underlines the importance of belonging, of being part of the crowd. At some point, being an individual will be important; right now it is more important to wear the most popular brand of shoes.

Classrooms geared only to individual achievement work against the basic need of the middle school learner to belong to the group. Students are often afraid to be high achievers or to let anyone know of their successes. Low achievers are equally out of step with the mainstream and easily suffer erosion of self esteem. Fragile egos can be assaulted daily by snubs, ridicule, and put-downs until motivation and achievement take last place to self-preservation at any cost.

Even though acceptance into the group is of paramount importance, the group itself is often dysfunctional. Healthy peer relationships are difficult when learners are not comfortable with their own identity. Security is more vital to the child than exploring and accepting differences. Affirmation of one's peers is rare; often the way to feel better about one's self is to be the master of the ultimate put-down.

Cooperative learning[6] techniques may be used to teach team-building skills, enhance self-esteem, practice social skills, motivate the reluctant learner, and foster learning. Students who have been labeled "slow learners" blossom in heterogeneous cooperative learning groups as they are guided by gifted students who, in return, become cognizant of the gifts of other group members. Some of the aspects of cooperative learning are:

1. Positive interdependence: Groups need to be structured so that the members realize that to accomplish mutual goals, each learner must fulfill an individual role and contribute to the group. United we win; divided we fail. Rewards are built in to the process to recognize joint effort and the achievement of shared goals.

2. Face-to-face interaction: Sitting knee to knee and eye to eye, students learn to communicate through giving explanations, drawing inferences from previous learning, and summarizing information that has been gathered.

3. Interpersonal skills: Students do not automatically treat each other with respect; social skills must be taught. Rewards can be given for "put-ups" instead of put-downs; first names should be used in communication; students must learn conflict man-

agement and decision-making skills and must be motivated to use them.

4. Individual accountability: The group cannot be successful until each member has mastered the material. The group goal will not be accomplished if the individuals are not held accountable. By ascertaining individual progress through frequent assessment, the group will be better able to support its members as they strive to achieve both group and individual goals.

5. Processing: Students need time to analyze the efficacy of their groups. Procedures that help them to reflect on their strengths and weaknesses will help them maintain and improve group skills.

A classroom structured for cooperative learning avoids the destructive aspects of competition. Positive interdependence means that one's self-interest is inextricably bound to that of others and that in the pursuit of both individual and group goals, ridicule and outward manifestations of prejudice almost disappear. Working on a project together and receiving praise from your peers cannot help but improve self-esteem and in turn improve one's ability to appreciate another's worth.

Meticulous advance planning and strict adherence to the basic elements of cooperative learning are the keys to effectively using this strategy. It takes time to structure a lesson for maximum benefit, but a well-designed and -executed plan provides the opportunity for effective skill building thereby insuring increased dividends from the next cooperative learning activity.

A traditional unit in general music centering on the life and music of Mozart will, after the quiz, tell the teacher whether each student has mastered the material in the test. Presenting the same material as a cooperative learning experience (e.g., compose letters as Mozart would have written them to his mother, wife, and moneylender; antique the final copies by dipping them in tea; complete and study a list of musical terms used in this unit; compare the death of Mozart as depicted in the movie "Amadeus" with extant newspaper accounts, and so on) will yield untold opportunities for sharing, affirmation, prejudice reduction, and motivation—plus absorption of the subject matter. Further, as the group studies together for their individual test, each helps the other, realizing that as each person's individual grade improves, the group will earn extra bonus points for an improved group average.

The following suggestions can be adapted to cooperative learning groups and designed so that each person in the group can be assigned a particular task that will contribute to the success of the whole:

- Instruct each group to write on a large poster five adjectives that describe the listening example assigned to your small group without writing down the title. Display each group's answers for the whole class to view, listen to all the selections and decide which modifiers match each example.
- Ask each group to describe the different timbres, pitch ranges, instrumental combinations, and rhythms in a percussion example. Using designated instruments, each group devises a percussion fragment that can then be performed either with the recording, alternately with the recording as a rondo, or in combination with the other groups as an entirely new composition with the form having been decided by the group.
- Assign a melodic fragment to each group. Using xylophones or other melody instruments, each group is to correctly execute the notation and learn to play the fragment. After each group plays for the class, the students decide in which order the fragments are to be played to create a unified song.

Teaching Strategy: Peer Teaching and Group Success

One of the cries of anguish from teachers the past few years has been, "How can I compete with the home entertainment system?" The solution lies in the answer to *this* question: What opportunities can the teacher offer in the classroom environment that are not possible in the audio/video world of the average child? The answer is peer-group experiences and hands-on opportunities in the creation and performance of music.

Most music teachers have had happy experiences working with or participating in choral or instrumental performing groups. Comparing the caliber of those experiences with a performance of fifteen fledgling guitarists playing a twelve-bar blues pattern may seem far-fetched. Many people, however, may never have the opportunity to participate in a successful musical performance unless they are provided with a group of supporting players or singers. Observing the reaction of a group of middle schoolers who have actually made music together for the first time is convincing proof that something significant has happened. Seeing a thirteen-year-old boy's reaction to being able to play guitar chords that fit a familiar recording is worth the effort of planning for the group experience and keeping up with broken strings.

The grading system used in an active, hands-on music course should be based on the level and willingness of participation displayed by the student. If this type of assessment process is employed, playing, singing, group projects, and group problem solving can be endeavors students pursue willingly. Singing in the eighth grade? Yes! Singing in all grades can be fun to the students if they have a reason to be singing the songs chosen. They will be even more willing if the songs they sing are somewhat familiar. Today's students are very familiar with many folk songs and with classic pop hits from the past twenty or thirty years. Current editions of graded music books include many of these types of songs and careful investigation will also reveal quite a number of singable tunes in today's market.

Keyboard and computer experiences lend themselves beautifully to one-on-one peer teaching. With groups of students playing guitar and working at the computer and the keyboard at the same time, activities and materials must be provided that can be self-taught. Careful planning, organization, and thoughtful use of peer teachers can allow one teacher to supervise the activities of a diversified group situation.

Setting up an active lab environment takes a substantial initial financial commitment by the school board and a lot of work on the part of the classroom teacher. However, once in place, the average yearly cost of consumables for the music lab is extremely low compared to costs in other exploratory areas like art, home economics, and industrial arts. At Ridgeview Middle School in Atlanta, the music lab instrument inventory has been expanded gradually on a yearly basis with either local or county funds. A formal request noting the successful experiences and enthusiasm of the students is submitted each year with specific needs outlined. Whenever possible, requests have been granted. Guitars and some keyboards (which are more expensive) have been provided by the local system, because the philosophy of the system is compatible with the hands-on philosophy of the middle school approach. Requests that have received the quickest turnaround on the local school level have been ones that indicated that students with low self-esteem or with learning problems would work tenaciously and with great success at a keyboard with earphones where they could work alone. While students must still share keyboards in classes of thirty as others are working on guitar or (only one) computer, the system works well enough that many children each year go into private study on guitar or piano or purchase an instrument.

If we are to avoid exhaustion and frustration as middle school teachers we must find various ways to help each child realize a satisfactory level of musical accomplishment and understanding. The teacher's willingness to explore and apply current learning theory is as important to affective teaching as knowledge of the subject matter. An understanding of the nature of the middle school learner is crucial to being able to manage the process of learning. If the environment is correct and musical opportunities are appropriate and successful then teaching music in the middle grades can be exhilarating and gratifying, and the music class becomes a learning experience that is rewarding and life enhancing to the students.

Notes

1. This may be the most disconcerting of all contradictions. Trying to remember that this is a child just trying on the cynicism of an adult can be very difficult during a confrontation.
2. Middle schoolers can show adult anger one moment and seek comfort and affection the next.
3. A user-friendly, practical approach is offered by Bernice McCarthy in *The 4Mat System,* published by EXCEL, Inc., 200 West Station Street, Barrington, Illinois 60010, 1980. Good sources for learning theory are: Dunn, R., and Dunn, K. (1978). *Teaching students through their individual learning styles: A practical approach,* Reston, VA: Reston Publishing Co., Inc. Butler, K. A. (1986). *Learning and teaching styles in theory and practice.* Maynard, MA: Gabriel Systems, Inc. Gardner, H. (1983). *Frames of mind: The theory of multiple intelligences.* New York, NY: Basic Books.
4. For further information see Keirsey, D., and Bates, M. (1984). *Please understand me. Character and temperament types.* Distributed by Prometheus Nemesis Book Company, P.O. Box 2748, Del Mar, CA 92014.
5. Some of the ideas in this section on critical thinking may be attributed to Dr. Lisa De Lorenzo, Montclair State College, Upper Montclair, N.J.
6. For further information about cooperative learning we suggest you read Johnson, D. W., and Johnson, R. T. (1984). *Circles of learning: Cooperation in the classroom.* Washington, D. C.: Association for Supervision and Curriculum Development.

SCHEDULING

BLOCKS, WHEELS, AND TEAMS
Building a Middle School Schedule

June Hinckley

Of all the changes associated with the advent of the middle school philosophy, many consider scheduling practices to have had the greatest effect on the delivery of music instruction. In school programs based on the traditional junior high philosophy, music is taught every day for the same length of time. Students have uniform daily schedules in which they go from class to class and teacher to teacher. This arrangement is the same as that used in high school scheduling—hence the name junior high school.

Middle-level scheduling practices, on the other hand, emphasize flexible scheduling and the grouping of students within a grade level into academic teams to encourage peer-group identity and rapport. In *An Agenda for Excellence at the Middle Level,* the National Association of Secondary School Principals' Council on Middle Level Education suggests that the culture and climate of schools should support "excellence and achievement rather than intellectual conformity. To achieve this, schools must...provide opportunities for students to achieve and demonstrate excellence in a number of domains (i.e., the arts, athletics, academics, crafts). Make certain that every student in the school has a reasonable opportunity to excel at something."

June Hinckley is a fine arts and instructional specialist for the Florida Department of Education in Tallahassee.

The agenda also supports the need for exploratory experiences. It describes the young adolescent as "being interested in virtually everything, but nothing very much." One technique commonly used to achieve this flexible scheduling is the exploratory "wheel" of short courses. Middle school students typically sample a variety of subjects—from foreign languages to specialized music topics—as they take part in "wheels" designed to involve entire classes of children in useful and intriguing sequences of four- to nine-week experiences. Of course, exploratory courses should not be allowed to substitute for a strong sequential exposure to the art of music, but they do form a significant component of many middle school schedules.

Effects on Music Offerings

Many music educators believe that every student in the middle school should have access to a variety of music classes—not just general music and ensemble classes. The broad array of course offerings that is emphasized in the middle school philosophy ensures that the learning needs of musically interested and talented students can be met along with the aesthetic and expressive needs of the general school population.

In a few schools that have focused strongly on developing an integrated curriculum, the general music program has become a part of the academic core, and music teachers are included as members of academic teams. On the other hand, though sequential general music instruction is recommended for all curricula through grade eight (in MENC's *Opportunity-to-Learn Standards for Music Instruction),* general music has recently become less widely required and less widely available as an elective in grades 6, 7, and 8.

In the minds of some, this loss of emphasis on general music over the last twenty years has been compensated for by the increased number of schools offering instrumental music.[1] A suggested reason for this increase is that introductory band and orchestra are often offered as exploratory courses included in the "wheel." Also, some school systems put forth the rationale that the variety of exploratory music courses offered in middle schools will attract students even though there is no requirement to take music courses.

Problems may occur where the inclusion of other elements, such as advisory periods and interdisciplinary units, has absorbed a great deal of school time. In some schools, these changes have meant that music teachers only see band students every other day or that the wheel requirement interrupts sequential instruction in music. Where the schedule does not allow multigrade grouping, advanced choir may no longer be made up of the best seventh and eighth graders in the school.

Middle-level schools are intended to better meet the needs of the child in the middle of his or her most active years developmentally and to help make that transition from childhood to adulthood easier. If they are to make good on this promise, then creative scheduling for academic and elective classes is essential.

Creating a Good Music Schedule

How can a teacher work to improve the music schedule? The first thing is to know who actually designs the schedule. It may be the principal, or it may be the guidance counselor or another teacher. The next step is expressing interest to that person about the schedule. This may need to be done several times. Then, before you actually begin the task, read up on middle school scheduling practices so that you can really be a help to those responsible for building the schedule. No two schools have the same schedule, but looking at other scheduling models may be helpful to you.

If your offer to assist in scheduling is accepted, it is important to be interested in the total schedule. Your suggestions will not be taken seriously if your interest seems self-serving. Even if resolving a conflict with an advanced algebra class means losing the best soprano in school, it may be wise to concede the issue and work out an independent schedule with that student. You will now have the opportunity to discover the rhyme and reason for your school's schedule.

Whether or not you assist in building the schedule, remember that every teacher in the school wants the best schedule possible for his or her own situation. It may, therefore, take several attempts to achieve the ideal schedule for the music faculty. Being patient is important: part of the art of being a team player in the middle school is determining when to stand up for your program and when to compromise. Arguing on behalf of students' needs will carry the day far better than arguing for your program. A rule of thumb is that any compromise should be in the best interests of the students.

The effort of creating a good schedule involves time away from teaching, and such time is hard to find for busy music teachers. If the schedule is really vital to the success of the music program, however, then the time spent is worth the loss of an extra sectional rehearsal. A student's middle years are a critical time of decision making regarding music study. Chances for a young person to have a wonderful continuing experience with music may be lost forever if a student loses the chance to be in a music class–or if the class itself is lost because of scheduling conflicts.

Common Scheduling Practices

- *Teaming and block scheduling.* A common method for scheduling academic core courses is to group approximately 150 students into interdisciplinary teams, forming a cohesive group taught by several teachers with different subject area specializations. These teams often select names for themselves like the Hawks or the Dolphins, and they function as social as well as instructional units. Frequently math, science, language arts, and social studies classes are scheduled as a unit; this unit is allocated a daily block of time that may be two hours or more. This gives the teachers involved a great deal of flexibility in organizing the time given to each subject, the ability to group and regroup students into smaller classes within the team according to academic need, and the opportunity to provide interdisciplinary instruction. Though teachers of electives are seldom involved as members of the team, they should try to be considered as resources for team planning.
- *The integrated curriculum.* Music, like other subjects, traditionally is taught by a subject-area specialist. The music specialist's goal is to develop performance skills, appreciation, or general music knowledge. The middle school philosophy encourages a more integrated approach to instruction. It holds that if students see connections across content areas, then instruction will have more relevance. Using this integrative approach, the music teacher can become a part of a team and pro-

vide general music instruction within the block schedule, assist with planning interdisciplinary units, or, at the very least, be a guest teacher when an instructional unit would be enhanced by music examples.

Music teachers who have worked with academic teams have found it rewarding. They report, however, that they had to work to become included as a part of the team. Because so much effort is made to develop an esprit de corps among the teachers in the academic teams, other teachers may be viewed as "outsiders."

Music can be the focus of instructional units involving an entire grade level or the whole school. In one middle school where the chorus was planning a production of *Scrooge,* all the students read Dickens's *A Christmas Carol* to prepare for the performance. Another year, the choral production of *The Electric Sunshine Man* (about Thomas Edison) generated a unit on "Great Men of Science" and a school science fair.

■ *Advisory programs.* Middle-level experts encourage scheduling an advisory or homeroom period for students in the middle grades.[2] This is often done during the first few minutes of the day or around the lunch period. Advisement periods allow students to discuss issues of general concern, develop personal skills, or work on special projects. This is the time often used for schoolwide projects such as Earth Day and holiday projects and programs, or interdisciplinary units such as "Technology in Our Times."

■ *Redesigning the exploratory wheel.* The wheel can be offered in each year of a student's middle-level education (to allow for sampling a wide variety of subjects) or just during the first year (with the hope that these experiences will facilitate choosing electives later). Obviously, if the courses in the "wheel" are to operate as recruiting devices, they must be offered early in the student's middle-level experience and must be of sufficient length and interest to attract students when the opportunity comes to select elective courses. In Manatee County Schools in Florida, for example, students take an allied arts wheel that includes woodwinds, brass, chorus, strings, and art in the first semester of sixth grade. Thirty-one to fifty percent of the students now taking music in grades seven through ten credit their exposure to music in the wheel for their participation in music as an elective.[3]

There is no set group of courses that schools offer as a part of the exploratory "wheel." Schools that offer minicourses on the wheel might offer "The History of Rock Music," "Electronic Music," or topics of local or cultural interest such as "Greek Music-Making Traditions." Other schools let students create their own "wheel" from a list of possibilities.

Schools that require students to choose between the wheel and music ensembles can put the music program at an unfair disadvantage. The potpourri of choices provided in the "wheel" can be immensely attractive to students at this age. Committing to one class for a whole semester or year and exploring subjects for short periods are inequitable choices.

■ *Electives.* Although the middle school philosophy supports exploration of many topics, it also encourages the development of "excellence and achievement rather than intellectual conformity."[4] Time for electives is essential if students are to be able to pursue their own special interests and talents in any depth. The block, the wheel, advisory periods, and regularly scheduled physical education can coexist with a vital elective program—one that includes music electives. Obviously, the more periods offered and the larger the music staff, the more variety and flexibility a schedule can have. MENC recommends that no fewer than eight periods a day be offered, but a schedule using eight or nine is preferable.[5]

Limitations on the staff time and facilities may restrict the number of offerings, but a good music schedule should include as much variety as possible. Piano or guitar classes may meet the needs of self-conscious middle-grade students better than traditional large-ensemble courses do. Interested music students might enjoy jazz ensembles or MIDI keyboarding. In one school, enrollment in general music classes increased when the teacher retitled it "From Bach to Rock."

■ *Other options.* Within these strictures, the schedule is limited only by creativity. Bob Spear, principal of Powder Mill Middle School in Massachusetts and a national consultant on middle-level scheduling, suggests that schools do not need more organization—they need more invention. He also maintains that there is no such thing as one best schedule for all students and teachers. A good schedule is one that enhances the learning process.

It is possible to schedule more creatively if the focus is placed on instructional needs rather than the number of periods. One technique Spear suggests is laying out the school day in ten-minute segments. The scheduling pattern he uses is extremely flexible and looks much like a mosaic when it is drawn up. Class lengths vary, and all classes do not meet every day.

Spear recommends scheduling "singleton" courses like advanced band, chorus, and orchestra first because they require multigrade grouping and generally involve a large number of students. If scheduled when more than one grade-level team has an elective slot in the student schedule, multigrade grouping is possible and the number of conflicts is reduced.

One schedule Spear suggests has music ensembles meet three times a week for an extended period. Students take other courses on the alternating days. MENC recommends, and most music teachers would prefer, that classes meet every day. If, however, schools have fewer than eight periods a day, meeting on alternate days is certainly preferable to losing students altogether. A compromise, such as meeting the woodwind players on two days, with the brass and percussion meeting on another two and with the whole group on the fifth day, may also work well and will allow the teacher to give more individualized instruction if classes are very large (see figure 1).

Rotating schedules are more structured. They also provide more scheduling options for students. One version of a rotating schedule has two courses paired to alternate with each other. For instance, a guitar class and a computer class may trade schedules each week, one meeting on Monday, Wednesday, and Friday and the other on Tuesday and Thursday. Alternately, the first arrangement may hold for a month before the schedules are switched. Some schools have one set of Monday, Wednesday, and Friday electives and another set of Tuesday and Thursday electives (see figure 2).

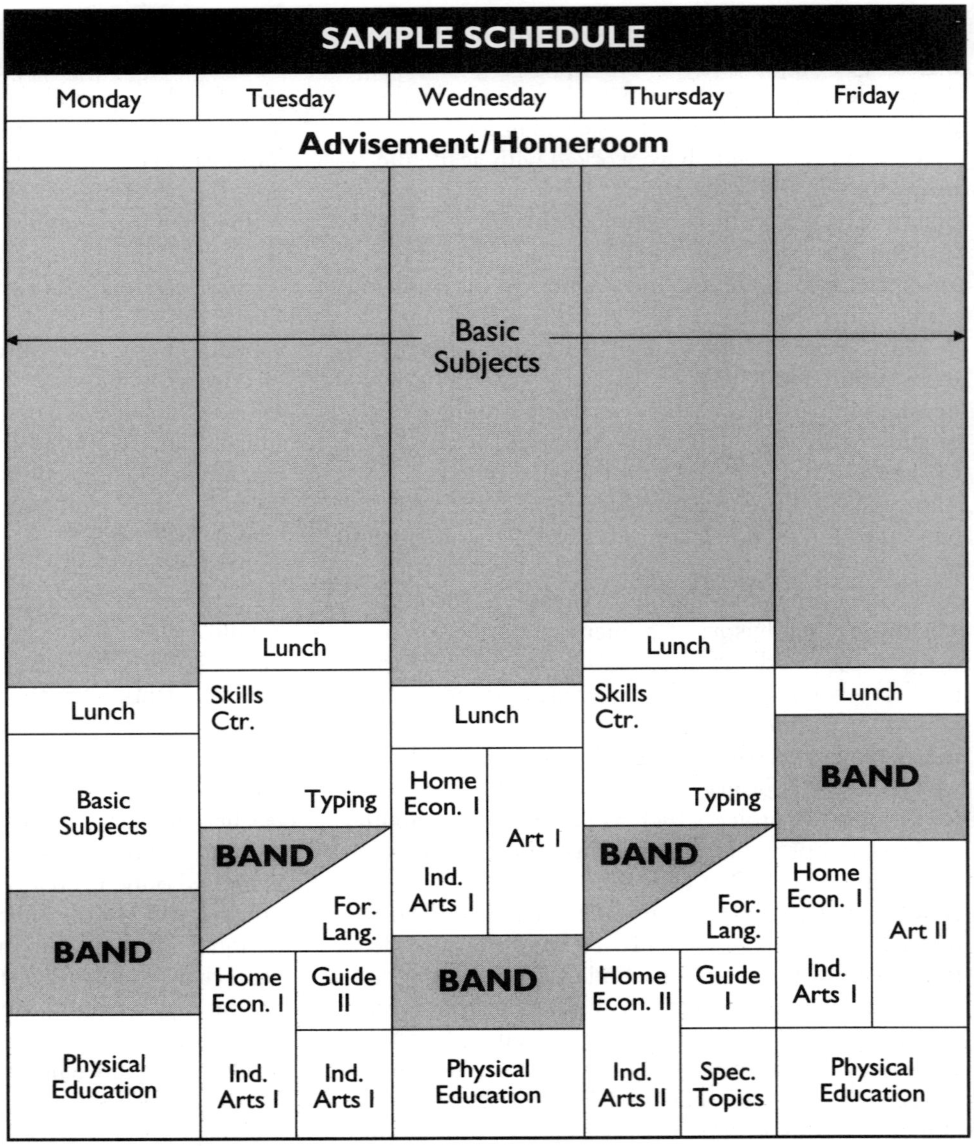

Figure 1. A sample middle school schedule

Building the Schedule

A middle school master schedule can make use of several options. It can use block scheduling, an exploratory wheel, minicourses, and advisory periods. It can also use varying class lengths, alternating classes, a "school within a school," a mosaic schedule, lunchtime curricular activities, and enrichment activities such as those suggested in the sections on the integrated curriculum and advisory programs.

An effective middle school master schedule may be based on one or more of these options. It must, however, be developed in recognition of the following principles:

- It is, most important, student-oriented
- It is a blueprint for the instructional programs of the school
- It assures that elective and required courses receive equal consideration
- It provides a balanced and comprehensive program
- It is based on input from teachers, staff, and students
- It allows students of different ages to be grouped together
- It gives equal status to each program, grade level, and team
- It strengthens interdisciplinary teams
- It provides for exploratory courses

Exploratory courses and mini-courses allow students to sample varied musical interests. Rotating and mosaic schedules allow a larger variety of course offerings to be scheduled so that students can pursue sequential music study in greater depth. Interdisciplinary units that are centered around or

8-PERIOD SCHEDULE – 6th GRADE					
	Monday	Tuesday	Wednesday	Thursday	Friday
1	Math	Math	Math	Math	Math
2	Science	Science	Science	Science	Science
3	Soc. Studies	Soc. Studies Reading	Soc. Studies	Soc. Studies Reading	Soc. Studies
4	English	EN Elective	English	EN Elective	English
5	Elective	Elective	Elective	Elective	Elective
6	Elective	Elective	Elective	Elective	Elective
7	Lunch	Lunch	Lunch	Lunch	Lunch
8	PE	Swim	PE	Swim	Early dismissal

M-W-F Electives	T-Th Electives
art band PE swimming skills computer Spanish theater general music ethnic studies	art chorus PE swimming skills computer Spanish theater class piano beginning band dance study skills video production career education media-yearbook social studies electives English electives science electives

Figure 2. A sample 8-period schedule

include music show how music connects with other content areas and all of life. All of these concepts that emphasize sequential, exploratory, and integrated study are important types of instruction for students in their middle years.

Schools that follow the traditional model of scheduling by periods, as most do, need at least seven periods for a viable elective program. The more periods offered and the larger the staff, obviously, the more opportunities students will have to include music class in their schedules. Variety among courses is essential to meet the differing needs of students in the middle years. Not all students want to perform with a large group in front of an audience, but most students would like to be able to make some kind of music. Music teachers can use the special scheduling configurations found in middle schools, such as advisory periods, lunchtime mini-courses, and the integrated curriculum, to reach and teach more students.

More creative scheduling practices demand more teacher time and input and greater faculty flexibility. Creating a good schedule that allows students time to study music as well as art and home economics is a creative challenge. This special effort will be rewarded, however, if more students' social and academic needs are met through music study, if the faculty is involved in solving the scheduling challenge, and if the instructional goals of the music program are well achieved.

Notes

This article is an edited reprint of June Hinckley's article, "Blocks, Wheels, and Teams: Building a Middle School Schedule," which appeared in the February 1992 *Music Educators Journal*.

1. Alexander, W. M., & McEwin, C. K. 1989. *Schools in the middle: Status and progress*. Columbus, OH: National Middle School Association, 16–18.
2. Alexander, W. M., & George, P. S. 1981. *The exemplary middle school*. New York: Holt, Rinehart, and Winston, 97–99; Kindred, L. 1968. *The intermediate schools*. Englewood Cliffs, NJ: Prentice-Hall, 193–205; Lounsbury, J. H., & Vars, G. F. 1978. *A curriculum for the middle school years*. New York: Harper and Row, 50–51.
3. Doane, C. 1990. *A preliminary report from the Florida task force on middle school music*. Tallahassee, FL: Florida Music Educators Association, 4.
4. National Association of Secondary School Principals. 1985. *An agenda for excellence at the middle level*. Reston, VA: National Association of Secondary School Principals, 3, 7.
5. Music Educators National Conference. 1994. *Opportunity-to-Learn Standards for Music Instruction: Grades PreK–12*. Reston, VA: Music Educators National Conference, 10.

SCHEDULING MIDDLE-LEVEL MUSIC

Ronald Williamson

The Ann Arbor Middle School is a large suburban school. Unlike many suburban schools, though, Ann Arbor Public Schools have a population of various cultures. Some form of music is required in the sixth grade in the Ann Arbor school district, but music is an elective in the seventh and eighth grades.

Except for the quality of the teaching staff, the school schedule has the greatest impact on the ability of a school to meet the varied needs of middle-level students. A schedule permits students access to a school's curriculum. The structure of the day and the ease with which students are able to access the program is determined by the structure of the school schedule. The placement of courses during the school day and their relationship to each other determines whether all students are able to take equal advantage of the curriculum.

The problem with school schedules is that they must balance the diverse and often competing needs of the students with multiple curricular areas. The many demands on the schedule often result in a construct that reflects the negotiations and give-and-take that must of necessity take place when considering both these needs.

Such compromise often results in the perception by various constituent groups that their particular needs have not been addressed, when in fact the schedule reflects a process of maximizing opportunities for students. Music staff often feel the unique needs of their curricular area have not been provided for while other staff often feel that the entire schedule has been constructed around the music department. Neither point of view is usually accurate, but the *perceptions* create barriers that must be overcome in order to serve students well.

Ronald Williamson is executive director for curriculum and instruction for Ann Arbor Public Schools, Ann Arbor, Michigan.

Scheduling Process

A first step in scheduling must be the opportunity for the school staff to discuss, and help establish, the priorities of the schedule. This includes a review of the school's mission and commitment to serving the youth of the community. The school schedule is a powerful tool, and it is imperative that it is seen by all staff members as a mechanism that supports the mission of the middle-level school.

Issues such as block-scheduling, common planning time, composition of interdisciplinary student teams, and the structure of the elective program require discussion and thought regarding their impact on both the schedule and the other components of the program. Thoughtful deliberation and discussion about the priorities of the program and its impact on students is essential prior to the actual development of the schedule.

Every schedule must take into account the local constraints and parameters that impact its structure. Among these constraints are the school's physical plant, the number of teachers, teachers shared with other schools, class size requirements, size of the lunch room, and grouping practices. It is critical to identify all of the local parameters that either inhibit or facilitate the schedule and develop strategies for assuring that they are accounted for in the schedule.

The location of singletons, courses that meet only once during the school day, and doubletons, courses that meet twice, must also be considered in developing the schedule. These courses have the potential to conflict with many other courses because students only have one or two opportunities to take each course. If a student chooses to take two singleton courses and they are scheduled during the same class period, there will be a conflict. Either the conflict must be resolved through a change in the schedule or the student will need to select an alternate course.

For the music teacher, the placement of singleton courses is of primary importance since most performing music courses are singletons. In the middle-level school there is the added variable of the location of blocks of time for the core teams. The scheduling of team time during the day affects the students' access to the components of the elective program.

The scheduling process requires the systematic adjustment of both the schedule of classes and the selections made by students. The priority must always be on adjusting the schedule to maximize student access to the curriculum; however, changes in student course selection are often necessary. When such adjustments must be made it is important that they be made in consultation with the student, parent, and appropriate staff.

Implications for Music Programs

For music staff, as well as other elective teachers, it often seems as if a middle-level program provides diminished opportunities for students in electives. Conflicts often arise over the implementation of interdisciplinary teaming and the use of blocks of time, grouping practices, and the offering of an exploratory program for students. Research, however, demonstrates the effectiveness of interdisciplinary teams, heterogeneous grouping practices, and the concept of exploration at the middle level. The implementation of these programs does *not* diminish the value of opportunities for students to strengthen and refine their skills, particularly in performing music classes.

The implementation of core academic teams with block-of-time scheduling does not, in and of itself, preclude the offering of performing-music classes that provide for students of distinct skill levels. The myth of middle-level-school scheduling is that one component must take on greater importance than the other. This is not true. The two components support and enhance each other. The use of teams permits every middle-level student to develop a sense of belonging and connection to the school. This enhances student self-esteem, and often promotes increased academic risk-taking on the part of students.

Teams and advisory programs are designed to provide support and encouragement to all students. When the staff—in both the core teams and the elective areas—work together, teams are able to support and encourage students who participate in music. This collaboration often includes correlation of curriculum, discussion of student issues, and open dialogue regarding ways to encourage greater student participation in the music program. Likewise, the implementation of heterogeneous grouping practices does not necessarily inhibit the ability to provide instruction for all students regardless of their skill level. Grouping too often results in tracking, where similar groups of students have a similar schedule for all or most of the day. Such tracking, it has been demonstrated, does not serve students well.

The grouping and regrouping of students for instruction can provide for the necessary skill development and enrichment that are critical to a music program. The blend of heterogeneous teams, with skill grouping in certain curricular areas, enhances the overall instructional program for students while not tracking them throughout the day. Teachers often express concern that offering an exploratory program for students will restrict the ability to offer performing music classes. This is another myth that must be discarded.

Exploratory programs are designed to assure that every student, regardless of background or experience, has a similar opportunity to experience all the components of a school's program. This often means that all students will take the same courses in art, music, foreign language, or other curricular areas. As a result of exploratory classes students elect subsequent courses based on knowledge of their own skills and interests, as opposed to the experiences of their parents or friends. Many times this results in greater representation of students of all ethnic backgrounds, genders, and socioeconomic levels in the exploratory areas.

The exploratory concept thus enhances the overall quality of an elective program. Exploratory courses offer opportunities for middle-grade students to test their skills in many different areas, areas in which they may not have had previous experience. An exploratory program, however, should not replace the opportunity for students to elect courses in performing music and other elective areas. The purpose of exploratory programs is to build interest in the curricular program; therefore, beyond the exploratory course, schedules must continue to provide students with options that permit them to study their areas of interest in greater depth. As in all programs, the critical consideration for staff is to focus on serving students, rather than on maintaining specific curricular offerings. Serving students well results in high quality programs. Without a focus on student needs no program will maintain a quality experience for long.

Strategies for Consideration

In developing a middle-level schedule there are several options worthy of consideration. These options address the perceived conflict between utilization of core teams and the associated blocks of time, and the needs of students in the elective program.

6th GRADE	7th GRADE	8th GRADE
Core Block (2) + Advisory	Elective	Elective
Elective or Exploratory	Core Block (2) + Advisory	Core Block (2) + Advisory
Lunch	Elective	Elective
Core Block (2)	Lunch	Elective
Exploratory	Core Block (2)	Lunch
Elective or Exploratory	Elective	Core Block (2)

Figure 1. A flexible middle-level schedule

The first consideration is that not every team or team schedule must be alike. While it is very common for teams at different grade levels to have different schedules, it is less common for teams at the same grade level. Flexibility in team schedules provides more chances for students to access the elements of the elective program.

An example illustrates this point: At one middle-level school in Michigan the morning schedule for all core teams in the seventh and eighth grade is similar—the core block is scheduled during second and third hour, while electives are scheduled first and fourth. This permits students at both grade levels to take electives either separately by grade, or cross-grade. In the afternoon the seventh grade schedule is different from the eighth grade schedule. Thus, time is available for grade specific electives (see figure 1).

This flexibility is the first step in designing a schedule that takes into account the varied needs of every curricular area. This model permits the maintenance of grade specific blocks-of-time yet provides options to group students across grade levels for instruction in certain content areas.

The second consideration is to acknowledge that not every course at every grade level must meet on a daily basis. Middle-level schedules are often constructed to look much like the schedule of a comprehensive high school and little like the schedule of an elementary school. The elementary model, however, is a concept that provides both greater flexibility and increased options for students when used at the middle level. For example, each day of the week might have different schedules. This permits the location of the blocks during the day, their relationship to electives, and blocks for other grades and teams to vary. It also permits the alignment of certain class periods so that students in performing music courses, between teams or across grades, and other courses may be assembled without totally disrupting the remainder of the schedule. It acknowledges that the music teacher may not require the total band or orchestra to meet on a daily basis, but that the program may benefit from the potential to work with ensembles and other small groups at various times throughout the week. Likewise, teachers on the core teams may welcome the opportunity to restructure their blocks of time. This flexibility provides options to group and regroup team students for instruction, to work with small groups of students, and to offer enrichment opportunities.

Other scheduling concepts may also provide increased options for students. These include the use of "alternate day classes," courses that meet during the same class period but only on alternating days. One course may meet on Monday, Wednesday, and alternating Fridays, while the other course meets on Tuesday, Thursday, and alternating Fridays.

The key to successful scheduling is a willingness to put aside the traditional vision of a schedule, including all of the traditional paradigms regarding the length of class periods, the frequency of class meetings, and the structure of both core team and elective time.

There are no perfect schedules but there are countless examples of fine middle-level schedules. The key to the success of a schedule is the thought and planning that takes place before the development of the schedule, and the willingness of all staff to maintain a focus on serving students rather than on maintaining specific programs.

References

Carnegie Council on Adolescent Development. 1989. *Turning points: Preparing American youth for the 21st century*. Washington, D.C.: Carnegie Council on Adolescent Development.

Center for Research on Elementary and Middle Schools. 1990. Implementation and effects of middle grades practices. *CREMS Report*. The Johns Hopkins University (March).

Garvin, J. 1986. Common denominators in effective middle schools. *Schools in the Middle*. Reston, VA: National Association of Secondary School Principals.

Johnston, J. H., & Markle, G. 1986. *What research says to the middle-level practitioner.* Columbus, OH: National Middle School Association.

MacIver, D. 1990. Meeting the needs of young adolescents: Advisory groups, interdisciplinary teaching teams, and school transition programs. *Phi Delta Kappan, 71,* (February): 458-64.

Williamson, R., & Johnston, J. H. 1991. *Planning for success: Successful implementation of middle-level reorganization.* Reston, VA: National Association of Secondary School Principals.

Williamson, R. 1993. *Scheduling the middle-level school to meet early adolescent needs.* Reston, VA: National Association of Secondary School Principals.

SCHEDULING FLEXIBILITY IN MIDDLE SCHOOL

Karl A. Kumme

Silas Deane Middle School, in Wethersfield, Connecticut, was created from the merger of two grade seven-through-nine junior high schools and the formation of a four-year high school. To complete the transition from junior high to middle school, the departmentalization of the junior high was abandoned in favor of a team-teaching approach: the five hundred students enrolled are divided among four teaching teams of approximately 125 students each—two teams each for grades seven and eight. The assignment of students to a particular team is accomplished in such a way as to assure heterogeneity.

The schedule for Silas Deane Middle School contains five periods for the instruction of the core curriculum (math, science, social studies, language arts, foreign language/developmental reading), two periods for the unified arts, and a "flex" end-of-day multiuse period, so called because of the flexibility it offers staff to provide students with a wide variety of services (see figure 1). Flex is not part of the regular instructional schedule, but is intended to give students and teachers time for extra help sessions, both remedial and enriching.

The unified arts—art, music, physical education, life management, and technology education courses—are scheduled during daily back-to-back periods. Seventh- and eighth-grade curricula are kept sequential and distinct—grade eight unified arts classes meet during periods six and seven, and grade seven unified arts meet during periods three and four. Team meetings for core curriculum teachers are held during these back-to-back periods.

Karl A. Kumme is the instructional supervisor for music, K–12, in the Wethersfield (Connecticut) Public Schools.

Because the unified arts classes are scheduled during four periods of the day, three music classes, one each of choral, instrumental, and general, run concurrently. A minimum of three teachers and teaching stations is therefore necessary to operate the program. The music program is staffed by 2.6 full-time–equivalent teachers (i.e., one full time and three part time). The teaching assignments of the part-time instructors are filled out at either the elementary or high schools.

Creating Successful Programs

The manner in which these disciplines are scheduled is significant in terms of each program's success. Individual, project-oriented work in art, home economics, and technology education is aided by block scheduling, which allows for class meetings in each for sixty consecutive days. Students would, for example, receive daily art instruction for the first twelve weeks (sixty days) of school; they would then switch to life management for the next twelve weeks; and end the year with twelve weeks of daily instruction in technology education. Music and physical education, which tend to benefit from regular, long-term instruction, meet throughout the year on a twice-weekly basis. These classes would be scheduled on alternate days during the second of the two unified arts periods (see figure 2).

The philosophy that guides the music program is that ongoing, sequential, and participatory instruction in music is essential to the education of every student. Students can best learn the materials and structures of

Monday–Friday Bell Schedule			
Period	1:	8:00 – 8:45	
	2:	8:48 – 9:29	
	3:	9:32 – 10:13	
	4:	10:16 – 10:57	
	5:	11:00 – 12:09	(lunch)
	6:	12:12 – 12:53	
	7:	12:56 – 1:37	
		1:40 – 2:20	(flex)

Figure 1. A schedule that incorporates a "flex" period

Grade Eight Team "A" Student Schedule

	M	T	W	T	F
Per. 1	Art	Art	Art	Art	Art
Per. 2	Music	PE	Music	PE	Dev. Rdg.

Grade Eight Team "B" Student Schedule

	M	T	W	T	F
Per. 1	Music	PE	Music	PE	Dev. Rdg.
Per. 2	Art	Art	Art	Art	Art

Figure 2. Schedules for the entire academic year

music, critical listening skills, elements of style and performance practice, and a historical perspective of their own cultural heritage, as well as an appreciation for and an understanding of other cultures through active participation in music making. This instruction in music should allow for in-depth study and development of skills, knowledge, and attitudes, as opposed to exploratory experiences.

It is important to note that, although the course offerings in music do not include the traditional general music or exploratory-type classes, the music curriculum is not performance driven. Rather, student participation in active music making is seen as the most appropriate vehicle for the transmission of that curriculum, and that performance is the normal outgrowth of instruction.

Electing Music Courses

Music courses are the only "electives" at Silas Deane. While all students must receive music instruction, the vehicle through which that instruction is delivered may differ. Students entering grade seven are asked to choose from among band, string ensemble, chorus, and an introductory piano/guitar course. Students entering grade eight may also select band, string ensemble, or chorus; however, they may choose either piano or guitar for in-depth, full-year courses.

Election of music courses takes place in the spring of the preceding year. Sixth-grade youngsters are asked, with their parents, to choose the music course that is most appropriate for them. All students have had at least two years of experience with instrumental and/or choral music in elementary school. This background, coupled with the recommendation of the elementary music teacher, assures to some degree the appropriateness of their choices. Recommendations for acceptance or change are made based upon the teacher's evaluation of student performance in grade seven. Generally, students are encouraged to stay within a specific track.

Students' course cards are sorted, by teams, according to their music choices. Those selecting chorus, generally the largest group, are further subdivided into groups of approximately twenty to twenty-five students each. Sections of band, orchestra, and piano or guitar are formed; depending on enrollment these could vary from two sections per grade to two per teaching team. These classes would normally consist of approximately fifteen students. Class size in piano and guitar is currently restricted to fifteen maximum because of equipment availability.

The music department believes that instrumental and choral music are not mutually exclusive; rather they are important complementary experiences. Participation in both choral and instrumental music is encouraged and facilitated by cooperative instructors who "share" students between classes and flex rehearsals. Students who play instruments select band or string ensemble class, then attend a chorus flex on a day when their instrumental ensemble is not meeting.

Flex Time

The end-of-the-day flex period allows for a large-group rehearsal of performing ensembles. Because this period is free of grade or team restriction, it is the opportunity for band and string orchestra rehearsals that draw students from both grades. Typically both performing ensembles would rehearse twice weekly. The fifth flex period during the week is an opportunity for the instrumental instructor to offer ensembles such as jazz band or string quartet or provide practice facilities, extra help, or additional computer access.

Students are assigned to specific flex rehearsals according to the ensemble(s) with which they participate. For attendance purposes, students assigned to band, for example, would be identified as attending band flex every Monday and Wednesday; students playing in the orchestra might rehearse every Tuesday and Thursday during flex.

The large choruses are met by halves. There are typically one hundred twenty or more students in both the seventh and eighth grade choruses; flex rehearsals would therefore involve sixty-plus students in each rehearsal. Flex assignments here are determined by the section of biweekly chorus class the students attend. Just prior to performances, all students in each group will attend both flex periods to allow for rehearsals of the complete ensembles. Four flex periods per week are therefore used for the rehearsal of the large choruses.

The fifth weekly, or "Funky Friday," flex is devoted to a Chorale of forty students, selected by audition, from both seventh- and eighth-grade students. The Chorale is the only performing group in which participation is not open and nonselective.

Students in the guitar and piano classes may elect to participate in a rock band that is organized and rehearsed during flex time. While not every student in either course participates in this ensemble, the opportunity is provided for those with the interest and the requisite skills. The rock band does serve as a motivator for individual practice and skill development. Band, orchestra, and chorus students have also participated in this activity.

Many students are now entering Silas Deane with experience on both a stringed and a wind or percussion instrument. The elementary program in Wethersfield, which starts string instruction in grade three, has allowed an increasing number of youngsters to begin a band instrument as well in grades four, five, or six and to develop sufficient proficiency to perform in two ensembles. Typically, because string classes are smaller, students proficient to perform in two ensembles elect string class and perform in flex rehearsals of both ensembles. The alternate day scheduling (Monday-Wednesday band, Tuesday-Thursday string ensemble) allows this to occur. Moreover, when the instructor wishes to expand the string ensemble to an orchestra with winds and percussion, band students are available to fill those roles without missing their band rehearsals.

The strength of this scheduling lies in the flexibility of being able to accommodate the traditional performing ensembles while allowing for smaller group instruction in those areas of music study traditionally reserved for the general music class. The twice-weekly classes allow instruction in all facets of music and musicality through the student's chosen medium; the daily flex periods allow for large ensemble experience and rehearsal and special-interest pursuits. Because of this fortuitous combination, all students receive a minimum eighty minutes of music instruction per week; most receive at least one hundred twenty, many as much as two hundred minutes every week.

In any situation, a cooperative and flexible school administration is a necessary ingredient for success; we are fortunate at Silas Deane to work with innovative, creative administrators who allow their staff the freedom to be innovative and creative as well. While this particular format of middle school scheduling is certainly not unique, we believe that this adaptation of curriculum to schedule has allowed the music program at Silas Deane Middle School to serve its students in the most beneficial and universal manner.

EXPLORATORY COURSES

SAY YES TO MUSIC ELECTIVES, SAY NO TO ELECTIVE MUSIC

Sandra L. Stauffer

In 1990, the Center for Research on Elementary and Middle Schools published the results of a national study of schools that serve early adolescent students. The researchers found that only 25 percent of school buildings in the United States that include seventh-grade students are grade 6–8 middle schools, and less than 40 percent of the nation's seventh-grade students are enrolled in them. All other seventh-grade students are enrolled in schools that can be categorized into thirty different grade-level structures, ranging from K–12 schools to buildings that house only one grade (Epstein & Mac Iver, 1990).

Myriad Programs and Philosophies

Middle school general music programs are as diverse as the schools early adolescent students attend.

Sandra L. Stauffer is an associate professor of music education at Arizona State University, Tempe.

Some diversity may be attributed to differences in school structure, but general music programs are also affected by scheduling practices, administrative philosophies, and curriculum plans. For example, a study of Maryland middle/junior high schools revealed that general music is required for all students, including those who participate in ensembles, in only one-fourth of the state's schools. In 36 percent of the schools, only those students who are not members of performing ensembles are required to enroll in general music classes. Students meet an "arts requirement" by completing either a general music course or a class in another one of the arts in 9 percent of the schools, and in 11 percent, there is no general music requirement. Other schools have a range of different plans (Saunders & Stauffer, 1989). Teaching styles and preferences, published curriculum materials, student attitudes, community needs and sentiments, and other factors also affect general music classes either directly or indirectly. It is hardly surprising that the "typical" middle school general music program is so hard to describe.

The Role of Electives

What role do music electives play in middle school general music programs? When the middle school concept and philosophy emerged during the 1960s, one of the goals was to provide curriculum and experiences based on the needs and interests of early adolescent students. Instead of forcing middle-grade learners to conform to a high-school-like academic curriculum structure, the intent was to provide greater depth and breadth of understanding through study that included exploratory, experimental, and creative opportunities. Interdisciplinary approaches to learning and teacher teams for instructional planning, advising, and supporting students were thought to be essential to building a middle school community and creating an atmosphere that fostered self-esteem, confidence, and a sense of accomplishment. Today, curricular flexibility, exploratory and creative opportunities, interdisciplinary learning, and team planning remain watchwords of middle school philosophy.

When it began, the middle school concept was an education reform movement directed toward creating school communities sensitive to the characteristics and needs of middle-grade students. Like other reform movements, the translation from theory to practice and from discussion to the classroom has been slow. Researchers note that "most schools for students in the middle grades still look much like the junior high school or high school of the recent past" (Braddock, Wu, & McPartland, 1988). Also, as with other reform movements, some of the goals of the middle school movement have been misunderstood or inappropriately applied. In many middle schools, music and the other arts have suffered this fate.

"Exploratory" and "Creative" Courses

Perhaps the most unfortunate misinterpretation of middle school goals has occurred in the development of exploratory, elective, and creative opportunities for students. The original intent of the middle school philosophy was that these varied learning experiences should pervade the curriculum and be incorporated in all areas of study. In many middle schools, however, entire subjects or courses have been designated "exploratory," and often music and the other arts are relegated to this dubious status. Under the guise of "electives," mini-courses are developed in which students are introduced to or immersed in one of the arts (or another subject) for a quarter, a semester, or some other segment of the school year. Elective courses from various disciplines are then arranged into block or wheel programs in which students attend a class in a different area of study every six, nine, or twelve weeks. The result of this course of events, now evident in middle schools everywhere, is that instead of being a subject area of year-round study in which electives are offered, music has become an elective subject.

Fallacies to Combat

There are three fallacies to thinking that categorizes entire disciplines as exploratory or elective. First, "creative" and "exploratory" are adjectives appropriately applied to an approach to teaching and a disposition for learning in any discipline, but not to the content of a discipline itself. It is possible for any teacher in any subject area to structure learning environments in which students have opportunities to explore new ideas, create new solutions to problems, elect one of several paths to a goal, experiment with applications of what has been learned, and so on. The value of the arts in the middle school curriculum is not that they are the *only* suitable venues for creativity and exploration, but that the arts provide these opportunities in unique ways.

The second fallacy hidden in thinking that categorizes the arts as exploratory or elective is the notion that an exploratory experience is enough experience. This kind of thinking fails to recognize and value what can be learned and accomplished by students through year-round study in so-called "exploratory" subjects, and ignores the fact that learning in every discipline is ongoing and developmental. Exploratory learning strategies are appropriate for any subject, but there is no subject that is exploratory alone. At their best, exploratory experiences are windows of opportunity that occur *within the context* of the learning process and that are connected in some way to the subject-matter content. In the arts, "there is content...beyond superficial liking, warm feelings, and a vague belief in their inherent goodness" (Lehman, 1988), and there is a learning process that is more substantial than exploratory.

Third, categorizing a subject area as exploratory and segmenting instruction into short-term blocks ignores much of what has been learned about the needs and characteristics of early adolescent students. One of the basic needs of early adolescence is to feel competent (Lipsitz, 1984). Competence and self-esteem are linked to achievement—to doing well and feeling good about what one is doing. Relegating a discipline to short-term elective course status not only limits opportunities to build skills and understanding, but also denies students the stable, consistent environment required to develop the feelings of accomplishment, self-worth, and identity that are essential to personal growth. What message is sent to students about the value of what they are learning, the meaning and merit of their accomplishments, and the significance of their investment if they must move on to something else after nine weeks or less? Clearly, a short-term course in any subject area meets neither the academic nor the social/personal development goals of the middle school.

Fostering Sequential Learning

Music educators must oppose practices and positions that place music in elective course status at the middle school level. Little is gained in terms of student achievement and attitude or personal and social development by concentrating music instruction in short blocks and abandoning it for the rest of the year. Music educators, however, can and should support middle school general music programs that are based on or include electives *and* that provide continuous music instruction throughout the middle school years. Curricular structures that provide choices accommodating student interest and ability as well as sequentially organized instruction leading to insight and accomplishment are more in keeping with the spirit and intent of the middle school mission.

If a middle school general music program is built on a series of classes students elect throughout the year, what options should be included? General music programs reach a diverse population of students in terms of interest and ability and should offer diverse opportunities. Some electives will be dictated by the needs and demographics of the school and community. Attitude studies and daily experience, however, indicate that students prefer active music making experiences to lecture/discussion classes about historical or theoretical aspects of music (Thompson, 1991). Classes in which students actually participate in the practice of music, whether through performing/practicing, creating/producing, or describing/responding to music in active ways, are more likely to be successful not only because students are interested, but also because they are engaged.

Instrumental Approaches

Playing instruments ranks high as a desirable activity among middle school students (Boswell, 1991). For example, a keyboard approach in general music was preferred by eighth-graders to a nonkeyboard approach (Wig & Boyle, 1982). The researchers noted that "students participating in the keyboard laboratory program developed more positive attitudes toward music, more positive attitudes regarding their own musical skills and abilities, and more positive attitudes regarding themselves as persons." Greater gains in music achievement were also found for students in the keyboard group.

Although there is relatively little documentation of their existence or effectiveness, other instrumental approaches to general music and elective instrumental classes have been developed and are offered at the middle school level. These include guitar, recorder, handbell, keyboard percussion, and electronic keyboard classes. In some schools, introductory classes in band and orchestral instruments afford new possibilities for students who missed the opportunity to begin instrumental instruction at the elementary level and second chances for students who may have started on the wrong instrument. These approaches to general music are most effective when instruction focuses on meaningful musical experience and comprehensive musicianship, not just acquisition of technique.

Using Performance Electives

Performance-based music electives need not be limited to instrumental experiences. Although some teachers have abandoned singing in middle school general music, several researchers have found singing a preferred activity among middle-grade students, particularly when opportunities to sing occur in psychologically and socially safe environments (Gerber, 1987; Nolin, 1988). Vocal electives could include opportunities to sing special repertoire or to participate in all-male or all-female general music class sections. Student experiences in vocal music electives can also be extended outside the walls of the music room by integrating music study with the study of other subjects (theater, language arts) or by participating in community service projects.

In most middle schools, one or more of the typical large ensembles—chorus, band, orchestra—already exists. General music electives might include alternatives in the form of class-size ensembles that study and perform a special repertoire of music. Class ensemble electives could focus on a particular genre or style of Western music or the music of a specific ethnic group or non-Western culture.[1] In the latter instance, music study and performance can be made more effective by drawing on the music-making practices and cultural resources of the local community and by scheduling these electives parallel to the social studies curriculum and integrating instruction when possible.

Composing, Improvising, and Listening

Other electives can be based on composing and creating music or developing improvisation skills. Sound resources for student creative/composition activities have become limitless with the availability of ethnic and traditional instruments, environmental and "found" sounds, and so on. In addition, technology has placed electronic keyboards (and other instruments), synthesizers, sound systems, recording equipment, and computers in the hands of many middle school students. Teachers can capitalize on student strengths and abilities and draw on student interests in creative/composition electives. Critical in these experiences is an "outcome [that is] aesthetically pleasing...in order to be valued" by the students (Gibbs, 1989).

Other elective options can be built around listening and responding to music. If not limited to Western art-music traditions, the possibilities are endless. Various popular and vernacular Western musics can be studied, as can the music of numerous ethnic groups and non-Western cultures. Like the class ensemble electives described above, listening-based electives afford opportunities for integration with other school subjects.

There is a significant body of research that can guide planning and implementation of listening-based electives. Perhaps key to capturing and maintaining student interest is choosing music students find accessible (Hedden, 1988). The results of preference studies indicate that teachers should choose as a starting point music with fast tempi, distinct, driving rhythms, melodies that are conjunct and diatonic, varied dynamic levels, little pronounced dissonance, and a moderate degree of complexity (Finnas, 1989; Getz, 1966; Prince, 1972). In an extensive literature review, Finnas (1989) found certain teaching strategies particularly promising for introducing unfamiliar music to students. Among these, intramusical strategies involve having students identify, describe, and analyze the structural elements of music with vocabulary and terminology that grows increasingly complex as listening skills become more sophisticated. Activities-oriented strategies engage students in the music through playing, singing, or moving. Opportunities for repeated listening also seem to have a positive effect on student attitudes about and preferences for music (Getz, 1966; Prince, 1972).

Reaffirming Middle School Goals

Creating a series of music electives that provide continuous instruction through the middle school years does not guarantee the success of a general music program. One of the dangers is that a curriculum based on electives will become a mere smorgasbord of unrelated classes, and the goal of sequential, developmental instruction will remain unattained. The underpinning for elective courses must be a common curriculum with broad goals on which options can be built. Electives then become related to each other through curricular objectives and musical experiences. One option is to organize middle school general music classes around a tiered or sequential system of required and elective options. In any case, developing and implementing classes and schedules that best serve middle school students will require communication among music educators, other teachers, and school administrators. Fortunately, team planning is one of the goals of the middle school structure.

A curriculum of music electives that provide continuous instruction may be difficult to implement in small schools, schools with only one music teacher, or schools with little scheduling flexibility. Still, these problems need not preclude incorporating elective options into general music classes. Electives can occur within the context of a class by offering students a choice of activities designed to reach specific goals. In these models, students elect or "contract" to work on a specific activity during a designated "lab" time in general music classes. For example, a performance goal might be met by providing a choice of playing experiences on guitars, melodic percussion, electronic keyboards, or recorders. Cooperative learning techniques are particularly useful in these settings.

True music electives, as originally intended in middle school goals and philosophy, remain largely uncharted territory. Recently, the middle school concept has been revisited by various education organizations, and many of the original goals of the middle school movement have been reaffirmed, including elective and exploratory opportunities for students in the middle grades. Now is the time for music educators to reveal the fallacies in thinking that designates music an elective subject. At the same time, we must affirm the possibilities of electives within ongoing music instruction in the middle grades. Exploratory activities and elective courses should lead to new understanding, and that cannot occur if music instruction is abandoned after a few weeks. Music educators must help turn the education community away from the shortsightedness of short-term courses and toward a vision of student growth that occurs with consistent instruction over time.

Building new models for middle school general music will require commitment on many levels, for no single model is likely to serve the needs of all students and all schools. There must be commitment among music educators to the ideas of choice and restructuring the curriculum. Commitment will be required among teachers of other disciplines and school administrators to plan for and implement new courses and scheduling plans. There must be commitment among college music educators to prepare individuals who will be effective teachers and powerful advocates for music in the middle grades. Most important, commitment is required of everyone in the school community to the special needs and abilities of middle-grade students and to the role of the arts in their education and their lives.

Note

1. I have recently observed in public schools that offered learning opportunities as diverse as mariachi ensemble, steel drum band, class jazz ensem-

ble, small-scale musical theater productions, and Brazilian festival music. Although not all were middle schools, the possibilities for middle school electives seem promising.

References

Boswell, J. (1991). Comparisons of attitudinal assessments in middle and junior high school general music. *Bulletin of the Council for Research in Music Education,* no. 108, 49-57.

Braddock, J. H., Wu, S-C., & McPartland, J. (1988). *School organization in the middle grades: National variations and effects.* (Report No. 24). Baltimore, MD: Center for Research on Elementary and Middle Schools, The Johns Hopkins University.

Epstein, J. L., & Mac Iver, D. J. (1990). *Education in the middle grades: Overview of national practices and trends.* (Report No. 45). Baltimore, MD: Center for Research on Elementary and Middle Schools, The Johns Hopkins University.

Finnas, L. (1989). How can musical preferences be modified? A research review. *Bulletin of the Council for Research in Music Education,* no. 102, 1-58.

Gerber, T. (1987). Student perceptions of teachers and teaching. *Update: The Applications of Research in Music Education, 6* (1), 21-23.

Getz, R. P. (1966). The effects of repetition on listening response. *Journal of Research in Music Education, 14,* 178-192.

Gibbs, R. (1989). Another look at creative activities. *General Music Today, 2* (3), 22-32.

Hedden, S. K. (1988). Music listening in grades six through nine. *Update: The Applications of Research in Music Education, 7* (1), 17-18.

Lehman, P. R. (1988). What students should learn in the arts. In R. Brant (Ed.), *Content of the curriculum: 1988 yearbook of the Association for Supervision and Curriculum Development* (109-131). Alexandria, VA: Association for Supervision and Curriculum Development.

Lipsitz, J. (1984). *Successful schools for young adolescents.* New Brunswick, NJ: Transaction Books.

Nolin, W. (1988). Patterns of attitudinal development in general music classes. *Update: The Applications of Research in Music Education, 7* (1), 33-36.

Prince, W. F. (1972). Some aspects of liking responses to junior high school students for art music. *Contributions to Music Education, 29* (1), 47-55.

Saunders, T. C., & Stauffer, S. L. (1989). Music education in the State of Maryland: General music and vocal/choral music survey results. *Maryland Music Educator, 34* (4), 25-33.

Thompson, K. P. (1991). An examination of the consistency of junior high students' preferences for general music activities. *Update: Applications of Research in Music Education, 9* (2), 11-16.

Wig, J. A., & Boyle, J. D. (1982). The effect of keyboard learning experiences on middle school general music students' music achievement and attitudes. *Journal of Research in Music Education, 30,* 163-172.

EXPLORATORY COURSES IN THE FLORENCE PUBLIC SCHOOL DISTRICT

Laura E. Davidson

Florence Public School District One (FD1) is located in central South Carolina. Drawing from both suburban and rural neighborhoods, the district includes 14,631 students ranging from kindergartners through young adults. In this article, Laura E. Davidson discusses the multifaceted program and how it is supported by the administration and the community.

Let's start with the bottom line. The Florence Public School District, in the middle of South Carolina, includes twelve elementary (K–6) schools, three middle schools (7–8), three high schools (9–12), a vocational school, and an adult education center. We have twenty-eight music teachers specializing in the areas of elementary music, band, orchestra, chorus, dance, and drama. The district employs a music coordinator, who also teaches elementary music, band, and strings, and directs the music gifted and talented program.

Certain basic programs are line items in the music budget; these are funded by the district:

- Instrument repair and replacement
- Travel costs (high school)
- Music supply (per capita amount): all levels
- Piano accompanist for high school choral teachers
- Gifted and talented program funding (Education Improvement Act–state mandated)

Exploratory courses evolved in FD1 because teachers, administrators, parents, and students wanted more from the middle school arts experience. When the decision was made to offer exploratory courses in music, it was determined that the cost incurred in setting up the exploratory courses would be shared by the individual school, coordinators, special accounts, students' fees, and the South Carolina Department of Education arts curriculum grants program, called Target 2000. The exploratory courses are all nine-week sessions, with the exception of beginning chorus, which is a one-semester course. In the middle school, we teach guitar lab, keyboard lab, and a music appreciation course that we call "Fun with Music." A week-long mini-course, Introduction to Computer Composition, is offered each year by an artist-in-residence.

Laura E. Davidson is the music coordinator in Florence School District One in Florence, South Carolina.

Why Offer Exploratory Courses?

The development of exploratory courses in Florence District One began as an attempt by school administrators to empty study halls. School administrators and parents find music a worthwhile subject for children. Students placed in nonelected music classes, however, are not necessarily pleased to be there unless the class is interesting to them. The lack of success with the practice of placing students in nonelected music courses caused the FD1 music staff to devise new courses.

The first order of business was the revamping of general music. One middle school teacher created an interesting nine-week course in which the students learned about the development of jazz. After some initial reluctance, the students became involved in a style of music that they found they could really relate to. It came as quite a surprise to many students that the development of jazz was something they found interesting.

The next exploratory course was created because the

model Target 2000 middle school decided to launch a "keyboard lab." Each student brings a personal keyboard to school from home for one nine-week period. This experiment has been highly successful. The students learn basic music notation, chord transposition, and chordal accompaniment for simple songs. They also compare styles of music, are taught how to distinguish forms, and learn to recognize the relationship of style and form. Each student must purchase a textbook. The students in each keyboard lab class give a group recital at the end of the session.

The newest addition to exploratory courses is the guitar lab. Some students bring their own guitars from home. For those students who do not own one, the school provides instruments for use. Each guitar is checked out to a student for the nine-week period. The guitar lab has been the most expensive exploratory course to implement. The cost of instruments is shared by the school and the district. A small student fee is charged to cover string replacement. Each student is required to purchase a guitar method book for class and later personal use. Student purchase of this book helps keep school costs low and encourages students to continue guitar, since they have their own reference to the class.

FLORENCE PUBLIC SCHOOL DISTRICT ONE
319 SOUTH DARGAN STREET
FLORENCE, SOUTH CAROLINA 29506

RENTAL AGREEMENT–SCHOOL-OWNED STRINGED INSTRUMENTS

STUDENT'S NAME ____________________

SCHOOL ____________________

AGREEMENT OF PARENT OR GUARDIAN:

1. I hereby request to rent a school-owned stringed instrument at the rate of $25.00 per semester or $45.00 per year.
2. I agree to replace any strings that may be broken during the year, and to be responsible for any damage or loss that may occur to the instrument while it is in my care.
3. I also agree to return the instrument when requested, without refund of the rental fee, if satisfactory progress is not maintained by the student.
4. I understand that the rental of violins may be limited to one school year or two semesters.

PLEASE SIGN THIS AGREEMENT AND RETURN THE TOP COPY TO THE INSTRUCTOR

DATE ____________________

SIGNATURE OF PARENT OR GUARDIAN ____________________

ADDRESS ____________________ **PHONE** ____________

TO BE COMPLETED BY INSTRUCTOR:

Name of instrument ____________________

Inventory number ____________________

Size of instrument ____________________

Fee paid ____________________

Dates of payment ____________________

Issue date ____________________

Instructor's signature ____________________

Date of return ____________________

Condition upon return ____________________

Copies: Original/White: Instructor Second/Yellow: Parent or Guardian

Figure 1. School form for loaner instruments

A mini-exploratory course with which we have enjoyed considerable success involves the use of our artist-in-education program sponsored by the South Carolina Arts Commission. Tom Law of Columbia, South Carolina, brings fifteen Commodore computers to a different school each year to teach a week-long course in computer composition and graphics.

Sharing the Financial Burden

All exploratory courses we have in place can be implemented at little or no cost to the school if students bring instruments from home. We are looking for funding for permanent keyboard labs to avoid limiting our population to those who own a portable keyboard. Sources of funding that may be available include (but should not be limited to) state arts commissions, arts grants from national organizations, and business adopters.

A rental program in FD1 allows students with financial need to participate in the orchestra program. The school district maintains approximately 120 instruments for student use. A school rental program is easy to manage and makes music available to more students than would otherwise have the opportunity. After the instruments are paid for, the rental fee can accumulate for repair and replacement of instruments. Figure 1 shows the form we use.

Attracting Students to the Program

Recruitment for exploratory courses is very important. Class registration week can be the best shot at reaching students with information about these courses, and the positive attitude portrayed by the music teacher at this time is critical to fulfilling enrollment goals.

During preregistration week, we present concerts during the school day that include the traditional music classes—band, orchestra, and chorus—but we also now include a guitar, keyboard, or jazz band demonstration. Enrollments are increasing in all music classes. The increases are related to new interest in the entire music program, which was probably prompted by the new offerings.

The exploratory courses in Florence District One run for nine-week sessions, with the exception of beginning chorus, which is one semester. The subjects being taught at the middle schools include:

- *Beginning Chorus*—one semester of exploration of two- and three-part singing for seventh graders with an appropriate discipline-based arts curriculum (DBAE) that includes study in aesthetic perception (vocal skills), performance opportunities, historical understanding of the music performed, and critical valuing of music.

- *Guitar Lab*—a nine-week class for seventh- or eighth-grade students. Each student has a partner to learn with. The DBAE curriculum for guitar includes skill development (note and chord reading), performance opportunities, historical information about guitar and the music being studied, and critical valuing, including discussion of guitar as a "lifelong" instrument.

- *Keyboard Lab*—a nine-week class to which students bring in their own keyboard for daily instruction. As with the guitar lab, a DBAE curriculum is followed. Students give a recital for parents at the end of the course.

- *Music Appreciation*—a nine-week course that gives seventh and eighth graders an overview of specific musical styles and periods. Performance is not required. The main emphasis of this class is critical valuing of music and understanding its historical context.

Mini-Courses

Week-long courses offered within the regular music curriculum is another way to explore new areas of music. In South Carolina, we are fortunate to have an extensive list of artists who are approved by the state Arts Commission and who are qualified to do residence programs in schools. The first computer composition and music graphics residency was offered to Florence students as a one-week course. Students discovered an interest in composition and the connection to art that the computer can offer.

All our middle schools offer jazz education as a mini-course once a week on an after-school basis. The curriculum is currently being written for this offering. Teachers are introducing jazz styles and compositions within their players' abilities. In the 1992–1993 school term, jazz was added at one middle school as a full year course. It has been a very successful outgrowth of the jazz exploratory course.

Florence music teachers meet at least twice each year for in-service sessions. At these meetings, curriculum is a main item on the work agenda. Florence teachers spend much time and thought on curriculum materials to be used and evaluation processes that match their materials and curriculum.

Exploratory materials currently in use and available for student purchase include the periodical *Music Alive* (by subscription), Hal Leonard's *Learning Unlimited* (a guitar method), and the *Alfred Adult Piano Method*. All exploratory teachers use their music budget to purchase current popular literature to enhance their course offerings.

The exploratory and mini-courses in Florence School District One seem to be serving an identified need seen by parents, students, and administrators. Students are now electing music classes instead of being placed in them. Students are getting into and staying in the music program. We are meeting our goals of introducing music to students, creating interest in music, and having fun with musical learning.

Community and school support will determine whether we meet our final goal: to lead children into becoming lifelong consumers and participants of music. We have opened the window for many children; it is our hope that they will learn and enjoy.

CURRICULUM

INSTRUMENTAL MUSIC

DEVELOPING A SUPPORT BASE

James L. Byo

Band and orchestra directors are concerned about the current state and future directions of middle school instrumental music education. The conditions for music in the middle schools in the 1990s are in many cases vastly different than what they were a generation ago. The consensus seems to be that some changes are for the better, but many are for the worse (Dean, 1987; Rohner, 1991). To develop a successful music program, directors must overcome many real and perceived obstacles.

The experts have diverse opinions on how to deal with the problems that plague middle school bands and orchestras. Those who maintain a traditional perspective think they could make things right with more money in the budget, more periods in the school day, more parental support, more clarinet players, less television watching, less Nintendo playing, fewer required courses, fewer athletic opportunities, and elimination of the "wheel program," pop music, and electronic instruments. If this wish list could be granted, we would be thrust back into an era that presumably offered fewer obstacles to success. Obviously, a trip back in time is unrealistic, wishing is unproductive, and less-than-ideal conditions in the school are not likely to be remedied easily.

James L. Byo is professor of music education at Louisiana State University in Baton Rouge.

Another opinion suggests that to focus on "more of this" and "less of that" is to focus on external issues, many of which are outside the control of band and orchestra directors. Perhaps problems in middle-level music education could be solved if directors focus on what they *can* control, namely their approaches to music and to people. People who do this realize that what they do, how they do it, what they say, and how they say it define their ability to make music attractive to students. Their goal is to build a support base by influencing students, parents, and administrators musically and socially so that the music program will be perceived not only as attractive but as indispensable to the school curriculum.

Perhaps the most effective middle school instrumental directors are those who help students connect emotionally with music. These directors evidence a degree of intensity in their approach to the rehearsal. Research literature defines "high-intensity" teaching as "sustained control of the student/teacher interaction evidenced by efficient, accurate presentation and correction of the subject matter with enthusiastic affect and effective pacing" (Madsen & Geringer, 1989, p. 90). This definition encompasses three elements: classroom management skills (sustained control of the student/teacher interaction); knowledge of the subject matter (accurate presentation and correction of the subject matter); and style of delivery (enthusiastic affect and effective pacing).

Implied here is that high-intensity teaching extends beyond the ability to be enthusiastic. Teachers must supplement enthusiastic delivery with subject matter expertise and adequate classroom management skills to be considered "high intensity."

Classroom Management

Few would argue that a predominantly positive rehearsal atmosphere is more pleasant than a highly negative environment for ensemble directors and student musicians alike. But let's assume a worst case scenario—out-of-control student behavior or unacceptable performance quality or both. How can the middle school director possibly be positive under these conditions?

Effective directors think in terms of noticing student behavior and responding appropriately, rather than simply "being positive." They avoid the tendency to respond only to problems by noticing both appropriate and inappropriate behavior. They notice individuals who are sitting tall, paying attention, or playing with a good sound, just as readily as they recognize individuals who are slouching, inattentive, or playing with unacceptable tone quality.

The following principle is useful in the middle school environment: "If you do good things, good things will happen to you. If you do bad things, bad things will happen to you" (Madsen & Madsen, 1983, p. 6). In order to approximate a four-to-one ratio of approval to disapproval—the ratio at which fifth-graders are the most attentive (Kuhn, 1975)—effective directors structure a rehearsal environment that maximizes the chances that students will "do good things" (i.e., behave and perform appropriately).

For example, if the task is to introduce crossing the break on the clarinet or shifting on the violin, the band or orchestra director breaks the activity into small parts and presents one part at a time so that students are literally set up to succeed. As they succeed with each new step, the director is able to say nice things ("be positive") in response (Brophy, 1981; Duke & Madsen, 1991). Students are induced to feel good about their accomplishments, an outlook that is likely to extend to their director, their instrument, their ensemble, and the subject matter of music. When self-esteem is high due to perceived success on an instrument, students are motivated to pursue more and greater challenges (Bloom, 1985; Gottfried, 1985) and discipline problems are reduced.

Effective middle school directors are cognizant of how they use rehearsal time. They structure rehearsals so that students are actively involved in the music making process for a high percentage of the time. They help students learn by doing. In short, this approach provides alternatives to simply telling students what to do. Obviously, an appropriate combination of both—telling and learning by doing—is desirable. For example, so much of what students should be exposed to in music involves development of a musically discerning ear, a process requiring specific instruction (telling) that creates opportunities for students to interact directly with music during performance (learning by doing).

Rehearsal transition periods (times when the music stops and the director talks), "getting ready" time, and ineffectual balance of routine and variety in rehearsal activity can be traps for losing intensity and, consequently, student attentiveness (Witt, 1986; Yarbrough & Price, 1981). Effective directors avoid these pitfalls by speaking precisely and concisely, working at an appropriately brisk pace, and monitoring amounts of routine and variety in order to avoid too much of either.

Many directors who work with beginning instrumentalists adopt a drill routine when using a beginning method book (Dillon & Kriechbaum, 1978). Students are seated in like-instrument rows. A line of music is repeated (without losing a beat) as many times as necessary to complete a sequence alternating between everyone playing and single rows playing. When single rows are playing, nonplaying rows are involved in prearranged counting, tapping, note naming, or singing activities related to the exercise. What originally was an eight-measure exercise taking just seconds to complete becomes a much longer event giving the director time to assume a "notice and respond" role. The class-propelled nature of the activity coupled with the seating arrangement allows the director to move freely in and out of the group, working with individuals on embouchures, hand positions, and postures. This appears to be an effective way of keeping everyone actively involved while offering individual assistance in matters of performance.

Command of the Subject Matter

In addition to classroom management skills, command of the subject matters of music and teaching is required of the "high-intensity" director. Such command encompasses musicianship, instrumental pedagogy, music literature and analysis, conducting, learning theory, and psychology. Not all directors are able to develop the competencies necessary to be a highly effective teacher and musician; mastery in all areas is at best a difficult and ongoing challenge.

However, deficiencies in one or two areas sometimes can be overcome by strengths in others and a tenacious desire to succeed.

Directors at any level must possess a knowledge of the score that makes it possible for them to identify and correct performance inaccuracies. This level of knowledge seems one step removed from the managerial skills required to perform such basic tasks as arranging chairs and stands, ordering buses, and organizing meetings with parents. Knowing the score also goes beyond recognizing the need to make general rehearsal comments such as "watch closely," "listen carefully," "sit up straight," and "pay attention."

The directors who have the most to offer students bring to rehearsal a knowledge of the score that exceeds a strictly performance-based orientation. They understand the ways that the composer has manipulated structural elements in order to achieve unity and variety. They are aware of the work's historical context. They seek and find relationships among structural elements, historical context, and performance skills. They bring a multifaceted perspective that can be achieved only after thoughtful, searching analysis (Battisti & Garofalo, 1990).

In preparation of the score, they notice the theme in augmentation or a motive in sequence; they recognize a slight variation in melodic contour or the return of the first idea scored differently or the use of a suspension to heighten tension at the end of a phrase. Through these activities, they prepare themselves to make informed musical and pedagogical decisions and reduce the need to look at the score constantly during rehearsal.

Preparing the score in this manner can serve as a foundation for a comprehensive approach to the rehearsal, the object of which is to create opportunities for students to experience music not only as performers but as listeners, composers, arrangers, conductors, and as people who are able to think and talk discriminately about music (Garofalo, 1983; Garofalo, 1981). Indeed, ensemble directors who by some definition produce musically literate students bring to rehearsal a knowledge of music that is broader than is perhaps necessary to simply make a band or orchestra perform at or near its potential. They believe that technical proficiency on a third-clarinet part is a first and highly positive step in the direction of a music education; however, this proficiency does not constitute a music education.

Research shows that students who have been exposed to comprehensive musicianship principles applied in a formal, structured way to the rehearsal have acquired conceptual knowledge, aural skills, and performance competencies to a greater extent than students taught in a traditional manner (Garofalo & Whaley, 1979). There is also evidence that comprehensive musicianship can be applied in the rehearsals of beginning bands (Whitener, 1983), junior high bands (Gebhardt, 1974), and middle school bands (Parker, 1975) without having an adverse effect on performance quality.

For directors who have not indulged in detailed score analysis and want to get started, it might be best to focus on perhaps three or four substantial works per year. (Obviously, few directors have the time and energy to approach every score in detail.) Initial efforts in the direction of the musically comprehensive rehearsal might be better received by students if structural and historical elements are introduced unobtrusively, almost in passing. One way to accomplish this is to use musical terminology when speaking about the music (e.g., refer to the return of the first theme rather than letter N; or say, "Trombones, in the antiphonal section, listen to the style of the trumpets and imitate them exactly").

The director's pursuit of comprehensive knowledge in music is an ongoing process, a product of a personal commitment to professional growth. Effective directors seek opportunities to continually expand their musical horizons. They do this in a variety of ways such as regular listening with score in hand to many styles of music (not only middle school literature), reading research, and attending concerts, clinics, and conferences. Among the most effective directors, this professional attitude extends into the choice of beginning method book. Making informed choices among the many available band and orchestra methods is critical, especially when the choice represents a fundamental approach to music teaching and learning (Byo, 1988).

Knowledge of the subject matter extends to one's skill as a performing musician, including one's ability to model characteristic tone and articulation on secondary instruments. Research has shown that directors who are more skillful modelers on primary and secondary instruments and who choose to use these skills as instructional tools produce students who are more skillful performers (Sang, 1987). This is supported by Dickey (1991), who found teacher demonstration-student imitation strategies to be more effective than verbal instruction in middle school students' ability to imitate brief tonal patterns on an instrument by ear and their ability to move rhythmically to recorded music. A multisensory, nonverbal approach is put to practical use in a beginning band series by Froseth (1984) in which the teacher assumes the role of performer and model, and the student is led to experience music through listening, moving, singing, and playing activities.

Conducting is an area that warrants consideration as part of the middle school director's subject matter. Some might ask, "How can middle school students be expected to watch a conductor? They have enough troubles trying to read music and finger notes at the same time. They're certainly not ready to respond to anything other than large, time beating motions." In fact, research indicates something different. Middle school students are not only capable of seeing qualitative differences in conducting gestures but prefer expressive conducting over more strict conducting (Price & Winter, 1990). This would seem to indicate that conducting provides yet another means of communicating musically with middle school instrumentalists.

Conducting either sensitizes or desensitizes the ensemble. A conductor whose eyes are predominantly out of the score and whose motions change according to changes inherent in the music and in the sound of the ensemble will likely induce performers to be responsive and receptive to the conducting act (Yarbrough & Price, 1981). This atmosphere of positive interaction among the conductor, the performers, and the music can be established through the appropriate use of a repertoire of nonverbal gestures. The unfortunate alternative is to desensitize the ensemble through the constant, mindless beating of time and the exclusive use of large gestures.

On the other hand, should a rehearsal involving five second-year violinists be conducted? Should a beginning band always be conducted? Is there a point at which emphasis on watching the conductor might actually impede students' ability to listen and respond to the sounds being produced around them, not to mention the director's ability to teach? It seems that at certain stages it may be more important for the director to be away from the podium, perhaps in the midst of the group, absorbed in his or her role as listener and teacher, rather than as conductor (Neidig, 1990). Simply leaving the podium reduces the distance between teacher and students and allows the teacher to assess individual progress and offer immediate assistance. Effective directors recognize when such behavior will be most helpful to students. With large ensembles, occasional nonconducted rehearsal segments can encourage students to play together by listening rather than watching. This places responsibility for maintaining precision on the students and provides a stimulus for establishing a unified internal pulse.

Delivery of Instruction

In addition to having control of discipline and a command of the subject matter, high-intensity directors have ways of delivering information that are engaging. Some work at a fast pace and are overtly enthusiastic, highly animated, and dynamic. Others are able to achieve intensity in a less aggressive, more soft-spoken manner. Still others engage students by varying their delivery—using a loud voice, then a soft one; or a fast pace contrasted with a slow one. Low-intensity delivery might best be described as a presentation style that evidences, but is not limited to, nervousness, verbal tics, little vocal inflection, and poor eye contact (Cassidy, 1990).

There may be no more immediate or direct way to "sell" the instrumental music program than to have an engaging delivery. With calls for school reform, administrators are under pressure to ensure that students succeed academically. In many cases, if something in the curriculum is forced to take a back seat, it is music. A back-seat position can mean anything from band or orchestra being dropped from the schedule to these ensembles receiving low priority in scheduling and budgetary considerations. Under these circumstances, do your students and their parents perceive instrumental music as something to fight for? The answer may be inextricably related to the ability of the director to use an engaging manner to initiate and nurture the development of positive director/student relationships.

Successful directors deal with adversity by getting students and ultimately parents to respond in positive ways. These directors are well-liked and respected by students (perhaps initially for their engaging personalities, rather than their musicianship). They demonstrate an infectious enthusiasm for music and young people. They are able to exercise classroom discipline. They possess an in-depth knowledge of music and methods of teaching. Therefore, it is not surprising that they are able to attract and retain students despite the challenges of competing student interests.

The desire of students to participate in band or orchestra creates interest and devotion among parents. These parents provide a support system for the director by encouraging student practice, sacrificing time and money for private lessons and attendance at concerts, and volunteering services that benefit the total operation of an instrumental music organization. Administrators often respond to such active involvement from parents with support of their own. When the director behaves in ways that garner support first from students, then from parents, and lastly from administrators, problems of an external nature (e.g., budget, scheduling, competition with athletics) begin to take care of themselves. Effective directors understand that they cannot expect to automatically or unconditionally receive support from the top down (administrative support before parent and student support). Directors need to put forth extreme effort to build a support base. This begins with self-evaluation and is followed by the nurturing of student and parental support.

Thoughtful consideration of the three elements of teacher intensity—classroom management, knowledge of subject matter, and delivery—might stimulate some ideas about how an instrumental teacher can continue to grow as a musician and a teacher. Of paramount importance is the director's desire to grow, the ability to be objective in evaluating his or her approach to people, music, and teaching, and the willingness to adapt or change as necessary. Excellent teaching and musicianship on the part of the director (the process) will define the product: the best possible musical experience for students and one that is valued by parents and administrators.

References

Battisti, F., & Garofalo, R. (1990). *Guide to score study.* Fort Lauderdale, FL: Meredith.

Bloom, B. S. (Ed.). (1985). *Developing talent in young people.* New York: Ballantine.

Brophy, J. (1981). Teacher praise: A functional analysis. *Review of Educational Research, 71,* 5-32.

Byo, J. L. (1988). Beginning band instruction: A comparative analysis of selected class method books. *Update: The Applications of Research in Music Education, 7* (1), 19-23.

Cassidy, J. D. (1990). Effect of intensity training on preservice teachers' instruction accuracy and delivery effectiveness. *Journal of Research in Music Education, 38,* 164-174.

Dean, R. W. (1987). ASBDA national survey of the middle school concept as it affects school bands. Paper presented at the American School Band Directors Association National Convention, Interlochen, MI.

Dickey, M. R. (1991). A comparison of verbal instruction and nonverbal teacher-student modeling in instrumental ensembles. *Journal of Research in Music Education, 39,* 132-142.

Dillon, J. A., & Kriechbaum, Jr., C. B. (1978). *How to design and teach a successful school string and orchestra program.* San Diego: Kjos West.

Duke, R. A., & Madsen, C. K. (1991). Proactive versus reactive teaching: Focusing observation on specific aspects of instruction. *Bulletin of the Council for Research in Music Education, 108,* 1-14.

Froseth, J. D. (1984). *The comprehensive music instructor: Listen, move, sing, play for band.* Chicago: GIA.

Garofalo, R. J. (1983). *Blueprint for band.* Fort Lauderdale, FL: Meredith.

Garofalo, R. J. (1981). A new plan for concert band. *Music Educators Journal, 67*(8), 32-39.

Garofalo, R. J., & Whaley, G. (1979). Comparison of the unit study and traditional approaches for teaching music through school band performance. *Journal of Research in Music Education, 27,* 137-142.

Gebhardt, L. R. (1974). The development and evaluation of an integrated plan of study providing for increased musical perception and skills by students in the junior high school band (Doctoral dissertation, Indiana University). *Dissertation Abstracts International, 34,* 4312A.

Gottfried, A. E. (1985). Academic intrinsic motivation in elementary and junior high school students. *Journal of Educational Psychology, 77,* 631-645.

Kuhn, T. L. (1975). The effect of teacher approval and disapproval on attentiveness, music achievement, and attitude of fifth-grade students. In C. K. Madsen, R. D. Greer, & C. H. Madsen, Jr. (Eds.), *Research in music behavior.* New York: Teachers College Press.

Madsen, C. K., & Geringer, J. M. (1989). The relationship of teacher "on-task" to intensity and effective music teaching. *Canadian Music Educator, 30,* 67-94.

Madsen, C. H., & Madsen, C. K. (1983). *Teaching/discipline: A positive approach for educational development.* Raleigh, NC: Contemporary.

Neidig, K. L. (1990). How to fix the mistakes and still make music. *BDGuide, 4*(3), 7-10.

Parker, R. A. (1975). A comparative study of two methods of band instruction at the middle school level (Doctoral dissertation, Ohio State University). *Dissertation Abstracts International, 35,* 5451A.

Price, H. E., & Winter, S. (1990). Effect of strict and expressive conducting on performances and opinions of 8th-grade band students. Paper presented at the combined conferences of the Southern Division College Band Directors National Association and National Band Association, Tallahassee, FL.

Rohner, J. M. (1991). Assessing the future of music education. *The Instrumentalist, 46*(2), 14-21, 103.

Sang, R. C. (1987). A study of the relationship between instrumental music teachers' modeling skills and pupil performance behaviors. *Bulletin of the Council for Research in Music Education, 91,* 155-159.

Whitener, W. T. (1983). Comparisons of two approaches to teaching beginning band. *Journal of Research in Music Education, 31,* 5-13.

Witt, A. C. (1986). Use of class time and student attentiveness in secondary instrumental music rehearsals. *Journal of Research in Music Education, 34,* 34-42.

Yarbrough, C., & Price, H. E. (1981). Prediction of performer attentiveness based on rehearsal activity and teacher behavior. *Journal of Research in Music Education,* 29, 209-217.

STRATEGIES FOR INSTRUCTION

Janet M. Tweed

The community of Waunakee, Wisconsin, about ten miles from Madison, has experienced rapid growth in the past twenty years; its character is changing from rural to urban. There are approximately 550 students in the middle school, and the music program is well supported by the community and by parent groups.

Students in the beginning and middle years of instrumental instruction must be active participants in the learning process. They need to see a reason for what they are learning and have short- and long-term goals. To help students in these areas, instructors need a systematic, detailed plan. As more demands are placed upon students in the course of a school year, their instrumental instruction must be well organized and exciting. Students at the middle level, at so many physical, emotional, and intellectual changes, are also often at the beginning of their experience with music performance. They respond to many of the strategies that work with new students of all ages, but organization and attention to students' developmental and social needs are especially important when dealing with middle-level students. I have found the following strategies useful in my work with middle-level students. They will work with any method book; simply be certain that the material covered in the book meets your curriculum.

Individual or Small-Group Instruction

Starting with the first lesson, make sure students have the equipment and supplies they need to make their initial experience in instrumental music a positive and rewarding one. For example, they need a lesson book, a folder to keep all material in, a pencil, and an assignment sheet. They also need specific instrument-related items, such as mouthpiece brushes, reeds, instrument swabs, cleaning cloths, cork grease, slide grease, and valve oil. Take the time in the first lessons to show students how to put their instruments together, take them apart, and clean them. Be sure students understand proper posture and breathing before they produce the initial sounds on their instruments. To help learn posture, I show students the correct posture, then have them sit incorrectly and try to stand without shifting their body weight forward. Then I have them sit correctly and do the same. They learn immediately which posture is better. Next, I ask them to do this exercise while holding their instruments.

For breathing, help the students experience that in order to play a woodwind or brass instrument, they have to breathe differently from what they consider normal breathing. Have them exhale completely and then inhale for a specific count, hold for the same count, and blow out for the same count. Another good exercise is to tape a piece of tissue paper on the end of a straw and have the students blow the tissue straight out for as long as they can in one breath. Similarly, have students hold a small piece of paper on the wall by blowing a stream of air. Use students who have quick success with a new exercise to demonstrate it for the rest of the class.

Next, model for the students the proper way to hold the instrument, form the embouchure, and produce the initial sounds. If you are not proficient on a particular instrument, enlist the help of an older student who is; a fellow teacher or a community member may also be able to do this task.

Once lessons are established and the beginning physical and mechanical elements are understood, students are ready to learn more on their own. Make sure they understand the fingering charts in their books, so if they

Janet M. Tweed is an instrumental music instructor and the Waunakee Middle School music department coordinator in Waunakee, Wisconsin.

have a question at home, they can find the answer without waiting several days or a week to ask you.

Beginning players need to learn how to practice. I tell my students that practice should consist of six parts: doing warm-ups, practicing a skill or technique assignment, rehearsing concert or solo/ensemble music, playing a piece for their own enjoyment, cleaning and storing their instrument, and keeping a record of their practice time. Lesson assignments should always be written down by the student (and the teacher, in a lesson notebook) on an assignment sheet provided by the teacher. This sheet has spaces for the six categories of practicing, as well as for special instructions and enrichment activities.

Another vital element in the success of a child's instrumental experience—especially at the middle level—is parental involvement. Keep parents advised of your expectations for progress, and maintain contact throughout the year with newsletters, telephone calls, written progress reports, and performances by their children. I let parents know that they are always welcome to visit their child's lessons or rehearsals. I also ask students to record their practice times throughout the week and have their parents initial that record. This not only makes the students accountable for their time; it also makes the parents aware of their children's progress. A practice record also helps you determine when intervention is necessary regarding technique or practice habits.

In a group situation, it's sometimes difficult to give individual attention, but try to hear each student alone at each lesson, if only for two measures of an exercise or song. Each time you hear that student, evaluate a different concept (tone, breath support, instrument position, hand and finger position, embouchure formation). I jot down comments on each student on comment sheets in my teacher notebook each week, so I have an accurate, ongoing record for remedial and enrichment purposes, as well as for written reports to parents. I date the comments each time I make them.

Teaching a new song to a group requires a careful approach. I use a technique I call "sing-say-finger-play." The students sing the words with correct pitch, after I have modeled; then they sing the notes using correct rhythm syllables. They finger their instruments and say the names of the notes in rhythm, and finally, they play the song. If the book does not have the words to the songs, find them out and teach them by rote. If this is impossible, instead of singing the words the first time, you can play or sing the song while the students follow the notes in their books. By the time the students have gone through the first three steps, their chances for success in playing are much greater. Encourage them to use this method when they practice at home.

Because not all students learn in the same way or at the same rate, we must be sure that our teaching accommodates all learning styles—visual, aural, kinesthetic, or a combination. I try to present concepts and reinforce them using all of these styles. Know your own learning style, because you will probably teach the way you learn best; you will have to learn to use other methods to reach all students.

Students who learn at a slower rate than the majority of the class are always a concern to the teacher. Remember that some of these students will become the strongest, most musical players, but must have additional time to grasp both the physical and technical aspects of instrument playing. Watch for them, be alert for them, and nurture them.

In our school, we use several strategies to teach and reinforce the students who need extra help. I may record the lesson on an audiocassette so the student may practice with it at home. Sometimes older students serve as tutors during lesson time or rehearsal time. The high school students come to the middle school and work with individuals who need extra help during the school day; they also serve as tutors during the summer program we offer for students who need extra reinforcement, are absent for one or more lessons, or are switching instruments. Middle school students who are making excellent progress also may work with those who are having problems in a particular area. For example: when clarinets students begin to play across the break, there are always some who have trouble. A student who has mastered this technique can work with them and watch their fingers and hands and offer pointers.

Another way I support weaker players is by planning my seating chart carefully. I make sure that the strong players are between the weaker players. By careful seating, you have built in at least two very positive things: there will be a peer model sitting next to each person who needs extra help, and this peer is a nonthreatening person to ask questions of when they arise. Students can learn well from one another.

Students who learn quickly and are always looking for something more to play and learn also require special attention. I give them extra music from the wealth available for students at the beginning and intermediate levels. I notify the parents that their children need additional material because of their high achievement, and I give students the opportunity to perform for their peers and in public. I also direct them to musical opportunities outside the school.

Because writing is an important strategy in the learning process for all students, aiding instruction, reinforcement, and enrichment, I use several work sheets. For example, I have students record new rhythms they learn on rhythm dictation sheets. These sheets become a resource for them, and they allow me to check the students' understanding. I also use tonal dictation sheets right from the beginning to help students see, hear, and write intervals and to prepare them for pattern-recognition exercises.

Solo and ensemble experiences are very important parts of the instrumental program right from the beginning. When teaching an ensemble, make sure everyone learns every part, so they really understand the piece they are studying. Students will rise to the challenge of new notes, new rhythms, and new forms if we show them we have confidence that they can achieve it.

Rehearsal

Running a rehearsal, which usually involves a large number of students, requires different strategies from teaching a small-group lesson. Here are some techniques that have worked for me.

Give all students (including percussionists) the opportunity to play different parts on different pieces, and keep accurate records of who plays each part on each piece. *There should be no first-, second-, or third-part players in middle school.* Dividing them into sections does not challenge them and causes dropouts. You may be surprised at the achievements of the students who are not labeled but rather given equal opportunities to grow technically and musically.

If you have a flat floor in the band room, try seating the students in a circle or in a square, all facing in. Or try putting the percussion in the center and winds all around. Experiment with seating; each arrangement will produce a different sound. With different arrangements, students can sharpen their skills in listening for timbres and textures within the ensemble.

To help students prepare for rehearsal, I provide study sheets for each piece of music we play. I include facts about the composer and/or arranger, historical background, notes about the form, and musical terms to be learned through this piece (for example, staccato, legato, obbligato). These study sheets give the students a context for the music and the reasons for learning a particular piece. When they have that information, they can play their music with greater understanding.

Another way to keep students as informed as possible is to write daily objectives on the chalkboard. This makes the students aware of the reasons for a particular rehearsal; they learn that they have to work hard to meet the daily objectives in order for the music to come together well at the end.

In rehearsal, it's a good idea to remember that learning music is like learning a language. When teaching or discussing music with your students, always use musical terms. Instead of "It should get louder here," try "There should be a gradual crescendo in this phrase." If we use this language frequently, students will be able to expand their music vocabulary.

Assessment of student progress can be problematic in a rehearsal situation. I have found that using short work sheets, review sheets, and check-tests (short, ungraded quizzes—oral or written) helps me immensely. These sheets may contain information about theory, terms and symbols of music, and material covered in a unit. Students love to receive rewards such as colorful stickers on complete and corrected work; they are proud of themselves.

What is the role of performances in an instrumental music program? I think they should be outgrowths of a unit of study. They should be "informances," where the students and director share with the audience what they have learned in the particular unit. I have students announce selections and give some background on the piece being performed. Also, I let certain sections within the band demonstrate a particular skill or concept they have learned recently. In these ways, the audience is quite involved in what the musicians have been learning.

Finally, positive reinforcement is the most valuable tool we have when working with students. When they feel good about themselves and think they have the ability to achieve, they will surpass our expectations. If they hear only negative comments, they will soon lose interest, and we will lose them from the program. There is a rule in our program: The word "can't" is not allowed in the band area. Instead, students may say "I am not yet able to."

ALTERNATIVE APPROACHES TO MIDDLE-LEVEL INSTRUMENTAL MUSIC TEACHING

Robert A. Carpenter

Crestview Middle School is an urban school (Columbus, Ohio) with approximately six hundred students. One of its outstanding characteristics is its frequent use of technology in instruction.

Many instrumental music teachers find themselves in situations where traditional methods of instruction are extremely successful, and there is little need to investigate alternative instructional strategies or curricula. Some middle school and junior high school music programs imitate their high school counterparts and produce outstanding bands, orchestras, and choirs, all full of enthusiastic students. These programs enjoy widespread community support, and the students develop technical proficiency and musical sensitivity in these performing groups.

Other teachers, including myself, find the traditional approaches to instrumental music education less successful than they once were. In my situation, large-group instruction and classes oriented almost solely toward performance did not draw students as much as they did before. Also, because of scheduling issues, gaps in the curriculum, reduced funding, and a changing student population, I was challenged to explore different approaches to music teaching and learning at the middle level. I try to keep the best of the old and incorporate new techniques to involve students. This often means developing a balance between basic music instruction and performance preparation.

Robert A. Carpenter teaches instrumental music at Crestview Middle School in Columbus, Ohio.

As I see it, the more homogeneous the student population is, the better the traditional methods work. As the student population becomes more diverse—economically, ethnically, culturally—new methods and curricula need to be developed. A traditional "melting pot" approach to instruction treats players as interchangeable parts of a larger organization. This works as long as there is a high degree of similarity between individuals. In settings with more diverse student populations, individual differences contribute to a "mosaic" which allows students to capitalize on their unique qualities. Successful instruction combines some student-selected learning outcomes related to a discipline with some universal experiences.

Schedule

One obstacle to the development of performance groups has been the block schedule, which is designed to move students as grade-level groups. If a teacher wants to rehearse a combined seventh- and eighth-grade band, students have to be released from other classes. Some schools have accommodated this need by creating a "flex" period in their schedules. This allows students to participate in activities designed for more than one grade, including music ensembles. Another way to accommodate performing groups in a block schedule is to have a once-a-week floating period. This approach is used in my district. For example, one week the floating period happens Monday morning, the next week it is Tuesday afternoon, and so on. This means that students are not always excused from the same academic class; rather, each academic class is equally inconvenienced.

At the middle school where I teach, the students have ten periods of related arts per week. For the instrumental music program, which includes band and orchestra, the students are released from related arts for three periods each week. This allows students to participate in cross-grade musical groups without missing too many other classes.

The block schedule makes it difficult at times to add classes. For example, many students are interested in keyboard, but it would be hard to add a separate class for them. My solution has been to incorporate these students into beginning instrumental classes. They learn to read music with the rest of the class, and when they have acquired some basic skills, they play a band or string part on a synthesizer. They can play missing instrumental parts or reinforce parts that need more strength. This experience will not replace traditional piano lessons but it does allow students to participate in the school music program and learn basic musical skills using a keyboard.

Curriculum

Another problem relates to the curriculum. There is much more to music than the Western European forms and composers many curricula stress. Given a diverse student population, we need to teach the music of many cultures. To add to the curriculum, I had to learn more about the instruments and musics of various cultures by reading books, listening to recordings, and attending cultural events in the area. Now I incorporate that knowledge into my teaching.

One activity I use is to have students listen to a certain piece of music, for example, an African chant with strong rhythms, and then ask them to create their own music incorporating similar rhythms. Another technique focuses on common elements in the development of music across cultures. For example, we discuss the ritual or ceremonial use of music and musical instruments in various cultures. This helps students learn that music has different roles in different cultures. As a further exercise, I ask them to think about and compose music: what would music related to birth sound like if it were composed today in the United States? What about music for the ceremonies relating to death?

While developing creativity has always been used as a rationale for studying and playing music, in many instances, instrumental music programs have not helped students develop their creativity. If you and ten other students play third clarinet, the last thing the band director wants from you is creativity—your task is to play the part correctly, period. To counteract this tendency, I have the students do a lot of composing. They write melodies, I score them for band or orchestra, and we play them in a concert. Middle school students are inclined to think that the only real music is what they listen to on the radio, but the more they struggle with composition, the more they understand that music is more than that.

Current educational psychology contends that children in the middle grades want to be treated as individuals. To ensure this happens in my classroom, students can choose from a range of activities: some may work in small ensembles, some may listen to tapes, and some may learn keyboard skills with the aid of a computer. Some days I may listen to each one play a scale.

The amount of time devoted to different learning activities varies with the goals of instruction. If a large-group performance is imminent, there will be many large-group rehearsals for the preceding month. If the goal of instruction is solo or ensemble preparation, more time is given to individual or small-group instruction. At first, I was hesitant to allow students to have the freedom to work in that manner. With more experience, I have become better at determining the balance between whole-group, small-group, and individual instruction.

As I see it, once you free yourself from the belief that the point of instrumental music is to learn and perform a handful of new pieces each semester, you can teach all kinds of wonderful things and students can choose the musical activities that most interest them.

Funding

As the competition for existing funds becomes more rigorous, music teachers have to look for new sources while attempting to make better use of what they already have. On behalf of the school, I have applied for and received grants from arts agencies and corporations so students do not always have to go knocking on doors to sell various products. Also, local service clubs such as the Kiwanis, Lions, and Optimists are often eager to demonstrate support for school projects and programs. Unfortunately, their budgets usually are not large enough to completely fund large-scale innovations, but they may be receptive to a collaborative effort where the students raise part of the desired amount and each of the community groups donates a portion. This allows each group to participate without breaking its budget.

For example, early in my teaching I took a position in a school that had no sound equipment. Buying all new equipment with money out of the general budget was out of the question, so I prioritized the equipment needs and connected them to instructional goals. The students raised $500; then I approached a local service club, which contributed another $1,000. The PTA found another $250, and the principal allowed $250 from the general fund. This combination of funds allowed us to buy amplifiers, an electric piano, microphones, and a bass guitar. This was the beginning of the use of electronic music equipment, and each group felt that it had made a significant contribution to the program.

Technology

I use computer technology in several ways when teaching instrumental music. Students are very interested in music technology because it is part of their everyday lives–they see it used on television, and they buy recordings that demonstrate a variety of powerful technologies.

When students are learning solos, they need to rehearse with the accompanist, but this is difficult to arrange on a regular basis. Computer technology can help: the computer plays the accompaniments, and the students play the solos. They can rehearse with the accompaniments as often as they like, right from the beginning, and adjust the tempos as they become more proficient. I also use the computer as a rehearsal aid for small ensembles. For example, if all four parts of a quartet have been sequenced by the computer, when one student is missing, the other three can still rehearse while the computer plays the fourth part.

Computer technology is also useful when students work on interdisciplinary projects. They can create visual images in art class, compose music in orchestra class, and write poetry and scripts in language arts class. All this information can be stored in the computer and integrated into the final project.

Over the years, I have acquired hardware and software to support music instruction. At this point we have three Apple IIe computers with MIDI interfaces, one Macintosh Plus, and one Macintosh LCIII with a MIDI interface. The students also use a Roland D10 keyboard, percussion pads, and wind controllers. This equipment is placed around the band room and arranged into workstations.

The Macintosh computers support sequencing and notation software: to capture and edit musical ideas, *Performer* and *EZ Vision* are used. We use the *Composer* and *Finale* programs to generate parts that can be performed by the various ensembles.

Assessment

As I try to expand the traditional approaches to teaching instrumental music, I have found it necessary to use new forms of assessment which allow me to assess individual and social outcomes. For individual work, I have the students prepare portfolios, which can take the form of a folder or box containing written work or other paper documents (pieces the student has learned, students' compositions). I also use audiotapes and videotapes of their performances, made with equipment in the music room. These recordings demonstrate improvement in tone, musical performance, and stage presence. After recording, I listen or watch the tape with the student and make observations about pitch, rhythm, tone, tempo, and other elements.

This kind of assessment is useful to me, but it may even be more useful to people without musical background. Music teachers can hear students play or sing often and thereby assess progress. Parents, administrators, and other teachers who do not hear the students perform as frequently can see and hear progress on recordings.

In terms of assessing social outcomes, when students work in small ensembles (for performances or interdisciplinary projects), I have them assess each other's participation by using questions such as: was the work distributed fairly? Did each do his or her part? Were conflicts resolved in a reasonable way? Of course, I monitor the process to make sure they don't turn it into a popularity poll. By assessing the contributions of each member, students learn to pick the best members, who may not necessarily be their friends, for their group the next time they have the chance.

As students who enter middle school music programs change, teachers will need to investigate new approaches to instruction. We will have to see whether the present methods of grouping students help them learn academic, musical, creative, and social skills. Perhaps we will supplement bands and orchestras with other ensembles to provide avenues for more students to be involved and to learn to love music. Teachers will need to expand their knowledge of new technologies, deepen their understanding of the middle school child, and learn how to teach students of various cultural backgrounds.

VOCAL MUSIC

CHANGING VOICE

Lynne Gackle

Teaching choral music in middle-level education is some of the most challenging and rewarding work choral directors can encounter. In recent years, greater awareness has developed among music educators concerning the expressive use of the child voice. The link between teaching young children to sing and the success of our high school and collegiate choirs is the middle-level singer. At this level, the young adult voice emerges and expressive sensitivity starts to mature. Unfortunately, at this level we often experience a decline in enrollment in our programs because students have lost interest in singing. Girls and particularly boys often find singing uncomfortable and become frustrated with their emerging new voices. Their perceptions of their changing voices also change, and many times the singing experience is less pleasant than when they were younger. Also, boys may perceive singing as less than masculine–fine for children, but not for them now.

As middle-level choral educators, we must become experts on the adolescent voice. We must understand this young voice and its development as thoroughly as we understand the rudiments of music. We must also become as knowledgeable as possible concerning all facets of adolescent development: emotional, physical, and psychological. By understanding the development of the adolescent voice, we can better choose literature with which our young people will find greatest success.

Lynne Gackle is adjunct assistant professor of music education at the University of South Florida in Tampa.

When we combine this information with voice-building techniques, we can begin to train the young voice in a healthful, efficient manner. This means allowing the natural voice to develop to its fullest. We need to have in our mind's ear a concept of how healthy, developing voices actually sound. It is not necessary to try to make them sound "older" or become something they are not. We must help our middle-level singers understand that each voice is unique and therefore grows uniquely. A primary focus of our teaching should always be healthy, efficient singing that promotes vocal development.

Often, many beginning choral teachers approach middle-level teaching with a bit of anxiety because they lack hands-on experience with this young voice. Understanding this voice and its development is vital to successful teaching at the middle level. When the teacher combines this information with methodic organization of the rehearsal–considering both *musical* and *vocal* goals generated from carefully selected, quality literature–the young singer benefits from teaching that is more succinct, comprehensive, and consistent.

Symptoms of Adolescent Voice Change

Much study has been given to the male changing voice. Stages of change, characteristics of each stage, methods of classification, strategies for teaching boys whose voices are changing, as well as the psychological issues that affect adolescent boys have been researched (Finn, 1939; McKenzie, 1956; Naidr, Zboril, & Sevcik, 1965; Cooper & Kuersteiner, 1973; Swanson, 1977; Cooksey, 1977b; Groom, 1979; and Cooksey, Beckett, & Wiseman, 1983).

Only minimal information exists concerning the adolescent female voice. Recently, however, there has been increasing recognition that the female voice also changes, though not as dramatically (e.g., the octave phenomenon) as the male voice. Various facets of this change have been the focus of scientific study (Cyrier, 1981; Huff-Gackle, 1987; and Williams, 1990).

In both the male and female voice, the following symptoms of change may be present:

- insecurity of pitch
- development of noticeable register breaks
- increased huskiness
- decreased and inconsistent range capabilities
- voice cracking (breaking)
- hoarseness
- uncomfortable singing or difficulty in phonation

Physiological Changes in the Adolescent Voice

One of the first indications of voice change in the young voice is a slight huskiness or breathiness in the voice. Vennard (1967) describes the openness in the glottis (the space between the vocal cords) and notes that this gap or "mutational chink" represents a weakness due to immaturity of the interarytenoid muscles and is heard as a rustling of air through the opening. This characteristic is especially noticeable in the female voice.

Increased size of the larynx and vocal cords causes a general lowering in range capabilities. Weiss (1950) observed that the principal difference between the development of the male and female larynx concerns the direction of laryngeal growth. Prior to puberty, the larynxes of both sexes are equal in size. During pubertal development, the male larynx grows primarily in the anterior-posterior (front to back) directions, accommodating the lengthening of the vocal cords and resulting in the protrusion of the thyroid cartilage or Adam's apple. The female larynx increases more in height than in width. As the final stages of vocal maturation occur, the vocal cords of both sexes increase in length (though length is greater in the male), ultimately yielding greater range capability.

Other growth changes noted by Weiss include greater breath capacity due to growth of the chest cavity, lengthening of the vocal tract, and development of the oral-facial structures related to resonance. Weiss noted that these anatomical developments result in greater vocal power, depth, and resonance capabilities.

Adolescent physiological growth is predictable, understandable, and measurable. Some changes that can be used as indicators or predictors of voice change are overall physical growth, skeletal development, appearance of secondary molars, growth of pubic hair, growth of facial hair in boys, breast development in girls (the first observable characteristic in the developmental sequence), and the onset of menstruation (menarche).

Obviously, we as teachers are limited in our ability to observe all these physiological changes. But if we have a general knowledge of adolescent development, we can better anticipate vocal growth in our students. Given current growth trends, we may expect to find voice changes occurring earlier. Teachers are observing voice change in elementary school rather than middle school. Rutkowski (1985) observed that boys generally progress through the vocal stages outlined by Cooksey (1977b), but noted that they consistently entered the climax of change and the New Baritone stage one year earlier than originally reported by Cooksey. According to Tanner (1972), the average age of menarche in the 1940s was fourteen. He notes that menarche is occurring three to four months earlier each decade. If Tanner's research findings are correct, the average age of menarche now is approximately twelve.

In both male and female voices, the speaking voice gradually lowers, signaling vocal maturation. Research indicates that postmenarcheal adolescent females exhibit not only higher incidence of voice breaks and

Comparison of Male and Female Adolescent Voice Change

Feature	Male Voice	Female Voice
Pitch (Lowest)	Lowers an octave	Lowers a third
(Highest)	Lowers a sixth	Rises slightly
Resonance	Lacks focus; husky, breathy	Lacks focus; husky, breathy
Range	Lowers and decreases	Stays within the same basic range; tessituras decrease and fluctuate; range finally increases
Register Development	Lift points change; falsetto becomes apparent	Lift points change; adult passaggios become apparent
Vocal Instability	Yes	Yes
Quality	Changes dramatically	Changes slightly, mostly in timbre, weight, and color
Laryngeal Growth	Greatest growth is in width	Greatest growth in height

Figure 1. Male and female vocal changes

increased breathiness in the singing voice, but also a lower singing range and lower speaking pitches than did premenarcheal girls, suggesting that the onset of menarche may be associated with a period of vocal instability in addition to a lowering in average speaking pitch (Duffy, 1970; Williams, 1990).

See figure 1 for a brief comparison of male and female voice change.

Stages of Voice Change: Males

Cooksey (1977) described six stages of voice maturation (figure 2).

Figure 3 shows the average ranges and tessituras for the stages of voice change outlined above. Because the ranges given are averages, some slight variances may occur from one individual to another.

Cooksey, Beckett, and Wiseman (1983) conducted a three-year, longitudinal study of the male changing voice that confirmed the validity of these classification guidelines. They used criteria of total pitch range, tessitura, voice quality, register development, and average speaking pitch.

Stages of Voice Change: Females

Gackle (1991) has studied the adolescent female voice for more than a decade. Using criteria similar to those of Cooksey, Beckett, and Wiseman (1983) and based on years of observation, Gackle identified developmental stages for use as guidelines in classifying the adolescent female voice (figure 4). (The author is in the second year of data collection for a five-year longitudinal study to determine the validity of these classification guidelines.)

Figure 5 (next page) indicates the approximate ranges and tessituras outlined above. Again, the ranges are averages and therefore, slight variations may occur from one individual to another.

A Formula for Success

The obvious question is, "How do we take this information and make it useful within the classroom?" Our goal as middle-level choral music educators is to provide an enriching choral experience. We can create a formula for success by integrating four elements: classification, literature selection, voice building, and organization.

Stages of Voice Changes in Males

Maturational Stage	Voice Classification
I	Unchanged (premutational)
II	Midvoice I (initial period of voice change)
III	Midvoice II (high mutation period)
IV	Midvoice IIA (climax of mutation and key transitional period)
V	New Baritone (stabilizing period)
VI	Settling or Developing Baritone (postmutational development and reexpansion period)

Figure 2. Six stages of male vocal change

Stages of Voice Changes in Females

Maturational Stage	Voice Classification
I	Prepuberty (unchanged)
IIA	Pubescence/Premenarche (beginning of mutation)
IIB	Puberty/Postmenarche (peak of mutation)
III	Young Adult Female/Postmenarche (timbre begins to approximate that of the adult female)

Figure 4. Four stages of female vocal change

Quarter notes indicate average tessituras.

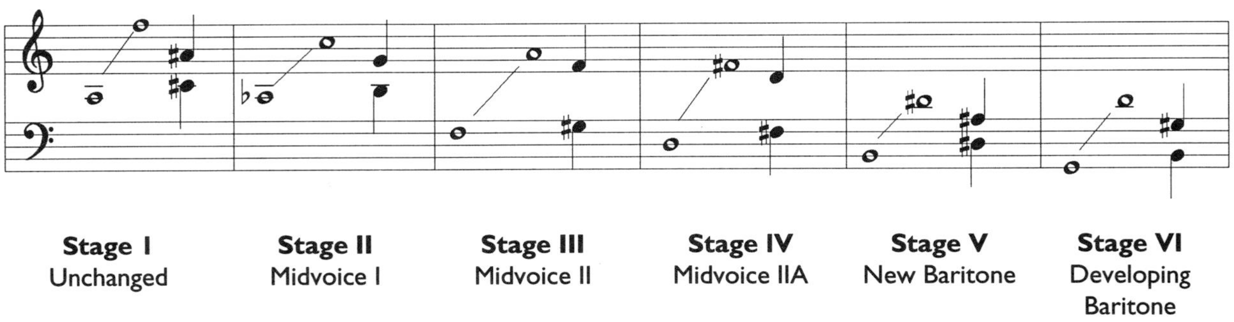

Figure 3. Average ranges and tessituras during male vocal change

Classification of the adolescent voice. The first step to success in the middle school choral program is correct classification of the young voice. The aim is to classify the young singer's stage of development based on range, tessitura, vocal quality, register development, and speaking pitch. When we understand what stage of development each singer is at, we can better select range-appropriate literature. We can also combine this information with voice-building techniques to train the young voice in a healthful, efficient manner. Figure 6 is adapted from Cooksey (1992) and shows the composite ranges and tessituras that are most appropriate for adolescent voices (approximately grades six–ten) and is based on the stages of development outlined by Cooksey and Gackle. "Composite" refers to the notes that are held in common (that is, within each range) by each stage of vocal development (male and female). Specific stages are indicated below each voice part.

Once the vocal ranges of each stage are understood, the information can readily be applied to other voicings. For instance, notes held in common by all voices (whether at actual pitch or an octave apart) include only from about B to G (A), with a comfortable tessitura of only from approximately B to F. Obviously, the composite unison singing range is quite limited and therefore finding limited range literature is quite difficult.

Some other composite ranges identified by Cooksey include two-part and three-part music (see figure 7, next page).

Publishers are currently answering the need for more music for middle school through the use of the "three-part mixed" voicing. This differs from the SAB voicing in figure 7 in that the third part generally spans from about G below middle C to F above middle C. A composite voicing for three-part mixed music is shown in figure 8 (next page).

While the availability of more quality three-part mixed literature is a blessing for most middle school programs, where Midvoice II and IIA classifications abound, it is important to remember that in junior high programs with older eighth and ninth grade boys, this voicing presents a problem for the new and developing baritones. The tessitura is obviously too high. In that case, the soprano line may be doubled an octave lower, or one may find more success with carefully selected SATB literature which accommodates the ranges of the older developing male voices.

It is important that teachers listen to their students at regular intervals in order to evaluate their vocal development. The change process, though gradual, occurs at different rates in different individuals. By using the criteria previously mentioned (range, tessitu-

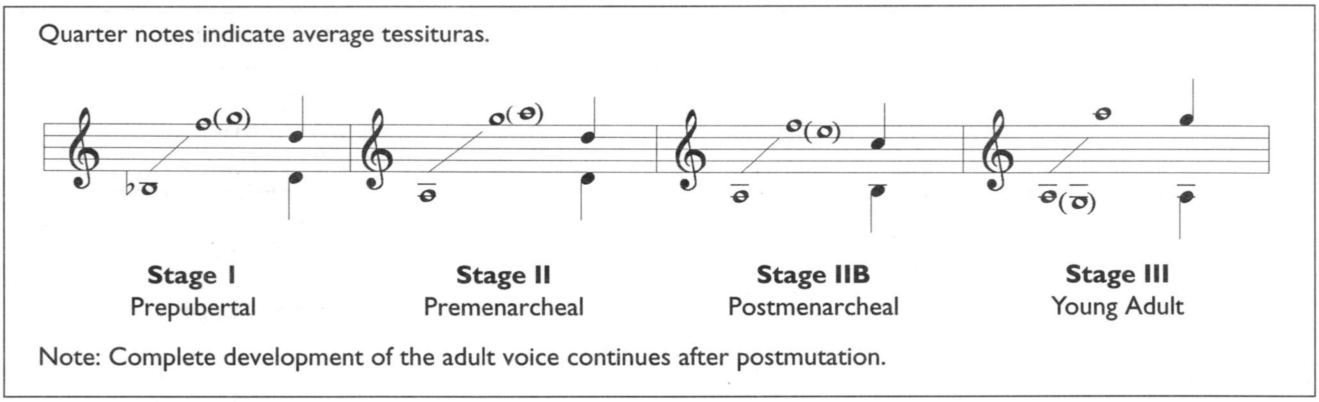

Figure 5. Approximate ranges and tessituras during female vocal change

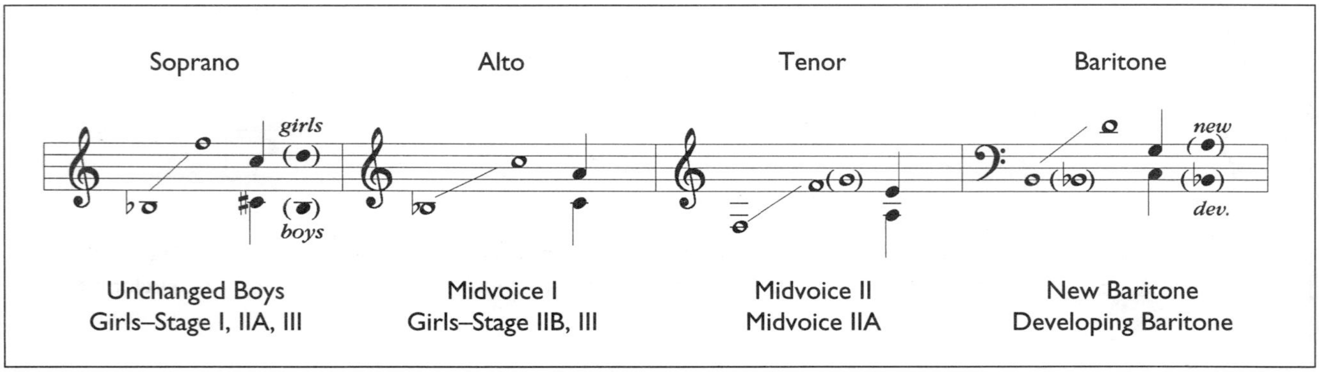

Figure 6. Composite ranges and tessituras for specific voice parts

ra, speaking pitch, vocal quality, register development), teachers can assess the young voice throughout its mutations.

Considerations for literature selections. Once the developing voices have been classified, selection of range-appropriate literature becomes more obvious. In addition to range-appropriateness, other considerations for choosing literature include:

- tessitura of each voice part;
- agility requirements (because the developing voice is often unstable, negotiating large intervals can be difficult and uncomfortable for the young singer);
- frequency and difficulty of register changes;
- length of phrases;
- appropriateness of text.

Finding quality literature that reinforces good technique and aids in the development of good vocal habits should be a key goal of the selection process.

Voice building. The third component of the formula for success includes the use of voice-building techniques within the choral rehearsal. This is especially important when working with young singers. The incorporation of vocal exercises derived directly from the music is an efficient rehearsal method that allows for maximum stylistic, textual, and ultimately, expressive considerations to be realized in the performance of the music (Corbin, 1983; Coker, 1984).

Through the use of a systematic approach to vocal development–including consistent techniques for relaxation, correct posture, breath management,

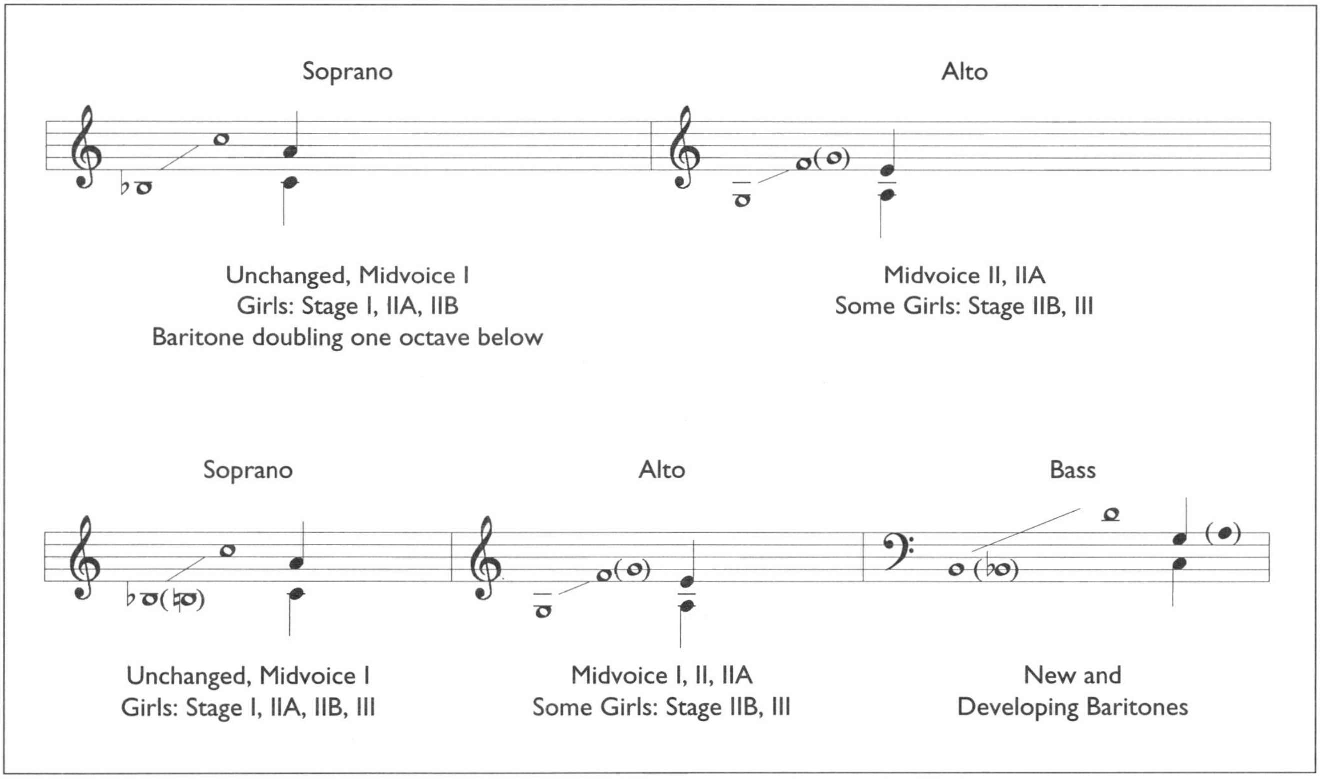

Figure 7. Composite ranges for two- and three-part music

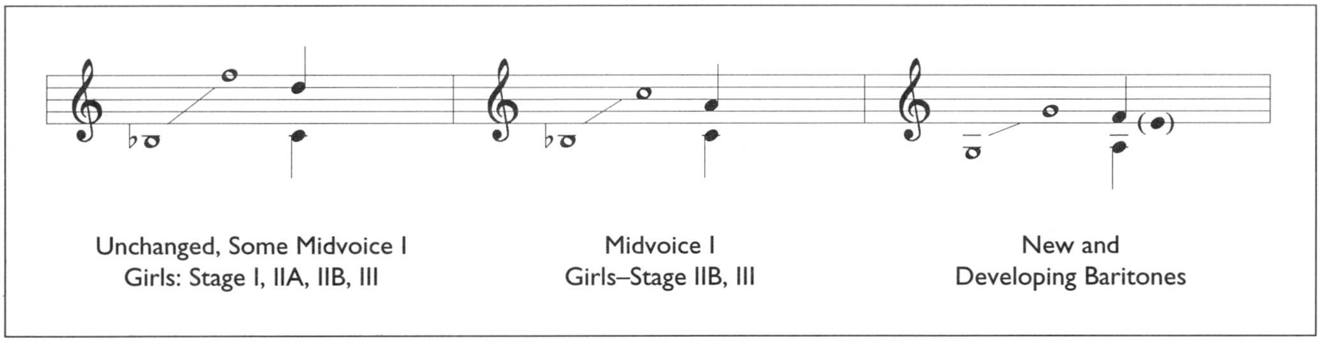

Figure 8. Composite ranges for three-part mixed music

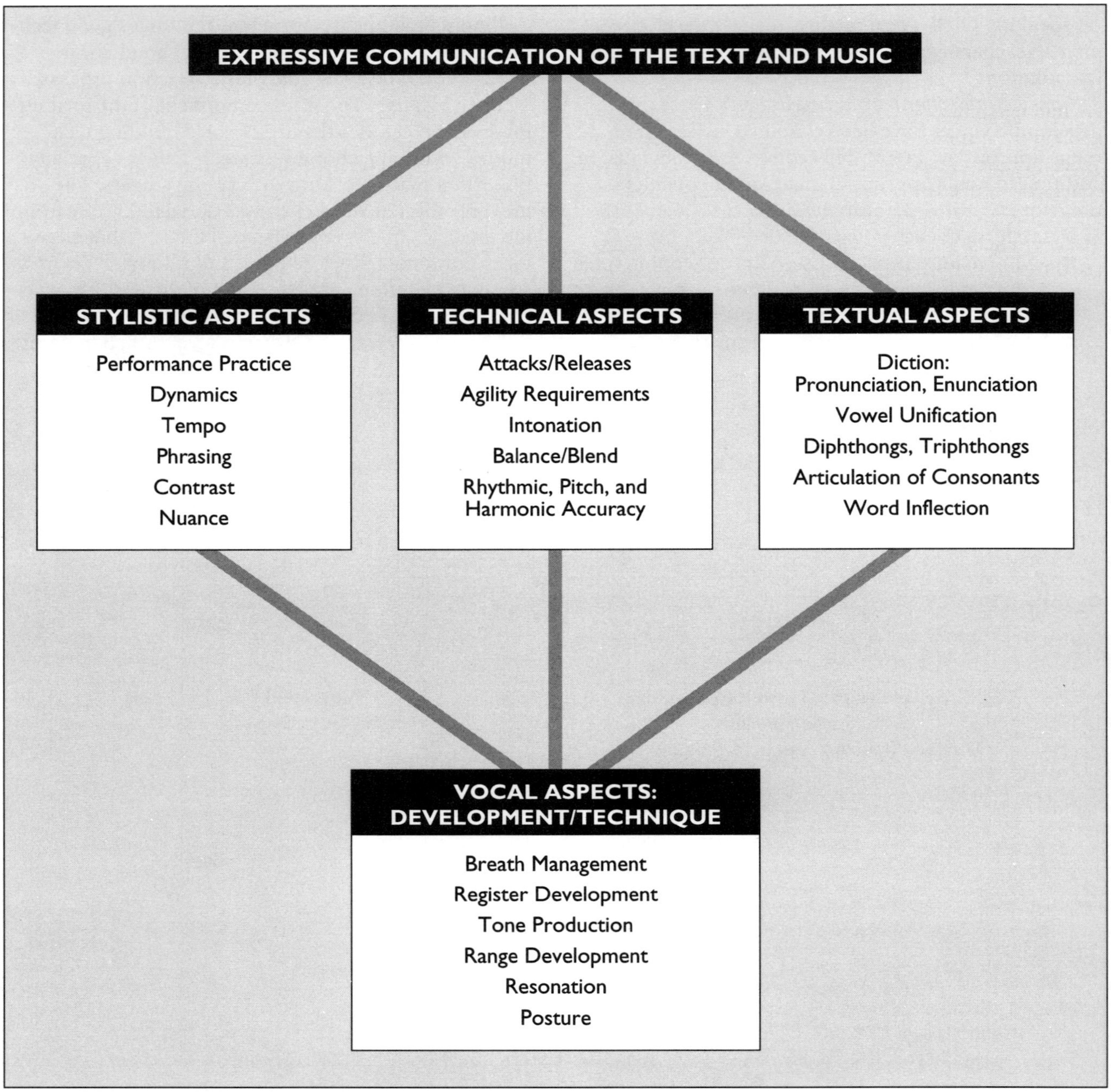

Figure 9. Aspects of expressive communication of the text and music

breath/voice connection, breath/tone connection, development of resonance, agility and range extension, and diction (vowel unification and articulation of consonants)–skills can be attained that not only encourage expressive, beautiful singing, but also foster healthy vocal development and hygiene. These goals are basic to the choral art. The need for such goals is never more apparent than during these strategic adolescent years. Figure 9 indicates the relationship between the musical and vocal aspects leading to expressive communication of the text and music.

It is virtually impossible to achieve correct style without the development of vocal technique. Figure 9 shows how the development of such skills is basic for all stylistic, technical, and textual aspects involved in expressive singing. For example, imagine singing a sustained, legato phrase from a Renaissance piece without first understanding the basic skills involved in breath management. Too often, we discuss the "breathing process" for the first two weeks of school and then assume that our students understand the concept and will use it from that point on. But singing is a psychomotor function that involves coordination between the brain and various muscle groups. It is unfair to expect students to grasp such concepts without adequate time for building and reinforcing those skills.

A football coach would never assume that the players had mastered exercises for strengthening, running, and agility within the first two weeks of a season. Voice building involves a similar approach. We are coaches—vocal coaches. In fact, we are probably the only voice coach or teacher that most of our students will ever encounter. It is our responsibility to instill good technique, encourage development of individual ability, and help students acquire good vocal habits.

Organization. Finally, by organizing our rehearsals according to specific objectives, we can create a more efficient, accountable method of teaching. Through identifying *musical* and *vocal* objectives we can create lesson procedures that include consistent rehearsal techniques that facilitate musical learning, encourage healthy vocal development, and help to create a musically sensitive instrument—the middle school chorus.

References

Coker, T. (1984). Choral warm-up exercises as a key to teaching music literature and vocal technique (Doctoral dissertation, University of Southern Mississippi, 1984). *Dissertation Abstracts International, 46/06,* 1549A. (University Microfilm No. DA 8518316).

Cooksey, J. M. (1977). The development of a continuing, eclectic theory for the training and cultivation of the junior high school male changing voice—Part II. *Choral Journal, 18* (3), 5-16.

Cooksey, J. M. (1992). *Working with the adolescent voice.* St. Louis: Concordia.

Cooksey, J. M., Beckett, R. L., & Wiseman, R. (1983). *A longitudinal investigation of selected vocal, physiological, and acoustical factors associated with voice maturation in the junior high school male adolescent.* Paper given at the 1983 National American Choral Directors Association Convention, New Orleans, Louisiana.

Cooper, I. O., & Kuersteiner, K. O. (1973). *Teaching junior high school music* (2nd ed.). Conway, AK: Cambiata.

Corbin, L. A. (1982). Vocal pedagogy in the choral rehearsal: The influence of selected concepts on choral tone quality, student understanding of the singing process, and student attitudes toward choir participation (Doctoral dissertation, Ohio State University, 1982). *Dissertation Abstracts International, 43,* 2485A.

Cyrier, A. (1981). A study of the vocal registers and transitional pitches of the adolescent female. *Missouri Journal of Research in Music Education, 4* (5), 84-86.

Duffy, R. J. (1970). Fundamental frequency characteristics of adolescent females. *Language and Speech, 13,* 14-24.

Finn, W. J. (1939). *The art of the choral conductor* (Vol. 1). Evanston, IL: Summy-Birchard.

Gackle, L. (1991). The adolescent female voice: Characteristics of change and stages of development. *Choral Journal, 31* (8), 17-25.

Groom, M. D. (1979). A descriptive analysis of development in adolescent male voices during the summer time period (Doctoral dissertation, Florida State University, 1979). *Dissertation Abstracts International, 40,* 4946A.

Huff-Gackle, M. L. (1987). The effect of selected vocal techniques for breath management, resonation, and vowel unification on tone production in the junior high school female voice (Doctoral dissertation, University of Miami, 1987). *Dissertation Abstracts International, 48(04),* 862A.

McKenzie, D. (1956). *Training the boy's changing voice.* New Brunswick, NJ: Rutgers University Press.

Naidr, J., Zboril, M., & Sevcik, K. (1965). Die pubertalen veranderungen der stimme bei jungen im verlauf von 5 jahren [Pubertal voice changes in boys over a period of 5 years]. *Folia Phoniatrica, 17,* 1-18.

Rutkowski, J. (1985). Final results of a longitudinal study investigating the validity of Cooksey's theory for training the adolescent male voice. *Pennsylvania Music Educators Association Bulletin of Research in Music Education, 16,* 3-10.

Swanson, F. J. (1977). *The male singing voice ages eight to eighteen.* Cedar Rapids, IA: Igram Press.

Tanner, J. M. (1972). Sequencing, tempo and individual variation in growth and development of boys and girls aged twelve to sixteen. In J. Kagan & R. Coles (Eds.), *Twelve to sixteen: Early adolescence* (pp. 1-24). New York: W. W. Norton.

Vennard, W. (1967). *Singing: The mechanism and the technic.* New York: Fischer.

Weiss, D. (1950). The pubertal change of the human voice. *Folia Phoniatrica, 2* (3), 126-159.

Williams, B. B. (1990). An investigation of selected singing- and speaking-voice characteristics through comparison of a group of pre-menarcheal to a group of post-menarcheal girls (Doctoral dissertation, University of North Texas, 1990). *Dissertation Abstracts International, 51(05),* 1544A. (University Microfilms No. DA9027739).

THREE KEYS TO TEACHING STUDENTS WITH CHANGING VOICES

Jeanne Julseth-Heinrich

Madison Junior High School enrolls 1,100 students, and 460 of them participate in the choral program. At this urban school, all seventh- and eighth-grade students are required to take a music course.

The junior high voice is a valuable instrument. In my twenty-four years of teaching junior high choirs, I have gained some insight on how to keep these voices going. There are three keys to guiding these young voices and maintaining students' self-esteem in the process: choose quality literature, monitor the voice on a daily basis, and exercise the voice as it changes.

Choose Quality Literature

Quality literature is the textbook from which we teach; that's why it is so important to choose literature carefully. Pieces that have stood the test of time work best. Four-part literature, especially at the eighth-grade level, is the best avenue to quality voicing for the changing middle-level voice. Girls will be challenged by the soprano and alto lines, and a boy can go through all four parts during his voice change. This means that no one is forced to sing in an impossible range.

Renaissance madrigals provide a fine source of quality literature. Madrigals are very rhythmic. The students enjoy that aspect, as well as the interesting texts. When the texts are in foreign languages, there is added interest.

Jeanne Julseth-Heinrich teaches vocal music at Madison Junior High School in Appleton, Wisconsin.

There are other advantages to using madrigals. The harmony parts are predictable; students can sing them with confidence. The bass part usually outlines a solid I–IV–V progression with just a hint of chromaticism to make the part interesting. The tenor line lies in the boy's upper register, and with its six-note range, boys whose voices are beginning to change can usually sing it. The altos and sopranos explore the upper registers of their voices. Finally, the repetition of the "fa-la-la" sections gives the four parts an opportunity to tune to each other.

To help students understand the concept of tuning to each other, I ask pairs of students within the same section to stand facing each other. Each watches the other's mouth, paying special attention to vowel formation. This exercise also works for two groups of students within a section; for example, the first row can turn around and face the second. Another technique I use to help the choir sound as one is to practice unison octaves. The sopranos and the tenors sing octaves and try to blend the sound, and the altos and basses do the same.

Monitor the Voice Daily

Listen to each singer daily. You can do this by standing near students when they are singing with the entire group, by having them sing in a trio or quartet, or by asking each one to sing alone. Once a quarter, I hear each student individually, either in person or on a tape. I ask them to sing exercises for me, and I listen for signs of vocal change: breathiness, huskiness, or changes in tone quality. If a student is absent, he or she makes a tape at home and brings it in so I can monitor the progress.

I also use tapes to keep track of the students' vocal development and for grading. Each quarter, students must prepare a tape on which they sing several exercises and their own part on two songs to demonstrate that they know the music. When I am listening to the tape, I use a short form to rate the student's mastery of correct notes, rhythms, intonation, and vowel formation. I give each person a written critique.

Taking the time to listen to each singer sends a clear signal that you value all the voices in the choir. This small detail can give hope to students who may feel discouraged by their changing voices. I tell the students that just as their bodies are changing, so are their voices. Boys' voices change the most, of course, but girls need to be aware of vocal change as well.

Have the students monitor their own voice changes. Keep a worksheet in each choir member's folder. Let them keep track of their highest and lowest notes. I also ask them occasionally to describe the sound of their voice or the sound of their section, listening for vibrato, breathiness, and tone quality.

Another technique for students' monitoring of their voices is "voice mail." To earn extra credit, they sing with each other on the phone. For example, I will ask a leader in the soprano section to call a singer who is having some difficulty. I give them a specific assignment, such as "Work on the intonation of these four measures." I use "voice mail" on a regular basis, but the pairs of students are random and for that day only. I ask students to limit the calls to five minutes. Because the sound is going directly into the ear, it is easy to listen carefully and give feedback on the quality of the sound.

Exercise the Voice as It Changes

Our bodies need daily exercise, and so does the singing voice. Choral warm-ups should include exercises that give the voice flexibility, volume control, breath control, and latitude in range. To help students through the vocal changes, I say things like "Never sing louder than beautiful," and "Breathe from the bottom of your feet." Also, I try to help them see the differences between speaking and singing. As they are walking to choir class, I tell them to say "I'm going to choir now" very slowly, exaggerating every vowel and consonant. This helps them mentally get ready to sing.

The choir should also take time to sing unison, familiar songs. Rounds and canons help keep middle-level voices flexible and most important, together, because of the repetition of particular vowels. The choir is a team. A changing voice alone can be soft and breathy, but with a group, it becomes a voice of power and unity.

Students who sing out of tune need special exercises. For example, I have them match my pitch using the vowel "oo," then move to "ah," then to "oh." They should not sing with the choir until you have worked with them—other choir members can be very cruel when placed next to an out-of-tune singer. I write a student who is out of tune a note or speak with him or her briefly after class. Sometimes during class I will send a weaker singer into the practice room with a stronger singer and ask them to do specific exercises. Another approach is to record exercises on tape, and ask the student to practice at home.

In addition to working on exercises with them yourself, assign a "telephone tutor" to the out-of-tune singer. The tutor calls the person and sings pitches; the weaker singer tries to match pitch. Again, with the sound going directly into the ear, the telephone can be an effective tool in helping students learn to sing well.

All choral instructors at the middle level need to keep their expectations high. When students have experiences of success, their self-esteem and confidence levels increase, and they learn that they can sing well even during the awkward time of vocal change.

GENERAL MUSIC

PRESENT AND FUTURE

David E. Myers

The music education profession places great importance on general music for early adolescents. In its Statement of Beliefs (MENC, 1991a), MENC says that "general music classes should be required of all students through grade eight including those who participate in performing groups" (p. 2). The report of the National Commission on Music Education (1991) declares: "Every child in every school must receive a balanced, sequential, high-quality program of music" (p. 30). And MENC's Future Directions (1991b) calls for "high-quality music programs in America's middle schools" (p. 4).

Over the last three decades, during which junior high schools have given way to middle schools, developments in early adolescent general music have emphasized intrinsic musical values and aesthetic expression. The association of music education with fields such as aesthetics, learning theory, and developmental psychology has spawned programs that integrate musical knowledge, expressive outcomes, the nature of music learning, and the developmental characteristics of students. The instructional value of the activities approach, i.e., listening, singing, playing, creating, and moving, has been strengthened theoretically by relating these activities to concepts that define musical understanding.

David E. Myers is associate professor of music and education and chair of the music education division at Georgia State University in Atlanta.

Recognizing the diversity of musical idioms and cultures represented in the daily lives of students, general music educators have broadened the range of music in the classroom. They have responded to adolescents' interest in a wide variety of learning tasks by incorporating individualized, small-group, and large-group learning opportunities. Many general music programs now include computer-assisted instruction, guitars, keyboards, and recorders, offering hands-on musical development and educational attainments that transfer to students' other musical experiences.

MENC's efforts, such as the Goals and Objectives Project, Comprehensive Musicianship, and the Manhattanville Music Education Project, have provided important avenues of progress in general music. Through these programs, music educators have become more cognizant of planning sequential learning tasks, teaching through inherently musical behaviors, choosing literature of high quality, and fostering musical expression and creativity. The guiding force underlying these developments has been the commitment of music teachers to the musical growth, musical independence, and aesthetic sensitivity of all citizens.

The Status of General Music in the Middle Grades

Despite its major evolution from a singing program to a comprehensive music learning approach, middle-level general music struggles with the persistent perception that it falls short of its potential. In 1952, MENC advocated junior high general music that used exploratory experiences based on listening, singing, playing, reading, and creating. But Britton (1961) observed that general music too frequently was taught only to students who chose not to elect performance groups, and that it was taught either with an elementary orientation, or by teachers who turned it into a choral ensemble.

MacDonald (1990) believes general music in the middle grades is regarded lightly by teachers, administrators, and students. Her view may be supported by studies suggesting that contemporary Americans often do not value music as a subject worthy of study (Barton, 1989), and that they fail to see music as involving participatory effort (Balfe, 1990). Similarly, Goodlad (1984) found that many students considered music a relatively unimportant school subject. MacDonald calls for "philosophical consensus among school professionals and patrons about the value of general music to the young adolescent" (p. 19).

Boardman (1990) thinks general music fails to attain the well established and widely accepted goals developed over the last fifty years. She argues that the too-often disparate skills and activities fail to produce "independent musicians—creative, critical thinkers, sensitive to the musical contributions which make up their heritage, open to the musical expressions of others, and able to make knowledgeable judgments about music" (p. 14). Lehman (1988) contends that general music based too much on teacher idiosyncrasies and short-range activities has compromised important long-term outcomes.

General Music and the Structure of the Middle School

Given the above observations, which are independent of implications associated with the administrative unit where early adolescent learning occurs, it is clear that forging a role for general music within a middle school structure can be difficult. According to one survey, only 31 percent of middle schools require music for seventh-grade students (Alexander and McEwin, 1989). Nationally, only about half of all seventh- and eighth-grade students participate in general music (MENC, 1990).

Though the middle school movement began in the 1960s, there has been considerable diversity in the ways local systems have implemented programs. Many middle schools have focused on the organization of the environment for learning—features such as interdisciplinary teams, teacher advisories, block schedules, and exploratory courses. However, some observers express concern that these represent only a change in form from the junior high school, and do not address the substance of the middle school program (Lounsbury and Clark, 1990).

If general music is to be a viable subject in the early adolescent curriculum, it is essential that music educators be actively involved in implementing both structural and substantive features of the middle school. It is not enough for students to take only one six-week, exploratory, general music class during three years in middle school; nor is it appropriate to substitute performance for the general music class. Administrators, students, and parents cannot be permitted to think that "exploratory" is descriptive of nonsequential, nonbasic subjects in which one merely "dabbles." General music educators must not be regarded as isolated specialists, but as team players who are integral to providing a total education.

The concern for substance is reflected also in reports such as *An Agenda for Excellence at the Middle Level* (NASSP, 1985) and *Middle Level Education's Responsibility for Intellectual Development* (NASSP, 1989), which have stressed the importance of intellectual activity and the need for comprehensive intellectual development, including musical intelligence (NASSP, 1989). General music, like other components of the middle school program, must allow for teaching and learning to be carried out in ways that support students' multifaceted development. *Inside Grade Eight* (Lounsbury and Clark, 1990), for example, reports that many eighth-grade students do little critical thinking and find little relevance to their own lives in the content and methods of classes. Weaknesses such as these must be addressed if the middle school is to fulfill its enormous potential.

Principles for General Music in the Middle School

The following principles are based on the primary tenets of middle school philosophy and structure and contemporary theory and practice in general music for early adolescents. Because the nature of transescent students and the desired qualities of teachers of adolescents are covered elsewhere in this volume, these principles focus on the structure, content, and method of general music as they relate specifically to the middle school environment.

1. *General music in the middle school is a course for all students, regardless of musical background, intelligence, or academic achievement.* For many, this assertion raises immediate questions regarding the range of student ability and achievement in a given class. However, heterogeneous grouping is consistent with the middle school goals of respect for diversity and of the implementation of creative strategies to meet diverse student needs (NASSP, 1985). Among the strategies recommended are individualization, focused small-group

learning, and student participation in goal setting (Carnegie Council on Adolescent Development, 1989).

In general music, there are tasks, such as singing, that can cut across the entire spectrum of innate abilities and involve *everyone* successfully. Moreover, participatory music learning allows assignment of tasks according to individual capabilities, for example, playing a repeated, "straight" rhythm versus playing a changing, syncopated pattern. When using guitars, some students may play chords on instruments pretuned to require only strumming, some may play simplified chords, some may play only the bass line, and others may play fully fingered chords. This kind of interaction among peers of different backgrounds and abilities fulfills important social development needs among early adolescents.

No sacrifice in content is required if the general music program is based primarily on conceptual understanding and expressive growth, as opposed to skill development. Skills at many levels can combine to create an expressive outcome. Students with limited skills may understand concepts at advanced levels without necessarily performing at advanced levels. Conversely, high levels of performance can be a foundation for very basic musical understanding.

Students may be engaged in higher-order thinking appropriate to their individual development. Some students may require explicit criteria for making judgments, while others can benefit from a more open-ended approach. Within the class, students may sometimes be grouped so that those able to synthesize information at a high level may be assigned one task, while others requiring more systematic or concrete steps can be assigned another task. Some students may be able to express their ideas through prose, or through standard or devised notation; others may do so more effectively through circling selected pictures, or by choosing and organizing representational icons supplied by the teacher.

Student groupings within the middle school should be flexible and open to consideration and dialogue among teachers working on a given interdisciplinary team. Thus, if particular groupings of students will serve learning needs better at certain times or in certain situations, the team should be able to make such decisions in the students' best interests. It is imperative that the general music teacher participate actively in this decision-making process.

2. *General music instruction in the middle school integrates three main components: the fundamental structure of music, the nature of learning in music, and the developmental traits of early adolescents.* There is no substitute for learning that is musically valid, musically energizing, and musically satisfying. The subject of general music class is *music,* and it must be taught within a musically enlivened environment. If students cannot make relationships between what happens in music class and their natural intrigue regarding music, they will find little value in the class.

Basing music learning on the fundamental structure of music means that universal concepts and elements form the building blocks of understanding and experience. Regardless of the context, for example, instruments of the orchestra, music of many cultures, music of many composers and eras, music of the Beatles, or improvisatory styles, the content that must be examined derives from the fundamental qualities of pitch, duration, timbre, texture, and expression. How does the music sound, and why does it sound the way it does? Extramusical influences and topics, such as aspects of composers' lives, the cultural contexts in which music occurs, and the evolution of musical instruments are of greater interest when the music provides the impetus for knowing about them.

The nature of music learning must reflect the fundamental quality of musical art, that is, music learning is founded on *aural and kinesthetic response.* Mursell (1958) said that musicality is "responsiveness to the tonal and rhythmic patterns which are the substance of the art of music" (p. 161). Gordon (1980) and Froseth (1983) have defined approaches to music learning based on the stable, fundamental aural content of music. Though not specifically musical, the work of Jerome Bruner (1960) has guided the curriculum development in general music that emphasizes recurrent musical experience as a foundation and reference for the development of musical understanding.

Despite the importance of cognitive change through adolescence (Inhelder and Piaget, 1958; Broughton, 1977), the need for an experiential base in music learning does not diminish as the learner matures. Performing, creating, and listening are essential learning behaviors at every level and in every music learning context, because they are the avenues of musical understanding and transmission across cultures and generations. Obviously, the level of sophistication expected should be consistent with the learner's development.

The psychosocial, physical, and cognitive developmental traits of the early adolescent, documented elsewhere, are at the heart of much of the form of the middle school. General music teachers must plan instruction—the substance of the program—so that levels of knowledge and thinking, difficulty of learning tasks, interactions, and evaluation strategies fit the needs of this age group.

Most important, these three areas of a teacher's knowledge and understanding—structure of music, nature of learning in music, and developmental traits—must be integrated, rather than viewed as isolated aspects of general music teaching. Current research suggests that effective teaching involves two primary components: (a) knowledge of subject and what students should learn and (b) effective delivery and sequencing (Madsen, 1990). A classroom environment that meets students' developmental needs is only appropriate if it also ensures that valid music learning can occur. Similarly, music teaching that fails to engage students in developmentally appropriate tasks will be ineffective, regardless of how musically worthwhile the content may be.

3. *General music should address tangibly the general educational welfare of students.* A primary value of general music in the middle school curriculum is its potential as an expressive medium that complements learning in other subject areas. Earhart (MENC, 1962) wrote that one of the failures in music education was in "not connecting and coordinating music with all other areas of human interest and experience" (p. 26). Gardner (1983) has documented the importance of experiences that foster development across a broad spectrum of intelligences. Studies suggest that carefully implemented programs incorporating the arts in the learning of other subjects increase the quality of instruction, enhance students' creativity, and improve students' self-concepts (McGowan, 1988).

The early adolescent frequently is caught in a web of conflicting emotions and feelings, sometimes exacerbated by low-level cognitive tasks dependent on verbal language. Music, as a nonverbal experience linked with emotional response and release, provides an avenue for exploring the expressive dimensions of concepts across the curriculum. For example, if seventh-grade students are studying American history, what historical references can be discovered through the medium of organized sound? What are the origins, qualities, and characteristics of African-American spirituals? Of the blues? How have composers such as Virgil Thompson, William Schuman, Aaron Copland, and Leonard Bernstein captured the vitality of the American spirit? What is the panorama of musical cultures that expresses the diversity that is America today? In how many different styles and forms have American musicians given voice to their feelings about major historical events?

Beginning with these questions, the general music teacher does not merely teach songs or listen to music "about" historical events. Rather, through direct experiences that engage students in *musical behaviors and thinking,* the teacher expands awareness of the expressive dimension of experiences that have been a part of American history and offers a basis for a more comprehensive understanding of historical events. The planning of such experiences should occur through the general music teacher's participation on an interdisciplinary team.

4. *Learning in general music should be relevant to musical life beyond the classroom.* One of the most frequently cited missions of the middle school is to ensure relevance of in-school learning to young adolescents' total lives (NASSP, 1985). Beane (1990) suggests not merely catering to the passing fancies of students, but recognizing "the shared interests [adolescents] have as individuals and as participants in the larger world" (p. 2). More than 30 years ago, music educator Allen Britton (1961) voiced concern that music education "operated at a certain distance from the wellsprings of American musical life" (p. 215). More recently, John Goodlad (1984) found that people's real-world experiences of the arts are not reflected in the ways arts education programs are taught in schools.

For the general music teacher, this may mean serious consideration of the opportunities students have for immediate application of what they are learning. If a student wants to play familiar tunes on a keyboard, what are the essential pieces of knowledge and skill? If accompanying simple songs on the guitar is the goal, what does one need to know and be able to do? How can one go about creating an original melody or identifying a particular musical style? One's ability to make music independently, or to think musically, no matter how simple or crude the effort, is often the driving force that inspires a desire for continued learning.

Middle-school students also need abundant opportunities to see applications of music skills and concepts in the lives of others and to appreciate the variety of musical expressions reflected in an ethnically diverse world (Shehan, 1985). Though they initially may prefer music with which they are most familiar, the opportunity to visit with community musicians or professional artists in small-group settings permits questions the middle-school student might be reluctant to ask in large groups.

Because early adolescents may tend to attribute success in music more to ability than to effort (Asmus, 1986), it has been recommended that teachers offer more effort-related encouragement. Student interchanges with musicians who can testify to the role of effort in their own musical endeavors and opportunities to work successfully with such individuals on musical tasks may be effective in helping students develop stronger self-concepts regarding their success in music. In turn, their motivation and achievement may be enhanced (Schunk, 1983).

5. *General music instruction should lead toward the discovery of musical concepts through perception of musical qualities and events.* The importance of exploration, self-discovery, and individual development are hallmarks of the middle-school philosophy. In music, the term "exploratory" can be interpreted as a general approach to learning for the young adolescent. Hands-on experimentation and creative sound experiences are essential (Morris and Thompson, 1989). While parameters for creativity and problem-solving may vary widely for students at this age, teacher guidance

should inspire many acceptable products and solutions (DeLorenzo, 1989).

Ideally, the flexible structure, individualized approaches, higher-order thinking goals, and enhanced self-concept objectives of the middle school should match many of the suggested classroom components for fostering creativity (Kratus, 1990; Davidson, 1990). Sharing of decisions and perceptions regarding original efforts among peers and other musicians is important, as is developing a musical vocabulary to describe music events. Learning through listening should focus students' attention on expressive and formal qualities that can be discovered and compared in many representative examples (Hedden, 1988; Pogonowski, 1989). Middle school students should have opportunities not only to solve, but also to formulate problems (Broughton, 1977).

Teachers who establish strong role models of inquisitiveness, problem solving, and creative approaches to learning are important in the middle school. Learning *with* students, rather than seeming to have all the answers, will appeal to young adolescents. General music teachers must communicate excitement about the world of music and musical thinking and must be willing to share their ideas with students. They must be open to new musical developments, especially in the area of technology, and demonstrate critical thinking about these developments on the basis of high musical standards.

6. *Assessment in general music should reflect the nature of music learning and should not be reduced to easily graded tests of information.* Eisner (1990) has urged educators to move beyond "the simplistic, the merely measurable, and the superficial" (p. 13). One current approach to assessment is the use of a portfolio containing a student's work (Fowler, 1990). Another is the emphasis on demonstration via musical behaviors, using agreed-upon criteria, as opposed to simple listings of information. These approaches are consistent with efforts to engage middle-school students in higher-order thinking, active learning, and creative problem solving.

A student and teacher together might review an original work-in-progress to assess incorporation (at appropriate levels) of qualities such as varying melodic contours, repetition and contrast, and dynamic variations. Rather than grading note accuracy in a guitar performance of "Merrily We Roll Along," the teacher and other students might assess the extent to which the performed tune sounded like real music, that is, obtained a flow of notes, was singable, incorporated expression, and used an appropriate tempo.

The general music program must be evaluated against broadly stated goals and outcomes, rather than against specific student achievements. Tools must be developed to determine whether students are growing in their musical maturity and competence, whether they are expanding their awareness of their cultural heritage through music, and whether they demonstrate interest in musical life beyond the general music classroom. Merely achieving short-term objectives does not link the program with broad outcomes, nor does it suggest the extent to which students are incorporating the art of music into their lives.

The Future of Middle School General Music

Whether general music plays a significant role in the structure and curriculum of the middle school depends on many factors, some under the control of music educators and some demanding the creative involvement of music teachers in cooperation with others. General music, in some form, seems to be an accepted subject in most middle school programs. However, its place in the curriculum needs to be strengthened if its full potential for the education of early adolescents is to be realized.

Decisions regarding the amount of general music required and elected, the specific content and strategies of general music, and the relationship between general music and more specialized music classes are generally made in local schools. What must be indispensable in such decision making is a commitment to the relevance of musical understanding in the present and future lives of young adolescents. To be a viable component of the middle school, general music must adhere to the highest aims of middle-level education. At the same time, general music must demonstrate its unique contribution to meeting the range of human needs represented among the children it serves.

References

Alexander, W. M., & McEwin, C. K. (1989). *Schools in the middle: Status and progress.* Columbus, OH: National Middle School Association.

Asmus, E. (1986). Student beliefs about the causes of success and failure in music. *Journal of Research in Music Education, 34,* 262–278.

Balfe, J. H. (1990). The baby-boom generation: Lost patrons, lost audience? *Design for Arts in Education, 92* (1), 29–38.

Barton, L. (1989). Arguing the cause of music education. *American Music Teacher, 38* (4), 78–79.

Beane, J. A. (1990). Rethinking the middle school curriculum. *Middle School Journal, 21* (5), 1–5.

Britton, A. (1961). Music education: An American specialty. In P. H. Lang (Ed.), *One hundred years of music in America* (pp. 211–229). New York: Schirmer.

Boardman, E. (1990). Needed research in general music. *Council for Research in Music Education, 104,* 5–15.

Broughton, J. (1977). Beyond formal operations: Theoretical thought in adolescence. *Teachers College Record, 79,* 88–97.

Bruner, J. (1960). *The process of education.* New York: Vintage.

Carnegie Council on Adolescent Development (1989). *Turning points: Preparing American youth for the 21st century.* Washington, D.C.: Carnegie Corporation.

Davidson, L. (1990). Tools and environments for musical creativity. *Music Educators Journal, 76* (9), 47–51.

DeLorenzo, L. (1989). A field study of sixth-grade students' creative music problem-solving processes. *Journal of Research in Music Education, 37,* 188–200.

Eisner, E. W. (1990). What really counts in schools. *Educational Leadership, 48* (6), 10–17.

Fowler, C. (1990). Recognizing the role of artistic intelligences. *Music Educators Journal, 77* (1), 24–27.

Froseth, J. (1983). *The comprehensive music instructor: Listen, move, sing, and play.* Chicago: GIA.

Gardner, H. (1983). *Frames of mind: The theory of multiple intelligences.* New York: Basic Books.

Goodlad, J. I. (1984). *A place called school: Prospects for the future.* New York: McGraw-Hill.

Gordon, E. (1980). *Learning sequences in music.* Chicago: GIA.

Hedden, S. (1988). Music listening in grades six through nine. *Update: Applications of Research in Music Education, 7* (1), 17–18.

Inhelder, B., & Piaget, J. (1958). *Growth of logical thinking from childhood to adolescence.* New York: Basic Books.

Kratus, J. (1990). Structuring the music curriculum for creative learning. *Music Educators Journal, 76* (9), 33–37.

Lehman, P. (1988). A music program for 2001. In T. Gerber & W. Hughes (Eds.), *Music in the high school: Current approaches to secondary general music instruction* (pp. 3–12). Reston: Music Educators National Conference.

Lounsbury, J. H., & Clark, D. C. (1990). *Inside grade eight: From apathy to excitement.* Reston: National Association of Secondary School Principals.

MacDonald, D. (1990). General music in education. *Design for Arts in Education, 91* (5), 15–22.

Madsen, C. (1990). Teacher intensity in relationship to music education. *Council for Research in Music Education, 104,* 38–46.

McGowan, J. (1988). A descriptive study of an arts-in-education project. *Journal of Research in Music Education, 36,* 47–57.

Morris, J., & Thompson, K. (1989). A different drum: Percussion ensembles in general music. *Music Educators Journal, 76* (1), 30–34.

Mursell, J. (1958). Growth processes in music education. In N. B. Henry (Ed.), *Basic concepts in music education* (pp. 140–162). Chicago: National Society for the Study of Education.

Music Educators National Conference (1952). *The function of music in the secondary-school curriculum.* Chicago: Author.

Music Educators National Conference (1962). *Will Earhart: Teacher, philosopher, humanitarian.* Washington, D.C.: Author.

Music Educators National Conference (1990). *Data on music education: A national review of statistics describing education in music and the other arts.* Reston, VA: Author.

Music Educators National Conference (1991a). *Issues in music education: Statement of beliefs.* Reston, VA: Author.

Music Educators National Conference (1991b). MENC future directions. Association document. Reston, VA: Author.

National Association of Secondary School Principals (1985). *An agenda for excellence at the middle level.* Reston, VA: Author.

National Association of Secondary School Principals (1989). *Middle level education's responsibility for intellectual development.* Reston, VA: Author.

National Commission on Music Education (1991). *Growing up complete: The imperative for music education.* Reston, VA: Music Educators National Conference.

Pogonowski, L. (1989). Teaching listening through critical thinking. *Music Educators Journal, 76* (1), 35–38.

Schunk, D. (1983). Reward contingencies and the development of children's skills and self-efficacy. *Journal of Educational Psychology, 75,* 511–518.

Shehan, P. (1985). Transfer of preference from taught to untaught pieces of non-Western genres. *Journal of Research in Music Education, 33,* 149–158.

LEARNING TO VALUE MUSIC

Colette M. Sherman

In Shakopee, Minnesota, a suburb of Minneapolis, 650 students in grades seven, eight, and nine attend Shakopee Junior High. All seventh- and eighth-grade students take classroom (general) music. These classes meet for fifty minutes, five days a week. Colette Sherman describes the curriculum and classroom activities, and discusses Shakopee's move toward outcome-based education.

At Shakopee Junior High, all seventh and eighth graders study general music. The seventh-grade requirement is eighteen weeks, five days a week. All eighth graders are required to take music for nine weeks, five days a week. An additional nine-week elective is also offered in eighth grade. Occasionally, a nine-week theory elective is offered for ninth graders. Band and chorus are elective courses and students in all three grades may participate in both. In addition, the music department offers a jazz band and a select vocal group; these groups meet before school.

The goals for classroom music are to:

- Further the student's knowledge and appreciation of music
- Develop an appreciation of music as a source of pleasure, the fulfillment of a need, and an expression of society
- Continue the study and practice of the elements of music
- Understand the history of music and the reasons different musical styles developed
- See the relationship of music to other disciplines
- Use the vehicle of music to pursue the study of other cultures and their music
- Provide opportunites for students to express themselves creatively
- Reinforce study skills (spelling, note taking, creative writing) as they apply to the music unit

Colette M. Sherman teaches classroom and choral music in grades 7–9 at Shakopee Junior High School in Shakopee, Minnesota.

Although there are no prerequisites, most seventh graders entering Shakopee Junior High have had six years of elementary music instruction. Because all students in the seventh and eighth grades are required to take classroom music, the classes contain students of various ability levels, including band and choir students. This is ideal. Cooperative learning takes place easily; students share information and skills with each other in a positive atmosphere. Band and choir students learn about elements of music and musical style that are difficult to address in a band or choir class, where the primary focus is performance.

Curriculum Content

The seventh-grade curriculum is an opportunity to explore several aspects of music, beginning with music as organized sound and proceeding through the elements of rhythm, melody, harmony, tone color, and form. Recorded examples show how the language of music is universal and can be applied to any composition. This listening repertoire is expanded the following year.

In the eighth grade, the curriculum focuses on different periods and styles in music: American folk and popular music, classical music, electronic and experimental music, the music of cultures around the world, and musical theatre. Learning about musical periods and styles opens up many discussions concerning the role of culture in music making. Whenever possible, movements in art, literature, and music are linked to historical events.

Rather than follow a single music textbook, I have developed study guides for each of the units. Our school purchases textbooks for all departments on a rotating basis, according to the district's PER

(Planning, Evaluating, and Reporting) curriculum cycle. Textbooks are chosen for their ability to supplement the curriculum guides in terms of appropriate songs, multicultural resources, artistic content, examples from poetry and literature, and quality recordings. These guides are broad outlines that students use like workbooks; they fill them in as the unit progresses. The outlines are useful because although the content of the unit remains relatively constant from year to year, music examples or other details can be changed without rewriting the outline. Teachers have the freedom to insert their own content emphases and teaching styles. The study guides may include listening quizzes, staff paper for composing music or for melodic dictation, a chart of note and rest values or note names, or questions to accompany a filmstrip.

Within this broad framework, activities, articles, and worksheets are organized into a master file for each unit. The teacher uses this master file and duplicates worksheets and other materials as necessary.

Classroom Activities

Students love to listen to music, especially rock music. Whether they are clinging to a boom box or wrapped in headphones, it is clear that music energizes them. It also reinforces their values and somehow validates their inner thoughts and feelings. Students new to the program often ask "Why do we have to study music?" One answer is that music's energy can help connect and vitalize all their learning and make it more meaningful to them.

One key to successful music classes is providing a variety of activities. Whenever possible, students move out of their seats for a music making experience. Some of their favorite activities include:

- moving to the beat of a hand drum, stepping to quarter, eighth, and other note values
- stepping (and sometimes whistling) to a march
- playing examples at the keyboard to illustrate musical terms (for example, crescendo, staccato)
- working with a partner or small group to solve a musical problem or to create music
- taking the teacher's place in front of the class to clap an original rhythmic dictation
- going to the board to write notation and answers to homework
- using percussion instruments to create and perform accompaniments to songs as they listen or sing
- participating in contests within a class or between classes for clapping, singing, or other performing challenges
- dancing or moving creatively as a whole class or in small groups

Teachers strive to promote a student's connection with his or her feelings of self-esteem. They encourage but do not force students to participate in music making activities. Often some students will choose not to clap or sing at their desks, but will get out of their seats to walk to the beat or dance. It seems that movement activities that involve the whole class make it easier for individuals to feel less conspicuous in the group.

Music activities take place in a spirit of fun; students aren't permitted to put down a peer when he or she tries an activity and doesn't succeed. In some situations, they are even encouraged to make a mistake in order to teach a particular point. They get as much positive feedback for being correct as for being wrong; it's only important that they've tried to participate.

In addition to music activities, Shakopee's music classes have a study-skills component. A research project is a requirement in both seventh and eighth grades. Seventh graders write a report and present a demonstration on a musical instrument—one they play or one of their choice. Eighth graders study a jazz composer or style. In addition to improving study and writing skills, these projects are worthwhile because they give students an opportunity to explore a specific aspect of music in depth.

Three or four days a week a short homework assignment is given, usually in the form of a worksheet, to reinforce an aspect of the lesson or to review some aspect of theory. This also may have a study skills component, such as spelling (editing a news brief on a famous composer), or math (adding and subtracting note and rest values).

Students are encouraged to make connections: to their personal and social lives, to learning in other classes, and to world and historical events. They earn extra credit when they bring in music or other information that shows they have made an out-of-class connection with what was learned in music class. The credit is banked and can be redeemed for one night free of homework. Students begin to understand that what they learn in music class doesn't exist in a vacuum; it has importance in the rest of life.

Enrichment Opportunities

Two or three times a month, class time is taken to read articles of current musical interest. Teachers use articles from a newspaper or a magazine. These special interest topics give students extra knowledge of some aspect of the contemporary music scene. Students receive extra credit for bringing in music reviews and news clippings about music events and musicians.

The Minneapolis-St. Paul area offers many opportunities for field trips through several theatre and musical organizations that offer programs for young people. Attendance at a musical or theatre event gains added significance when it is planned with other departments as part of an interdisciplinary unit.

Structuring a Unit

Minnesota is moving toward an outcome-based education program. The goals for classroom music are aligned with the district's course, program, and graduation outcomes as specified in the state's "Model Learner Outcomes for Music Education."

The course outcomes for music class involve integrating music knowledge in a way that makes the student feel successful. Units are sequential, beginning in seventh grade with "Sounds and Rhythm." When planning a unit, four to six outcomes are created, each addressing a higher-level skill (following Bloom's taxonomy). The outcomes are practical applications of what the student has learned. A list of learner outcomes for "Sounds and Rhythm" is given in figure 1.

Each outcome is taught sequentially, but more than one outcome may be addressed during a single class period. The materials and activities are structured in a way that the learning is not only sequential within the outcome, but may relate to another outcome at the same time. For instance, the class may be working on tapping quarter- and eighth-note rhythms to a composition that also features a fermata and an accelerando.

As the unit progresses, short formative tests are given to test knowledge of symbols, note and rest values, terms, and compositions and composers. When students have mastered these concepts, they are ready for the final assessment, in which they demonstrate classroom learning and activities and go on to practical applications. The final assessment addresses all of the outcomes and may include listening and score analysis, as well as composing and performing music.

Separate study guides, review sheets, and formative and summative tests have been written for students with learning disabilities. Performance outcomes are adjusted to fit the student's abilities.

UNIT PLANNING GUIDE

Subject/Level: Music—Level 7
Unit Title: Sounds and Rhythm
Time Allotted: 23–25 class periods

Unit Outcomes

1. Recognize that environmental and electronic sounds can be used in music to achieve special effects by stating the probable intent of the composer in using those sounds.
2. Recognize the aspects of musical sound such as dynamics, pitch, tempo, and articulation, by identifying them as they are heard in music.
3. Identify, by ear, the major compositions associated with this unit, and list the composers of each.
4. Apply the symbols for musical interpretation by stating what happens to the music when these symbols appear in a score.
5. Perform a given rhythm pattern in 4/4 meter which consists of a combination of note values (whole, half, quarter, eighth), and rests (whole, half, quarter), by tapping the rhythm.
6. Use musical symbols associated with duration and dynamics by composing, notating, and performing a piece (in a small group) for three or four rhythm instruments.

Figure 1. A planning guide for seventh-grade music

Equipment and Facilities

Our music program makes use of a piano, AM-FM tuner, CD player, cassette deck, speakers, phonograph, VCR and monitor, and overhead and filmstrip projectors. Compact discs and filmstrips purchased for the program last several years, and the music program also benefits when the school media specialist purchases CDs and videos that have interdisciplinary applications. In addition, students bring in their pop cassettes and CDs; these are used in class when they relate to a musical concept or style in the unit. The music department has a computer with two megabytes of memory and an internal drive, with a MIDI-compatible performance synthesizer. To purchase the computer and keyboard, we used part of the instrumental music budget. The instrumental, choral, and classroom music groups share these resources. In addition, the school has a computer lab that the music students use to supplement their study of music theory. They also use the lab to type definitions at the end of each unit as a review. When the course is complete, they generate a printout of all the terms they learned.

The music classroom at Shakopee Junior High is part of a multipurpose area, which includes a three-tiered choir room, a classroom with thirty-five desks, five practice rooms, and a band room. Folding doors between the areas are usually kept open, allowing extra space for small group work or for movement activities.

A Personal Perspective

My primary goal is to help students value and enjoy music. Sometimes I ask them on a unit test how they can use what they learned in class in daily life. When I get answers like "So that we can understand people of other cultures better," or "So we can recognize music used on TV shows or in movies and know something about it," then I know that students are learning to value music. Often parents tell me at conferences what the students bring home from music class. One student reported that she had visited a Native American powwow and was able to have a discussion with one of the adults about the music as a result of a unit we had studied. When I hear these reports, I know I'm well on my way to accomplishing my goal.

SINGING THE MUSIC OF SEVERAL CULTURES

Simonia E. Milton

Fannie C. Williams Middle School is located in the suburbs of New Orleans. The ethnic makeup of this school is broader than other schools in the district, and as part of the general music program, students explore Asian, African-American, Hispanic, and Northern European cultural backgrounds. Each culture has a different way of appreciating music, and in class students explore these cultural differences and similarities. When students discover they have something in common (music), they begin to look at each other differently and appreciate each other.

I teach general music as part of the vocal music program at Fannie C. Williams Middle School. In our school, there are exploratory electives, which change each quarter. The music programs run through the entire school term. This continuity and consistency helps the students achieve more effectively.

The students in general music have varied artistic abilities and interests; some have studied music for several years, and some have not even participated in a sing-a-long at a church meeting. Singing is an integral part of the general music class. Some students possess beautiful voices, while others can't or won't sing, which makes classes interesting and challenging to me. Their listening skills and musical tastes also are at various stages of development. This mixture of students' abilities presents a challenge for me. My job is to enrich the experienced child and to wake up the inexperienced child. I must begin with an attitude of "we will succeed" and an enthusiasm of "they will excel to the end."

Simonia E. Milton is a vocal music specialist at Fannie C. Williams Middle School in New Orleans.

Our school year is divided into quarters. This suits my general music classes beautifully. Each quarter we study the music of a particular culture. The first quarter focuses on Northern European music and its development. The second quarter is devoted to the study of African-American music and its relationship to music of Africa. In the third quarter, we discuss Asian peoples and their music and customs. The music and celebrations of Hispanic peoples are the focus for the fourth quarter.

Every day my aim is to meet the musical and emotional needs of the children. I hope also to lay a foundation for their lifelong enjoyment of the music and an appreciation of all cultures.

The Daily Schedule

In teaching general music to a multiethnic class, I stress four areas of activity: listening, performing, writing, creating. Students listen to and analyze the music of the group under discussion; then they perform certain selections pertaining to that ethnic group. Performing includes: singing, playing rhythm instruments, moving, creating dance steps, and making costumes. They must write a report about the group, describing its customs and discussing how the music relates to its culture. The last assignment is to compose music in that style.

The class meets five days a week for fifty-five minutes. Each day I write the goal on the board so everyone knows what is expected. I write down each activity with a time limit next to it, which makes everyone accountable. Our goal is to stay focused on the tasks for the day.

The class begins with a five-minute review of the

previous day's lesson. If homework was given, we discuss it after the review and then I collect it for correction. Class continues with singing, which focuses students on the instruction for the day. Everyone is encouraged to participate in the singing, which lasts about fifteen minutes. Students sing for the sheer pleasure of it.

Every voice is important; I don't single out students who don't have good tone quality. We discuss changing voices and good vocal techniques during the first few weeks of school. The boys are seated together, so those whose voices are changing will not feel hopeless and left out. The girls sit together, divided into high and low voices. The students experience belonging, comradeship, and self-esteem.

The next part of the lesson takes about twenty minutes. In the first few days of each quarter, we review what we've learned in the previous quarter. Then we begin to explore the new culture and its music by studying the specific locale and some general historical background. A student reads a report he or she has prepared on the particular group and one of its composers. Students may create posters, charts, and other supplementary materials to enhance their reports.

The listening and appreciation phase of the lesson encourages the students to analyze the music completely. We listen to recordings and discuss them. To fulfill curriculum goals of critical thinking, the students answer questions from a ditto sheet about rhythm, melody, style, dynamics, lyrics, and instrumentation. We spend about ten minutes on this activity. In the last ten minutes of the class, I summarize what was introduced that day.

At the end of each quarter, each student prepares a notebook to be graded. I also use singing and listening activities to evaluate the student's understanding. As the culminating activity, we present a program and invite parents and administrators as well as musicians or other representatives from the various cultural backgrounds. Students prepare food from that particular culture. They perform the dances learned during the quarter and use rhythm instruments to accompany themselves.

The success of my teaching depends on staying in touch with the needs of students and the effect their culture has on their lives. I want to always keep the lines of communication open and let them know that despite our diversified backgrounds, we can all grow musically into productive, creative, functioning people.

For Further Reading

George, Luvenia. *Teaching the Music of Six Different Cultures*. Danbury, CT: World Press, 1988.

Potter, Jean. *Teaching Music Today*. Portland, ME: J. Weston Walch, 1977.

LEARNING TO PLAY THE DULCIMER

Emily McCullough-White

Approximately one thousand students in grades seven through nine attend Dater Junior High School in Cincinnati, Ohio. At this urban school, the general music classes meet each day for twenty weeks (one semester). One option in the general music program is learning to play the dulcimer. Emily McCullough-White developed this option and students have welcomed it.

Latchkey children, throwaway children, children having babies. These immediate and startling realities often face those who teach urban children. Education must reach beyond the "three R's" in order to serve the whole child in our nation's inner cities.

Several years ago, I was assigned as a vocal music specialist at a middle school in Cincinnati. Within a few weeks, I discovered that many of my students were the third generation of offspring from thirteen- and fourteen-year-old parents. Unlike less disadvantaged students in the city and suburbs, their experiences were limited to a twenty-block radius in the heart of the city. Lesson plans based on the music textbook couldn't effectively meet the needs of those young people. Our city-wide music curriculum began with grades three and four, but the basic skills and concepts were very sketchy. As an added obstacle, the reading levels of my particular students were several grade levels below their grades seven and eight.

Initially, I gathered folk songs and spirituals and focused on a vocally oriented music program, integrating curriculum demands as best I could. Although my guitar playing and singing gained a captive audience, I was not providing a challenging educational experience. I was entertaining my students, not involving them.

Emily McCullough-White is vocal music director at Dater Junior High School in Cincinnati, Ohio.

A vocal approach at this stage was indeed a gamble: the boys' changing voices and all the students' lack of background in vocal music on the elementary level were major drawbacks. Also, singing requires a great deal of self-expression. Such self-expression does not come easily to adolescents in general; it was particularly uncharacteristic of these young people.

A Dulcimer Ensemble

The situation cried out for a hands-on program. I wanted music to provide a magnet that would help keep my students in school. I decided that the Appalachian dulcimer would be ideal. Such a simple folk instrument would not make undue demands on student reading levels and offered the possibility of instant gratification.

My supervisor came to the rescue and provided six student-sized Appalachian lap dulcimers called "backpackers". These instruments are approximately one-third smaller than the traditional lap dulcimer. They have four strings, and are tuned in the Ionian mode, akin to the present-day major mode. (Due to limitations in students' experience, particularly ear-training, I did not expose my students to the other modes and tunings commonly used for the dulcimer.) They have two unison melody strings, or home strings. A middle string is tuned to the same pitch as the two home strings. The single bass string is tuned down a fifth.

My classes were relatively small, so I set up teams of two and three, sharing the six instruments in class. This arrangement was satisfactory, but as the students gained facility on the dulcimer, their desire for their own instruments increased as well. Once again, my supervisor was able to tap special funds, and we had a total of twelve dulcimers.

Students took pride in their instruments. I arranged extended practice time by allowing reliable students to check out instruments overnight. Classroom behavior began to improve dramatically, and an air of competition developed with the promise of taking an instrument home. Reliability, attitude, and effort in class were the major considerations in allowing a student to have a dulcimer overnight.

Finding an appropriate student book was a challenge. Many excellent dulcimer song books exist, but they were generally too difficult for these students. I decided to arrange my own dulcimer text, using the American folk songs and spirituals that had initially captivated the students. I also included tunes that would be appropriate for holidays.

My approach was quite simple. I triple-spaced the lines of text, and under the appropriate words, placed circled numbers corresponding to the frets on the dulcimer. Next to some circled notes, I added another number outside the circle. The inside number was for fingering the melody strings, and the outside number could be played on the middle string to add harmonic interest. This choice of songs and the simple tablature were a success. The students delighted in playing the familiar tunes over and over.

To teach the music, I sang a song phrase by phrase, so that the rhythms were established. Next, I sang the tune, phrase by phrase, using the circled numbers. The students echoed the phrases on their dulcimers. I must admit that I broke a cardinal rule of some dulcimer players by placing peel-off numbers on the fret board. This allayed the students' frustration at searching for the correct fret, which was counterproductive to reinforcing instant success.

As the students acquired skills on the dulcimer, their zeal for participation in music class became evident. They began to arrive at class on time, as I used the "first come, first served" policy; early arrivals did not have to share a dulcimer. Personal accountability and dependability were markedly improved. Being able to play the dulcimer provided a certain prestige for my general music students. Students who weren't even in my music classes showed up at my door, wanting to sign out a dulcimer. After I turned them down, they would try to talk me out of a dulcimer song book.

Performance Opportunities

Though I had not envisioned performance possibilities for these rookie dulcimer players, I knew the extra challenge was necessary. They needed to share their newly acquired musical skills. I scheduled the dulcimer ensemble for the December Holiday Concert, along with the modest choir of twelve singers. Two students from the general music/dulcimer classes were good singers and were included as soloists. They sang along with several dulcimer numbers.

I spent several rehearsals acquainting the students with performance skills: how to walk to assigned seats, how to sit while waiting, how to sit while performing, and how to hold the dulcimers. Those exercises were the ultimate test of patience, for both students and teacher! We talked about facial expressions and standing for applause. We practiced getting on and off the stage gracefully and quietly. One of the by-products of a music program that incorporates performance is the opportunity to develop self-discipline. These children, with their limited social skills and often severely disadvantaged home lives, met the challenge.

Just prior to the Holiday Concert for the students and parents, the dulcimer ensemble was invited to perform for a holiday presentation sponsored by our school system's Educational Center. I accepted the invitation with some trepidation, as I was uncertain about how well my students would adjust to a different environment. I worried about how my emotionally fragile dulcimer players would react to being surrounded by so many peers. These worries were important because the overwhelming amount of emotional baggage these children carry is always the paramount issue in trying to teach them effectively. Their extreme poverty seems to heighten the pain resulting from the severe personal traumas many have experienced.

The Educational Center concert was in the evening, and getting kids back to school at night could well require an act of God, if not a constitutional amendment. Pizza, a completely irresistible item to the adolescent palate, was the answer. I promised, "Any dulcimer player who will remain after school and perform in the concert would be served lots of free pizza and pop. Return your permission form and join in the fun!" It worked. A friend helped me transport the twelve newly trained instrumentalists a few blocks across town for their first concert.

The performance was a huge success. The only sign of their nervousness was that their strumming became tentative at times, but this minor problem was insignificant compared to what they had accomplished. They felt good about the experience and about themselves. Their skills and confidence would improve with practice.

I continued rehearsing their performance presentation skills as the time approached for performing in front of their peers. Walking on stage was becoming a part of their daily lives. The singers became old friends with the microphones. All our efforts paid off when the concert was well received by parents, teachers, and peers. People who already knew the gentle sound of the Appalachian lap dulcimer were charmed. Those new to the experience were absolutely captivated.

The students met and exceeded the goals I had envisioned for them. They were getting to class on time and staying in school. Their self-confidence was growing, and their attitudes and efforts had risen to an acceptable state for a middle school classroom. They started to display care and appreciation for the property of others. They learned skills applicable to every aspect of their education. Last, but certainly not least, they were making beautiful music!

The semester in general music ended in late January, and all my students went on to general art. New students arrived, happily anticipating learning to play the "dulcimore," as they called it. The hands-on experience in music provided a positive addiction for those urban children. By the end of the school year, the new dulcimer ensemble had presented three performances, including selections on the eighth-grade graduation program. Music had made an indelible mark on the hearts and minds of those young people.

When enrollment in this school declined, my teaching assignment was cut in half. I was reassigned to a large junior high school in another area, and felt sad to leave these urban children. The sharing of cultures and a love for music would remain with each of us always.

Developing A New Program

My relocation, I knew, would be very challenging. The vocal program I was assigned to had a long-standing reputation for excellence. The average student did not have to survive in extreme poverty as did those in my former assignment. However, a myriad of other similarities did exist: teen pregnancy, single-parent families, and a lack of positive role models for some students. I taught general music, as well as vocal music, so I started another dulcimer ensemble.

Though learning to play the dulcimer is not unduly demanding, some students preferred risking failure to performing poorly in front of their peers. I had to invent ways to cajole shy students into not giving up based on their initial frustration. No student was required to play solo. I accommodated extreme shyness by arranging after-school testing. The more reserved students eventually gained the confidence to play in a duet or quartet in class. Students who tried to attain even modest skill at playing the dulcimer set the foundation for tackling new tasks throughout their lives.

The first performance for the newly formed dulcimer ensemble was at a neighborhood church; a senior citizens' club wanted musical entertainment for their holiday luncheon. My students enjoyed planning for the performance, because they would be away from school all morning. The particulars of getting on and off stage with poise were rehearsed to perfection.

The preparations were more than adequate until the group took its position on stage and spied the audience. Few students had been in either elementary band or choir, so this was a new experience.

Such stressful conditions can elicit strange and unpredictable responses in the adolescent. Luckily, there was no inappropriate behavior, and the group performed fairly well—though they looked terrified. After the performance, they acted as if they had just completed a Carnegie Hall debut. The illusion was created by the thunderous applause of an enthusiastic, elderly audience, followed by homemade cookies and fruit punch. I praised my students for their excellent work. Their enthusiasm demonstrated their own feelings of accomplishment.

The choral program I inherited had different problems. Several sopranos, who could break your heart with their high, floating tones, had unfortunately developed a condescending attitude toward the lowly general music students. Imagine the chagrin of my concert choir when they discovered that I had invited the dulcimer ensemble to accompany the choir on its holiday circuit of the downtown hotels and skywalk. "Music is for everyone," I reminded the somewhat haughty singers. "You'll understand when you hear them play."

The forty-member dulcimer ensemble settled on an open stairway leading from the skywalk to a hotel lobby. The concert choir was situated on a mezzanine, just at the foot of the stairs. The dulcimer group was well-rehearsed and hungry for another audience. They sounded like ethereal harps as they strummed their eleven carols for the lunch time crowd of shoppers and business people. The boldest choir members quietly hummed along with the familiar tunes. Have you ever heard forty strummed dulcimers playing at once? It is a truly beautiful sound.

The music became too easy for those students. It seemed important that I refine and expand the tablature in the dulcimer book, as well as include more songs. The students would be further challenged by the simple harmony parts I added. Two-thirds of the group played the melody, and one-third played the harmony. They loved the new sound! I also introduced a method whereby they could begin to sound out their own tunes.

During the summer vacation, I spent many hours experimenting with songs that could be added to the student book. I also devised a method of rhythmic notation integrated with symbols for strumming, so the students could do more than learn by rote.

I completed two new student song books: one of holiday songs and one with many folk songs and spirituals. The students were eager to act as guinea pigs and provided feedback when I needed to make adjustments in the tablature. My hope is to devise a song book that will be appropriate for the music student who does not read music. A clear, yet challenging tablature is critical for a beginners' dulcimer text.

Conclusion

Is your general music course relevant to the students you teach? Have they had musical training in their school experience? Do your students need music as an academic discipline, or would their needs be better met by establishing a program that would focus on the by-products of a performance-oriented music program? Are young people neglected by not having a music history survey course during the middle school years? Should there be a general theory course for this age level?

These are just a few of the questions I have asked myself. The answers to these have evolved in the form of my personal philosophy of a whole-child approach: both the approach and the information taught must be relevant to the lives of the students. A hands-on lesson provides a lasting experience and is particularly appealing for this age of adolescence. Use of a folk instrument such as the lap dulcimer enables each student to develop personal creativity in addition to learning about music. When education is focused on the whole child, the possibilities are boundless.

From the premise of this holistic approach to education, I am constantly aware that what I am teaching is *the students*. The success of this particular program utilizing the dulcimer is due to my having capitalized on the experience level of my students. A program that is relevant to the student will succeed, and students will take with them a lasting love and appreciation for music.

RELATED ARTS

FINDING COMMONALITIES AMONG THE ARTS

Paul Haack

The experiencing, understanding, valuing, and usefulness of the art of music can be richly enhanced by knowledge of how it relates to the other arts and to the sociocultural context in which it is created. Music is not a self-contained entity, free of social and technological influences; nor does it exist in isolation from the other arts. Teaching music in relation to the other arts and in the context of the entire school curriculum, especially the middle-level curriculum, strengthens and gives witness to the claim that the arts are basic.

At the conclusion of the second edition of *A Philosophy of Music Education,* Bennett Reimer (1989) states, "The realization begins to dawn that we must change in a fundamental way without abandoning our fundamental devotion to music and to education, a change towards arts education" (p. 241). Though he cautions about specious arts relationships and espouses the continuing need for courses focusing on music, his final remarks call for consideration of a move "in the direction of transcendence beyond the limitations of music education as a separate field" to provide a brighter future for music and all of the arts in the school curriculum (p. 241).

Paul Haack is professor and head of the Division of Music Education/Therapy in the School of Music at the University of Minnesota in Minneapolis.

Understanding music in the light of other art forms enhances the process of music education in two essential ways: the true commonalities among arts give insight into the most basic meanings and functions of music and all the arts, and the differences among the arts help us better understand music for its uniqueness within all the artistic forms of human expression. Just as knowing another language helps us to understand our own language better and studying other cultures helps us to understand our own culture better, so studying music in the context of the related arts can lead to more effective involvement with music itself.

How the Arts Are Similar

To relate the arts in education effectively, it is necessary to understand how they are, in fact, alike and similarly influenced in their makeup. While most scholars have begun by looking directly for similarities, Susanne Langer (1957) began by looking initially at the differences. She considered all of the discrete aspects of each art discipline—basic media and materials, scope, time/space dimensions, and so on—and reached the conclusion that, while differences are greater than some might expect, there are basic similarities in artistic form:

> *But if you trace the differences among the arts as far and as minutely as possible, there comes a point beyond which no more distinctions can be made. It is the point where the deeper structural devices...all the organizing devices–reveal the dynamic form that we learn from nature as spontaneously as we learn language from our elders. These principles appear, in one art after another, as the guiding ones in every work that achieves organic unity, vitality of form or expressiveness, which is what we mean by the significance of art.* (p. 79)

We are familiar with these principles of deep dynamic form in the manner and feelings of tension-release, departure-return, stimulation-sedation, motion-rest, similarity and contrast, balance and imbalance, congruences and variations, and so on. Here we find similarities among the arts based on the great as well as the subtle rhythms, dynamics, and forms of feeling that are the prime analogs of the human condition itself.

How the Arts Are Similarly Influenced

Artistic work is not created in isolation from its sociocultural context. Artistic expressions and values are always related to their time and place of origin. Thus, art forms from varying media will tend to demonstrate similar values common to the cultural epoch from which they grow. This principle is not negated by the fact that relationships may be inverted or negative, as in the case of some social commentary and protest art or works representing subcultural values.

Thus, the arts relate in reflecting the values of a given time and place. Of course, at times the arts are more like headlights than reflectors, helping lead society in new directions. Nevertheless, the most basic commonalities among the arts can usually be found in the ways they express, through their deep dynamic structures, similar values through their differing media–values relating to such aspects as objective/formal or subjective/personal emphases, and classical or romantic styles, trends, or vacillations, as expressed through manipulation of the unique elements of the varying art forms.

Some Basic Concepts for Relating the Arts

The following concepts flow from the preceding ideas. The first two points relate more to the question of how and why the arts are similar. The remaining five points are concerned more with how the arts are similarly influenced:

1. All persons have biological and psychological needs for aesthetic experience.
2. Nature, including human nature, provides the broad parameters and the models for all art forms.
3. The more distinct styles and manners of artistic expression are determined by the cultural milieu.
4. The arts are related in terms of the contextual values they express and symbolize.
5. Artistic expression depends on (a) time and place, including socioeconomic, religious, political, technological, and general cultural factors (societal values); and (b) the temperament of the individual artist (personal values).
6. All artists are a part of their times, but can also influence and help create their times.
7. Artistic eras or stylistic epochs generally have three aspects: (a) the waning, dying past; (b) the flourishing, mainstream present; and (c) the experimental, promising future.

Some Empirical Research Background

While a number of related-arts curricula have been devised during the past thirty years–notably at the middle level–few have been researched or subjected to rigorous assessment. In fact, very few empirical studies have been done in this area, and most of these have been concerned with limited aspects of music and visual-arts relationships.

Wehner (1966) and Lawrence (1977) found that students' abilities to perceive common moods and "common elements," such as rhythm, color, texture, and shape in music and the visual arts, can be enhanced through appropriate pairings of examples and systematic instruction. They noted, however, that students' vocabularies may limit the effectiveness of instruction, and it may be necessary to develop students' verbal skills pertaining to the arts and aesthetics to make related-arts approaches advantageous. Also, common-elements approaches need to be employed with caution so as to prevent misconceptions, for example, the notion that terms such as "color" and "texture" mean the same thing in music and the visual arts.

Haack (1970) found that middle-level students who had studied the style concepts of Romantic and Classical with the help of examples from the visual arts (including architecture) were significantly more effective in categorizing musical examples than were those students who had spent all of their class time studying and listening to musical examples only. The notion that it is easier to see than to hear elements of style was supported in a later study, in which musically experienced subjects were found able to categorize visual-arts styles more accurately than musical styles (Haack, 1982). The suggestion is that it is more difficult to perceive properties such as balance, symmetry, repetition, simplicity, complexity, contrast, imbalance, and the like when they are embodied in sound through time than when they are embodied in the more stationary spatial images of the visual arts and architecture. Thus, the study of the latter can enhance perception of the former. All in all, we may be on safer ground examining art elements and expressions for their similar treatments in terms of the deep dynamic principles mentioned above than we would be in examining them in terms of a "common-elements" approach.

Some Current Practices

In his essay in this book, John Nyberg presents an excellent topically oriented approach to involving many students and many art forms in a creative process culminating in a "concert." In another project leading up to a concert, band students studied arrangements and compositions based on folk tunes of the old West and paintings (slides) of the West by nineteenth-century American painters. With the music and art teachers' help, students discussed and chose the images that they believed were the most appropriate, in style and expression, to accompany various portions of their concert's musical selections. Added sensitivity to musical expression was claimed as one apparent result. Later elaborations on this concert concept included the insertion of appropriate poetry readings between selections, and the involvement of a physical-education dance class in a hoedown selection.

On a grand scale, several schools have planned related-arts festivals. Unifying themes range from styles and values ("Feeling vs. Form") to eras ("Contemporary Expressions" and "The Jazz Age") to moods and feelings ("Blues" and "Race Against Time"). Dance, drama, and mime artists from the community as well as the school may be involved, and most plans call for a week-long festival. In one format, the general music class sets the theme and organizes and manages the entire production. Orchestras, chorales, concert bands, or jazz bands share the stage with language-arts students' poetry readings and dancers' thematic interpretations. On alternating nights, the dramatic arts take the center stage, and throughout the week visual-arts students' works are on display in the auditorium and cafeteria areas of the school. This programming also includes special-arts students and their work.

Several ensemble and general music teachers have combined efforts on stylistic-era units, for example, a unit on the Classical period that has the performing group and the general music class listen to recorded music examples and study exemplary paintings and architecture. The latter might be slides of paintings by Jacques-Louis David, slides of architecture such as the Supreme Court building in Washington, D.C., or local neoclassical structures photographed by the music teachers and general music students themselves. Teachers and students discuss commonalities such as emphasis on balance and symmetry, and relative simplicity in line, texture, and form. Then they contrast these formal/Classical values with the more dynamic and openly expressive Romantic-period styles of Gericault and Delacroix.

Students are asked to think about their own aesthetic values and to consider instances when the Classical style seems particularly satisfying or useful to them. At the same time, the ensemble students are working on a selection by Mozart, Haydn, Gluck, or an early composition by Beethoven. Their concluding exercise is a recorded performance with emphasis on stylistic authenticity. This recording is then reviewed and critiqued by the general music class.

Probably the most common formats for related-arts curricula over the past several decades have been "Related Arts," "Allied Arts," or "Arts and Humanities" class offerings. These have been topically or thematically based, elements based, chronologically based to go with the flow of history, reverse-chronologically based to begin where we are, psychologically based to begin with romanticism where middle school children may feel most comfortable, and so on. Recently, a unique format proposal for an "Arts in Daily Living" class was based on Alan Merriam's ten functions of music, extended to common functions of the arts: emotional expression, aesthetic enjoyment, entertainment, communication, symbolic representation, physical response, enforcing conformity, validation of institutions and rituals, stability of culture, and integration of society (1964, pp. 219–227).

Generally in related offerings, the commonly involved art forms have ranged from only music and the visual arts to dance, drama, and the language arts in general. At times, these offerings have included a significant historical/cultural component, and in these cases credit toward English or social studies requirements might be awarded. Staffing has ranged from a single teacher, sometimes assisted by incidental or call-in help from staff or community colleagues, to teams of teachers representing the various arts and humanities areas involved. Single staffing is expecting a great deal from a teacher, and team members that are in the classroom only one at a time may be less effective than team members that can interact with one another as well as the class. The latter arrangement, however, generally requires larger class sizes to justify the presence of several teachers. In some team teaching situations, classes may break into performance media groups for hands-on experience with the various arts.

Some Possible Future Directions

Although a variety of course types has been mentioned, at present there is not a great number of regularly offered related-arts courses in the middle schools. Despite anticipated growth in this curricular area in the middle/secondary grades in light of increased state arts requirements, action has been limited and there is need for the development and evaluation of new approaches.

Experimentation with curricula employing basic arts principles and/or related-arts functions as unifying contextual agents may be helpful, particularly because such approaches may make it possible to incorporate ethnic art forms and cross-cultural art relationships more effectively. Such an effort, however, will require some consideration and understanding of the various societal contexts involved so that the art examples can be studied and valued on their own sociocultural terms rather than with ethnocentric and chronocentric concepts. Such experiences can provide valuable multicultural insights with regard to arts relationships. For example, whereas in Western civilization it is common to hear rock, ballet, or operatic music without the dance or drama components, in some societies the relationships are so strong that such "partial" performances would be unacceptable.

Another direction for exploration is greater involvement of nonarts teachers. At the middle school levels, this could mean involving social studies and language arts teachers on teams or coordinating an arts-across-the-curriculum approach with them. The latter arts infusion/arts integration approach offers particularly rich ground for exploration. At the upper elementary school levels, we need to experiment with the arts training of general classroom teachers. Possible directions here include related-arts training for arts integration and application to the general core of classroom teaching, in which broadened, mutually enhanced understandings could result in a variety of subject areas.

The National Endowment for the Arts report on arts education, *Toward Civilization* (1988), clearly recommends that teachers in all grades and subject matter areas be educated to use the arts to contribute to their teaching as well as to show how their subjects can contribute to an understanding of the arts. This makes much sense when we consider the importance of understanding music in its technological and sociocultural contexts; and it is equally important to realize, for example, that teaching history without frequent allusion to the arts is teaching faulty history—history that is lacking in a vitally essential and influential endeavor.

Efforts in these directions will be pioneering, with all the risks that term implies; however, the rewards can be great. These include the satisfaction of learning more about the other arts, and the accomplishment of creating more efficient and realistic courses in which music is not treated like an entity that is isolated from the rest of the curriculum—and life. Few things will build collegial and administrative support for an arts program as will incorporating an interdisciplinary component into the goals and content of the program. When we music educators make a concerted effort to base our content in its social, historical, and technological contexts and to tie it to related-arts references, examples, and courses, we not only enhance music teaching/learning processes and foster more sensitive, expressive performances, we also demonstrate that we are an integral part of the basic middle school curriculum.

References

Haack, P. A. (1970). A study involving the visual arts in the development of musical concepts. *Journal of Research in Music Education, 18,* 456-461.

Haack, P. A. (1982). A study of high school music participants' stylistic preferences and identification abilities in music and the visual arts. *Journal of Research in Music Education, 30,* 213-220.

Langer, S. K. (1957). *Problems of art: Ten philosophical lectures.* New York: Scribner's.

Lawrence, J. (1977). Development of methods and materials for increasing perception of music, visual art, and literature through concepts about elements held in common. *Contributions to Music Education, 5,* 1-88.

Merriam, A. P. (1964). *The anthropology of music.* Evanston: Northwestern University Press.

National Endowment for the Arts. (1988). *Toward civilization.* Washington, DC: National Endowment for the Arts.

Reimer, B. (1989). *A philosophy of music education.* 2nd ed. Englewood Cliffs, NJ: Prentice Hall.

Wehner, W. (1966). The relation between six paintings by Paul Klee and selected musical compositions. *Journal of Research in Music Education, 14,* 220-224.

RELATED ARTS IN THE MUSIC CLASSROOM

John L. Nyberg

Brimhall School in Roseville, Minnesota, is a suburban school with approximately 750 students. Because its attendance area includes housing for foreign families attending the University of Minnesota, international students account for about 20 percent of the Brimhall enrollment. The school's related-arts program responds to the student body's rich, unique mixture and encourages children to discover connections among the arts.

My experience in relating the other arts to music has been in the writing and production of several musical theater pieces that I simply call "concerts." My original attraction to this form of student performance was prompted by a need for injecting incentive and enthusiasm into a tradition of lackluster spring concerts.

What are the other arts to which we attempt to relate? In my experience, they are dance, acting, speaking, painting, drawing, and costuming. Because of the sheer number of aspects involved, these productions have a tendency to resemble opera in the grand nineteenth-century tradition. That is, they involve a combination of singing, playing instruments, dancing, telling a story, pageantry, and ceremony. The impact on performer and audience alike is undeniable. I shall attempt to give my formula for putting such performances together.

The first ingredient is *planning*. A year or two is not excessive in planning these programs. A key element is choosing a topic or theme. For me these come from other curricular areas or my imagination. Sometimes a theme appeals to me because of the challenge it poses. Here is a list of the themes that have come to final production in the past:

- Election Year Revue–Current candidates and the history of election songs and slogans in the United States.
- La Música de las Americas–Hispanic, African, and Native American influences.
- Yipes and Tally Ho!–Excerpts from British musical theater.
- Tournament–Songs, dances, and pageantry from the Middle Ages.
- The Immigrant in America–Ethnicity as realized in the American mosaic.
- Minnesota: A Musical Tribute–History, geography, and current events of our state as told in songs, dances, and poetry.
- Neptune's Kingdom–Sailing songs, shipwreck, and under-water adventures.
- Gershwin!–The life and music of a great American composer.
- Airplane!–Songs, dances, and poems that tell the story of aviation and the exploration of the skies.

In addition, I have put together programs centered around the counties of Greece and Italy. At present, the foreign language curriculum in our school has provided the opportunity for building concerts around themes of the Spanish-speaking world, the French-speaking world, and our heritage of German language and culture. We have had, in addition, the challenge of constructing a concert around the music and literature of a non-Western culture: Chinese songs, dances, and visual arts were combined in a school production.

John L. Nyberg is a music teacher and curriculum consultant in elementary classroom music for Roseville Area Schools in Roseville, Minnesota.

The Art of Singing and Playing Instruments

As soon as I have decided upon the general theme to be used, I begin a search for musical materials from which to draw for the actual program. If the program is in February, we start working on some of the songs in October. When foreign languages are involved, more time is needed. My first line of attack in choosing songs is reviewing the wealth of materials found in current and out-of-print graded series music books. Folk songs from America and Western Europe are well represented in these books. Other sources are needed, of course, if the goal is music from such locales as the Balkans, Asia, or Africa.

Vintage American popular songs have been a wonderful discovery for me, and in searching for these songs I use the collection of the Minneapolis Public Library, which has them cataloged by subject area as well as title and composer. This collection was especially useful when we were planning our Minnesota concerts and the aviation concert.

In choosing songs, I look for variety in tempos and keys as well as literary value in the texts. I frequently discard much more than I actually use in a concert. Once the music is chosen, I decide which songs will use dance or other movement and which songs will be dramatized or enhanced with visual arts. Musical content and musicianship are at the center of my theories of performance in the school setting. The other arts, however, are not merely trappings, but integral parts of the whole process and product.

The Art of Dancing

My colleague in physical education helps find the dances to fit our needs. It has been my good fortune to work with this teacher over a twenty-year period, trusting and relying upon his musicianship and good judgment. Sometimes the repertoire of folk dance doesn't fill the bill, and we must create a new dance for existing vocal or instrumental music. We have come up with both folk-style dances, when appropriate, and more free-form structures at other times.

Simplicity is the key word in the dance area. In most cases, the dances are taught to the entire group in the physical education classroom setting. With everyone knowing the dance, we can make choices in casting that provide the widest opportunity for the students, and we do not have to worry about understudies in case of illness on the day of performance.

The Art of Acting and Mime

Most children are born actors, and if they are given the opportunity to improvise within a structure from an early age, their skills can develop into performances that have both grace and poise. I often tell children that I would *never* ask them to do something that would embarrass them in front of their peers or family. I like to keep the improvisatory feeling going as long as possible when using the spoken word and not set the exact wording until the speaker can really feel and interpret the words comfortably.

Many ballads and other folk songs have built-in stories, ready to be acted or mimed. These are good for practice in class before being selected as a component of a concert. My motto is "Opportunity for as many as possible to experience as many of the arts as possible."

The Art of Speaking

The art of speaking, whether in making simple announcements or in presenting a dramatic sketch, has always been the most difficult component for me to teach students. From my viewpoint, if every word is not audible and intelligible from the last row of the auditorium, the performance fails. Even in student performances, audiences are less forgiving of poor speech than of a little faulty intonation or a misplaced dance step. For this reason, I try to assign speaking roles as early as possible. I attribute the difficulty today's children have in public speaking to the lack of emphasis on memorization and oral speaking in contemporary language arts curricula. Music teachers must work around this problem by giving it extra attention.

The Art of Drawing and Painting

The visual arts that we integrate into our concerts are varied, depending upon the choice of theme. The visual aspect of these productions includes such items as programs, posters, scenery, costumes, and props. In addition, student work (from art classes) that relates to the theme is on display at the performance.

Student art work actually helped to solve a logistics problem at my school caused by a shortage of audience seating space. Because a typical cast in my concerts numbers about two hundred performers and the audience seating capacity is only 350, there is always a demand for more seats than available. So, several years ago we started a tradition of back-to-back performances. The concert is usually forty-five to fifty minutes long. On the afternoon of the evening performances, the teachers on my team work quickly to construct an art show and exhibit area in a small gymnasium. This area is also set up with a table of coffee and desserts, which are donated by parent volunteers. Parents and other audience members have the choice of attending either performance and viewing the art exhibit during the other one. For us, this has been a satisfactory solution to the space problem, with the extra benefit to the audience of viewing the students' work and enjoying a social hour. We usually schedule the first performance at 6:30 p.m. and the second at 7:30 p.m. This gives the performers a short break to reset the stage and take care of other important needs.

In my experience, it has been difficult to duplicate the energy of the first performance in the second. Children, and amateur adult performers as well, frequently perform above their actual level of competence, especially in the first staging of a work. This is one of the miracles of live performance and one that cannot be explained completely. The professional performer of any age is required to deliver the same high-quality experience to the audience time after time. Professionals work to achieve this feat; in school we do not have the time to do so. But, by giving two performances back-to-back we can explain to students something about the realities of live performance in the professional world.

Scenery for my concerts is limited by a small budget, a lack of storage space, and the need for portability. I try to create a colorful background for the performers and usually rely on paper from 36-inch rolls in one or two colors as the basis for this background. These strips are hung vertically using strong tape. They can be individually rolled up and clamped if the performance space is used, as mine is, for physical education or school lunch between rehearsals and performances.

The background can be enhanced with items from the students. In the aviation-theme concert, we used the students' original airplane designs on a field of sky blue. Sometimes we construct a large theme banner using the thirty-six-inch paper strips horizontally. Every theme demands a different alphabet for banners and program covers. These alphabets (or print styles) are available in books, and the art teacher helps us locate them.

A symbol for the concert theme, cut in silhouette, can be stunning against a solid background—we used flamenco dancer and toreador silhouettes for the Spanish concert. I sometimes ask for advice and help from the art teacher. When it comes to the actual design for the background, however, I like to have the final word and frequently do most of it myself. Of course, other teachers, teachers' aides, and students help me bring the design to fruition. For example, a sixteen by eight foot Venetian mosaic, constructed from foil paper for the Italian concert, required the help of all two hundred students to glue thousands of mosaic pieces to four sheets of plywood (painted with a flat black latex paint).

My theory of scenery for children is one of economy—less is more. Giving a hint of reality requires the use of imagination. The cinematic realism of television and film has made us lazy viewers. Children especially need the experience of using the imagination to nurture and stimulate creativity.

The Art of Combining the Above

The nature of these experiments in combining the arts is sometimes perilous and filled with added stress, which most school music teachers probably do not need or want. The sheer joy of seeing such a project take shape, however, more than compensates for the extra effort.

Flexibility is the key to success in these projects. I try to remain open to suggestions and ideas generated by students and other staff members. I always acknowledge to parents the importance of my colleagues in putting such a large project together. My colleagues, in turn, assume every year that they will have important roles and enthusiastically support my work in the music area. I am especially grateful to them for the successes we have achieved.

Finale

In conclusion, my efforts in mixing the arts and integrating one into the other have proved to be fascinating and highly satisfactory experiences. I am frequently queried by students on the very first day of school in September, "What will our concert be this year?" Depending upon the lead time in preparation, I put this question off as long as possible to heighten their interest. My usual answer is "I cannot tell you because it's top secret."

Astute critics of my work pointed out several years ago that the annual concert, though in fact an excellent product, is an undertaking rooted in a process—going through the necessary work and learning to achieve a goal. I believe that process should be our first concern in all arts education. When we combine the arts, students can see clearly how the final performance develops from rehearsals and from the bits and pieces we use to construct it. I have been further gratified to see a number of my former students pursue music and theater at the university level and in the professional world. But, it is not these few highly gifted students who make our work truly important—it is the students who will become adult consumers of art and music and who need an understanding of the creative process.

We, as arts educators, need to keep a vision of what the creative process can do and need to convince colleagues in other subject areas and administrators of our point of view. This in itself is an ongoing process and one that will ensure the future of arts education. Parents naturally love a good show involving their children. If we take the opportunity to tell these parents what we are attempting and why we work so hard to achieve it, they will come to support arts in the schools and to understand the importance of music, theater, dance, and the visual arts in their lives and those of their children.

JAPAN
Teaming the Arts

Sandra M. Tsurutome

The Alexander D. Henderson University School is a developmental research school serving grades K-8 and is part of Florida Atlantic University's College of Education. The University School has more than four hundred students from the urban areas of Palm Beach and Broward counties. It is a pilot school for the State of Florida Middle School Advisement and a member of the state task force for the Florida Performance Measurement System.

The cultural diversity of our student population demands that we develop curricula that address the uniqueness of this ethnic diversity and bring understanding and appreciation of these cultures into the classroom. The school can accommodate this pluralistic classroom by providing educational experiences that encourage and develop sensitivity to peoples from a broad spectrum of ethnic backgrounds. An innovative curriculum can contribute to global awareness and can cope with the diverse cultures found in the classrooms of the 1990s.

Curriculum

Multicultural (Ethnic Studies) courses at A. D. Henderson University School, the laboratory school located on the campus of Florida Atlantic University, focus on multicultural education at the middle school level. The result is a total program using a concept-oriented, interdisciplinary approach that emphasizes active participation by students. The program reflects the following characteristics:

- Focus on the life experiences and culture of the people
- Flexible, activity-oriented format
- Affective emphasis
- Common conceptual themes.

The goals of the program are to:

- Assist in the development of increased self-awareness and positive self-concept
- Develop an understanding of, and an appreciation for, the culture
- Promote the acceptance and appreciation of value systems and life styles of the culture
- Share the rich diversity of music, art, dance, and culinary heritages of the country
- Stress the commonality of human experiences among cultural groups.

Courses currently in the school curriculum are focused on Japan, China, Polynesia, 50th State, Israel, Mexico, and Black America. About 90 percent of our students elect an ethnic study class during their middle school years. Music is the common thread that runs through all of the units and provides the entrance to a world of exciting experiences. Students exit each course with a real sense of awareness and appreciation of the culture.

Sandra M. Tsurutome is professor of music and director of research for the Alexander D. Henderson University School at Florida Atlantic University in Boca Raton, Florida.

Getting Started

The following are general guidelines when designing a curriculum for classroom instruction:

- Involve other teachers, parents, and students in the planning

- Team, if possible, with other classes
- Identify the ethnic group represented in each class and use them as a resource
- Encourage students to share their unique cultural background
- Research thoroughly, using parents or other paraprofessionals as resources
- Invite experts from the community to speak on specific cultures and share experiences
- Update the program regularly
- Draw on personal experience
- Dispel stereotypes through discussion
- Check for understanding and learning.

A Typical Course: Japan

Our course on Japan is called "Japan: Teaming the Arts." It teams history, geography, mathematics, and language arts with the music, art, dance, and culinary practices of the culture. The teacher uses an interdisciplinary format to design a unit that is interrelated. A teacher can implement the unit alone or team with another teacher. The objectives for the unit on Japan are as follows:

- To provide information on Japanese history, culture, arts, and traditions in order to better understand and appreciate the culture aspects of Japan and their relationship to our community today
- To provide an awareness of the experiences of the Japanese-American in adapting to American life
- To acknowledge the contributions of Japanese-Americans
- To examine the social and economic impact of Japan on the current life-style of all Americans
- To share in the cultural experiences of Japanese-Americans through participation in various activities and important events
- To discuss common values shared by all people and those particularly associated with the Japanese
- To become familiar with the Japanese as an immigrant group who settled in South Florida and to study their impact on the community.

An introductory lesson on the geography sets the stage for the unit. The students relate to the country globally, and can compare and contrast it to the rest of the world. The seasons are highlighted in the accompanying activities, which often relate to nature. A sample lesson follows.

Geography. Japan consists of four main islands, which form an archipelago that runs north and south. It encompasses both a semitropical and semifrigid zone, providing the nation with weather of almost every sort.

The four seasons are clearly distinct. In the summer there is a rainy season called *tsuyu,* occurring mostly in June. It is the best season for farmers to transplant young rice plants in their paddy fields. After *tsuyu,* a very hot and humid summer sets in. Autumn is when the typhoon season often hits Japan. Generally, however, it is a time when the climate stabilizes and the leaves of the trees turn color and look beautiful. The winters are cold and dry on the east (Pacific Ocean) side and snowy and cold on the Sea of Japan side. The cherry blossoms bloom in spring, and all over Japan people have a common feeling for nature.

The attitude of harmonizing with nature is clearly evident in the daily life of the Japanese. A traditional house, for example, is made of wood, floored with *tatami* (straw mats), and divided into rooms by *shoji,* which are partitions made of wood and paper.

An expanded geography lesson could include map reading and could focus on the topography, cities, and population of Japan. Animal and plant life could also be discussed.

Language Arts. Students never outgrow the desire to have stories read to them. Japanese children's stories are an excellent source for understanding and expressing folklore. These stories tell what the people thought was important to pass on to their children and give information about the culture of the people as it existed long ago. The story used in this lesson is "Saburo," named after the main character, a boy who lived on a farm in Japan. This story is found in *Japanese Children's Favorite Stories,* edited by Florence Sakada (Rutland, VT: C. E. Tuttle Co., 1958). Other sources for folktales are *Little One Inch and Other Japanese Children's Favorite Stories,* edited by Florence Sakada (Rutland, VT: C. E. Tuttle Co., 1958); *The Dancing Kettle and Other Japanese Folktales,* edited by Yoshiko Uchida (New York: Harcourt Brace, 1949); and *Folktales of Japan,* edited by Keigo Seki (Chicago: University of Chicago Press, 1963).

Additional activities may include writing haiku poetry using themes about life on a farm, insects, animals, or the seasons. The class can be divided into four groups–spring, summer, fall, and winter–and each group can write haiku poems about its particular season. Then, the students can illustrate the verses.

History. Historically much of Japan's early culture came from China. The characters used in writing Japanese are called kanji (Chinese letters). The basic number of kanji for general use, taught to all Japanese school-age children, is 1,850. In the first six years of schooling, they are supposed to learn 881 of these, namely the "education kanji." The total number of kanji that have been used at some time or other is about forty thousand.

Many of the most fundamental characters began as pictures, and even now we can often see the connection between shape and meaning. Take for example the kanji for rain: *ame*. You can almost see water dripping out of the sky. It probably originated through an evolutionary pattern, shown in figure 1, ending with the form that is the modern representation.

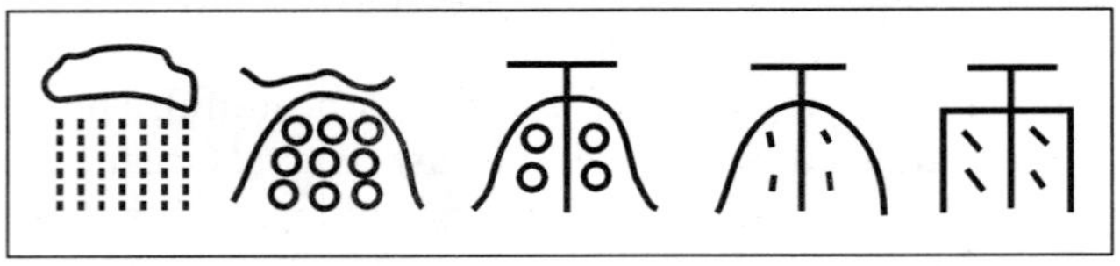

Figure 1. The probable evolution of the kanji character for ame *(rain)*

Music. Japanese music moves within strictly prescribed boundaries. Refinement rather than expansion is the trend. All of the selections in this unit are sung in the vernacular to introduce students to the sound of the language and to identify the key words, which then become part of a vocabulary lesson. The themes of each song deal with nature. Movement and instruments can be added later. A vocabulary puzzle can be constructed to test understanding of the text. All of the songs are traditional folk songs found in any Japanese children's songbook. Figure 2 is the opening of a song about a red dragonfly (prepared by the author).

Dance. A related activity would be to teach "Tanko Bushi," a folk dance of the people of Kyushu, the southernmost island. It tells the story of the coal miners. There are five basic movements repeated over and over:

1. The miners dig for coal with their shovels. They use their feet to help push the shovels deeper into the ground: *Step out with your right foot. With your hands, pretend to hold a shovel and dig. Repeat this movement. Do this movement twice on your left side.*

2. The miners throw the coal over their shoulders into loading carts. This is the second movement: *Take one step with your right foot as you hold your shovel and throw the coal over your right shoulder. Repeat this movement on your left.*

3. Digging coal is hard work. The miners pause to wipe the sweat that drips from their foreheads: *Step back with your right foot. Sweep your right hand, palm facing you, past your forehead, and put your left hand, palm down, out in front of you. Repeat this movement on your left side.*

4. The miners fill their carts and push them out of the mine: *Take a step forward with your right foot and push both hands out at chest level as though you are pushing a cart. Take a step with your left foot and repeat the hand movements.*

5. The miners clap their hands. Their long day is over, and their work is finished: *Put your hands to the side, palms down. Step with your right foot as you move your hands toward each other, crossing over, and then move them apart again. Bring your right foot back. Standing in place, clap your hands twice.*

Art. The art activities in this unit complement the theme of nature and children. One skill used is paper cutting—*kirigami.* In an activity that relates to the song about the red dragonfly, "Aka Tonbo," the children make a symmetrical design by cutting paper, which has been folded in half. The required materials are colored paper, pencil, and scissors. The process is the following: Fold a piece of paper in half. Draw half a dragonfly on the paper. Cut preliminary lines, and then cut out holes in the body. Figure 3 shows the folded paper and the final product.

A more advanced process would be to try a hexagon fold. The math concepts involved in this activity should be discussed. It is a more complicated project but can be accomplished if the design is broken into separate parts. These and other kirigami activities may be found in "The Magic of Kirigami" by Florence Temko and Toshie Takahama (distributed by Japan

Figure 2. The opening measures of the Japanese folk song "Aka Tonbo" ("Red Dragonfly")

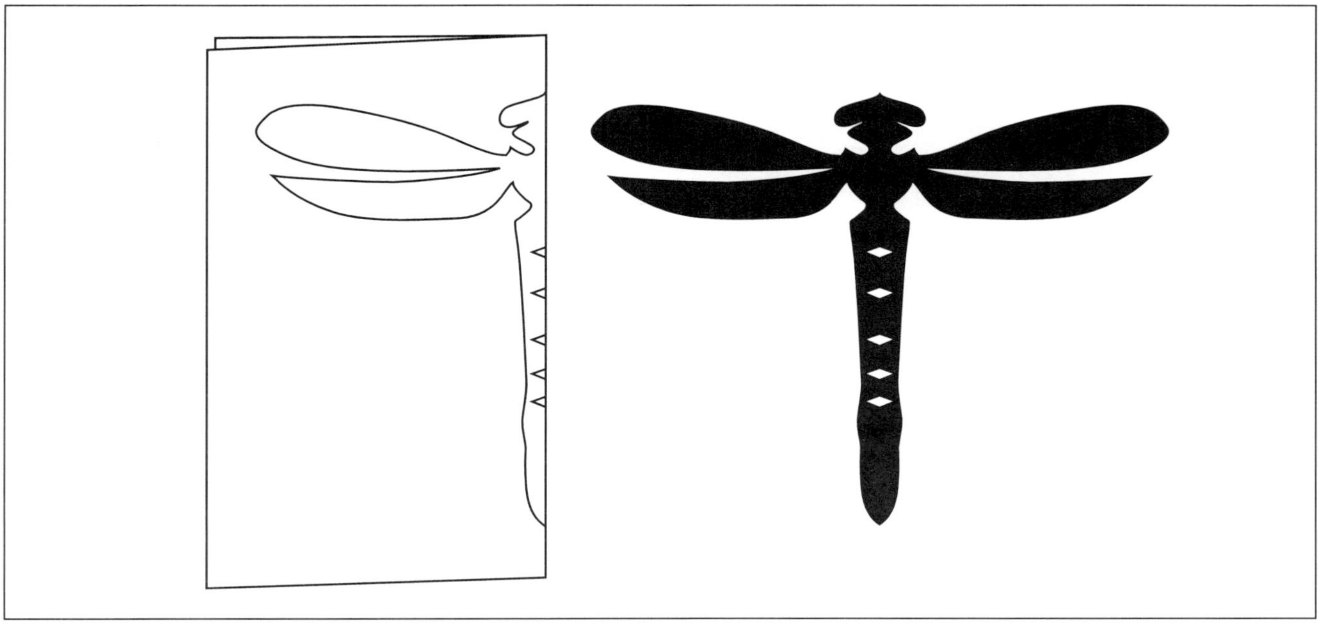

Figure 3. A dragonfly made by kirigami *(paper cutting)*

Publications Trading Co., 200 Clearbrook Rd., Elmsford, NY 10523).

Origami is the art of paper folding. The folded shape in figure 4 is traditionally called a *yakkosan* (manservant), but children enjoy making this figure and putting various faces and clothing on it. It can be used to represent Saburo and his family, the characters in the folktale that the children read.

For Further Information

There are no limits to the types of activities that can be designed to relate to this unit on rural Japan. Additional information and a bibliography of resources for teaching about Japan is available from Dr. Sandra M. Tsurutome, A. D. Henderson University School, 500 N. W. 20th Street, Boca Raton, FL 33431 (Phone: (407) 367-3977).

Figure 4. A human figure made by origami (paper folding)

TECHNOLOGY

TECHNOLOGY IN THE MIDDLE SCHOOL
A Powerful Potential

Brian Moore

The middle school movement seeks to improve the education of the adolescent. At the core of this movement lies the realization that adolescent learners are neither miniature high school students nor "big" elementary children, but rather unique and special people. Much of the discussion of the middle school concept focuses on the environment for learning. The inclusion of sixth grade, the team approach to teaching, and exploratory experiences that lead toward mastery help in fostering a unique environment for the adolescent learner. Technology can be a strong and motivating force in this environment by engaging adolescent learners and unleashing their creative potential. When technology is integrated into an arts curriculum such as music, the results can be even more astounding.

In today's world, technology surrounds us and has become an almost indispensable and often invisible aspect of our lives. Technologies that were on the cutting edge a decade ago, such as the microwave oven and the video cassette recorder, are now commonplace. We also see evidence of one area of technology enhancing another area; for example, the cellular phone has given rise to portable fax machines that can be used in a car. Even the use of the word *technology* has become more widespread and encompasses more than just computers.

Brian Moore is associate professor of music education in the School of Music at the University of Nebraska in Lincoln.

Technology in Education

For the educational community, however, technology is still largely defined in terms of the personal computer and is only now slowly branching out to other areas. While educational television has been with us for awhile, it has been the computer that has received instructional attention as a curricular area. In the early years of instructional computing, for example, we spent much time and energy in the teaching of LOGO, a graphics-oriented computer programming language. What is it about the computer that captured the attention of the educational community as a sole definition of technology?

The computer ignited the imagination of educators, who saw the potential of individualizing instruction based on "time to learn" since students could access and process information in a self-paced format. The application of previously introduced concepts and skills through drill-and-practice software allowed students to progress as quickly or as slowly as desired. Furthermore, the same technological platform could be used in many curricular areas. In addition to traditional areas such as science and math, software appeared in disciplines such as language, history, and music. The application of computer-assisted instruction in an arts curriculum was, in hindsight, a major step forward in the use of technology as an integrated resource within the school environment.

Computers and technology also seem to hold a special attraction for the adolescent learner. This interest on the part of students has been a motivating factor in educators' use of technology. The adolescent is a naturally curious and energetic individual. One does not need to spend much time in classroom situations with learners of this age to realize their need for structure with some flexibility, and for challenges that are within their reach. These characteristics are accompanied by an insatiable desire to be accepted as part of the group. The ways these attributes manifest themselves in adolescents' attraction to technology, both in and out of school, can be summed up in two words: culture and control.

Technology as a Facet of Our Culture

Adolescents have grown up with technology and accept it as a normal and expected aspect of life. From the Walkman to MTV, the personal use of technology is seamlessly integrated into their daily experience. Much of the technology that captures their attention relates to music. The consumer market for electronic keyboards has exploded in recent years. As a group, adolescents constitute an important and very large market for the purchase of recorded cassettes and compact discs. When asked to identify their preferred type or style of music, most middle school students will not respond with "rock" or "rap" but with the name of a particular group, radio station, or cable video station. Their listening to music goes far beyond the music itself, extending to sight, symbol, and sensation. The adolescents' need for acceptance is even evidenced in their need to be part of a music culture, be it through their immediate peer group or MTV.

With the introduction of computers in the school curriculum beginning in the early 1970s, students began to experience a technology that enabled and empowered their personal productivity and creativity. Student access to computers has expanded from solely school situations to now include home use. This has allowed students who have always had a keen interest in music (but have not found a matching niche in the school curriculum) to realize this interest and, in many cases, to demonstrate high levels of ability and talent.

Student Control over the Learning Environment

With the exception of elementary instrumental music, the middle school presents students with perhaps their first opportunity to control their destiny within school by choosing an elective. The exploratory nature of the middle school, coupled with its ability to provide students with choices in the form of electives, gives the adolescent a degree of control over his or her classroom environment.

Technology, especially that of the computer, continues this sense of personal control because learning experiences can be self-paced and, depending upon the software and activity, sequenced according to the desire of the user. Early instructional software was menu-driven, allowing the student to select from a listing of choices. Each menu item contained sub-menus and so forth; thus, the prominent feature of this learning environment was the ability to vary the amount of learning time. Students could progress through these sets of menus as quickly or slowly as desired.

Recent improvements in both hardware and software have yielded instructional software that is event-driven; activity or action determined by the user is the guiding factor in the learning experience. Rather than going through or backing up from a series of menus, the user simply does an action (event). In comparison to menu-driven programs, event-driven software is much more conducive to real-life activities and gives even more control to the user. Event-driven software is also a better metaphor for real-life activities such as the composition of music. Since we have no clear sense of the "best" sequence or approach to the creation of music, it would be inappropriate to design composition software with an implied hierarchy (menu) and sequence.

The ability of technology to match the desires, interests, and strengths of the user in solving a problem fosters an environment that considers not only the student's time needed to learn, but also his or her preferred style of learning.

The Adolescent's Attraction to Music Technology

Research and actual practice have often identified the dichotomy between "real" music and "school" music. Especially for adolescent students, music is one area with little correlation between personal interests and the kinds of experiences found in the school environment. This dichotomy emphasizes one reason why middle school students are so attracted to technology in music—the technology enables them to realize their interests in music in a way that schools have traditionally not addressed.

The traditional approach to school music at the secondary level has embraced group instruction and a focus on performance. While we, as teachers, acknowledge the strength of the performance ensemble as one means of musical education, most of our students do not elect such experiences. In order to realize their interests in music, they turn to other resources outside of public school music education.

The Marketplace of Technology and Music

One needs only to peruse the catalogs from mail-order software houses to realize the impact of music on the noneducational technology community. Music software is often listed side by side with other categories of software such as word processors, spreadsheets, and graphic design programs. An approach to music from a technical rather than an artistic perspective is reflected in the way some catalogs group software and hardware under MIDI (Musical Instrument Digital Interface) rather than under music. Music has emerged as an area of interest for the home hobbyist since the technology can enable people with little musical knowledge to realize their musical desires from the vantage point of listener, performer, and, most dramatically, composer.

Much of the hardware and software that has been developed for music composition requires little, if any, formal musical training to use. For example, many software sequencers that have been developed for the home market include in their documentation an appendix on "how to read music." The amateur musician with a good ear and a self-taught "single-finger" ability on a musical keyboard can quickly and efficiently create, edit, and save quite complex musical compositions. These compositions can be realized in full symphonic proportions given the capabilities of multiphonic and polytimbral MIDI instruments.

It is important to point out the ways in which the creative musical process can be enhanced or changed via the use of technology. One advantage is increased visual and aural contact with the musical product. Throughout the working and reworking of the composition, the user can quickly develop, change, and refine ideas, and then play them back and view them in either iconic or traditional notation on a computer monitor. Ideas that form the basis of the complete work can be sequenced in various orders and forms to create longer phrases. Traditional compositional alterations such as retrogrades, augmentations, and transpositions are easily done via sequencing software and hardware. Other types of alterations that are more specific to the software are also available, including looping (repeating any section of music), diatonic transposition (moving music up or down a line or space rather than a set interval), and pitch changes such as pitch bend and modulation (vibrato). An important advantage of making these changes via technology is the increased ability to make modifications at very high levels of precision.

A second advantage of using technology for composition is the ease of producing printed musical output. For many individuals, seeing the music in visual form is the best method for reviewing and reworking of ideas, especially as a piece nears completion. While producing professional-level notation takes a great deal of time and attention at the final editing stage, the initial entry of the notation and generation of parts shorten the tedium associated with creating hard copy of a musical work. The empowering aspect of the printing capabilities of technology is that professional, camera-ready scores of stunning clarity are possible via desktop music publishing.

The technology of MIDI software and hardware can provide a musical environment for personal creativity that, up to now, not even professional musicians have been able to enjoy. This is, in essence, a technology-based environment that enables the user to do things that would otherwise be near impossible.

Interestingly enough, this development has presented quite a dilemma for music educators. With such unlimited access to the creation and recreation of music with relative ease, certain concerns have emerged. Students have the potential of developing "bad" musical habits due to a lack of knowledge and evaluative abilities. Technology does not improve the ability to make music, but merely serves as a catalyst for musical creativity. Technology can accelerate the production of music, which could result in bad art in potentially large quantities.

The Challenge to Music Educators

Music has always been a technology-based art. From the psaltry and harp to the valved horn and synthesizer, the making of music, by necessity, requires some form of technology. The use of technology, however, does not necessarily result in a better musician. A student using a word processor to write a paper is not automatically a better writer. Technology changes the processes used to yield a final product, and because the technology provides a greater potential for generating output, new concepts are presented that confront and hence impact on the educational process. The act of musical composition can now be experienced by the youngest musician, and improvisation, long relegated only to relatively advanced jazz experiences, is not only feasible but welcomed by the young learner.

We have not made significant advances in our music curricula beyond the traditional approach of performance ensembles. If we are to reach the middle-level student, the school music curriculum must include creative experiences along with our existing, heavy focus on performing and listening.

The challenge for music education is thus twofold: to assess and to adapt. Software and hardware designed for noneducational markets must be integrated into an educational environment with specific curricular outcomes and goals. Before that can occur, we need to assess our current efforts as well as the potential of the available technology. Only then can hardware and software be thoughtfully selected and integrated in order to accomplish instructional objectives and goals. Simply having and using technology is not enough. Our focus needs to be on our desired musical outcomes—the products that result from the processes. For example, few music educators have approached ways to foster aspects of higher level thinking, such as musical creativity, within their everyday curricula.

Resources for Solutions

Few issues illustrate the need for education and industry to work together better than technology. Gifted and talented programs, special education programs, and curriculum are most often directly developed and controlled by the local district. Even textbooks, though published by professional houses, must go through formal adoption procedures either at the state or local level. It is conceivable that a teacher could develop an original curriculum and not rely upon the publishing industry to support the teaching and learning in a specific classroom. If the curriculum involves technology, however, independent development may not be possible. From the perspective of time, money, and expertise, the resources for the development of software and especially hardware are clearly not within the grasp of even the most affluent school districts. If educational technology, with its growing complexity and sophistication, is to be an efficient and effective resource, formal partnerships between the educational community and the private sector must be fostered and strengthened.

In order to develop technology that makes educational sense, we must give instructional needs precedence over technical concerns. In short, education should be the driving force behind the research and development of hardware and software for the teaching of music. Since the process of developing technology is hardware driven, design specifications, as well as the practical application of a software or hardware project, are usually guided by engineers and technical personnel rather than educators. As technology continues to grow in complexity, the level of educators' involvement in all phases of research and development will need to increase if the final product is to be efficient and effective in the teaching and learning of music. Industries that involve music and technology, such as the manufacture of electronic keyboards and computers, have certainly realized the importance of partnership with the educational community. Virtually all of the major technological corporations now have executives who have an education background and who perform a cooperative, liaison function for all levels of education, from preschool through college.

Future Directions

Perhaps the most important, lasting impact of technology has been in forcing educators to adapt to rapid change. Current trends and issues facing education, in one way or another, focus on the need for us all to adapt to change. The need to develop higher level thinking skills, the restructuring of schools, and the emergence of the middle school concept reflect the impact of change on our society. Solutions are needed for problems that did not exist a decade ago. Furthermore, a solution for a problem today will not last twenty years as it might have in the past. We will be called upon not only to adapt, but also to adapt at faster and faster rates.

Music education finds itself caught in this tidal wave of change. Our tradition of teaching music through performance ensembles is no longer sufficient to meet the needs of all our learners. Students are interested in performing music, but students—especially at the middle level—are also interested in creating music and making it more personal. It is clear that the status quo will not be efficient or effective in addressing the new problems and possibilities that we face. Technology will continue to be an important and driving force in addressing the need for improved teaching methods. "States are increasing their support for the arts, including music, through new graduation mandates. The integration of technology in the music curriculum, efforts to build student awareness of the music of other cultures, and projects to develop sounder means of assessing student progress in music are winning support" (O'Neil, 1990, p. 1).

One of the ways in which musical creativity can be fully fostered and explored is through the same technology that has created the need for a shift in our thinking. Technology becomes humanizing by providing opportunities for musical and hence aesthetic expression (Moore, 1989).

As music educators, we should view the changes in the world around us as the impetus for taking fresh and new views of what we do, how we do it, and for whom. The exciting challenge of technology and the middle school is to be active rather than reactive in our role as music educators. As we challenge our students, we also challenge ourselves. No amount of software or hardware can ever take the place of caring teachers since, after the family, we are the most important educator for the adolescent.

References

O'Neil, J. (1990, June). Music education: Experts take new look at performance, general music. *Curriculum Update,* p. 1.

Moore, B. (1989). Musical thinking processes. In E. Boardman (Ed.), *Dimensions of musical thinking* (pp. 33-44). Reston, VA: Music Educators National Conference.

APPLICATIONS OF TECHNOLOGY IN THE MUSIC CLASSROOM

Stephan P. Barnicle

Simsbury High School is a suburban Connecticut school with more than four thousand students. It offers its students music technology courses.

Have you ever wished that you could isolate the viola part of a Beethoven symphony for your students to hear and at the same time see in the score? Have you ever wanted to show your students a video on the development of an instrument, or the orchestra, or sonata-allegro form? Would you like to show them a video on the life of a composer, and answer any questions they might ask with immediate, accurate information?

Have you ever wished that you had an accompanist available at all times who could change tempos and keys to suit your students' needs? Have you ever wished that, when you sat at the piano, you could capture your creative ideas and turn them into printed scores?

Today's technology enables us to make all these wishes come true in the middle school classroom (as well as in classrooms of other age groups). So now the question becomes "How do we use these new tools in the classroom to meet our students' needs in understanding the art of music?"

First, consider what types of tools are readily available now, at reasonable costs, and how they can help us in our teaching. These tools can be divided into three basic categories:

- *Technology-assisted music instruction.* These applications help teachers and students in the traditional processes of music instruction.
- *Technology-based instruction.* These applications are made possible and desirable by the technological advances themselves. These applications are not traditionally taught in music classrooms or, perhaps, not taught with the ease now possible or at the grade levels now appropriate.
- *Classroom support.* These applications may not apply directly to the teaching and learning process, but they can help teachers be more effective classroom managers.

Stephan P. Barnicle is choral, orchestral, and music technology teacher at Simsbury High School in Simsbury, Connecticut. He is also executive director of the Simsbury Music and Arts Center, a summer program for students in grades 3–9.

Technology-Assisted Music Instruction

The first question usually asked about introducing new technological advances into schools is "How can it help me teach or help my students learn what is in our existing curriculum?" The answers are as varied as the tools available and the ways in which your imagination can apply these tools. One approach is to ask yourself what you would do "if" a certain condition could be met.

For example, what would you do "if" you really could show your seventh-grade students a video on the development of the orchestra or the life of a composer, and answer their questions with immediate, accurate information? With today's interactive video discs, all this information and much more is at your fingertips. While the library of discs is still quite limited, the scope of the information and the ease and speed with which it can be accessed is extraordinary. The question is, how would you choose to apply this resource?

As interactive video discs are introduced into classrooms around the country, teachers are finding them indispensable in general music situations where they have long been searching for ways to keep students interested in learning about the classics. As more discs become available, even more situations are sure to be found for their application.

Synthesizers. When a colleague of mine recently asked sixth-grade students in a rural Connecticut school to bring in electronic keyboards if they had them, enough keyboards were brought in so that every student in each music class had a keyboard to use. By following this kind of example, we can meet our students where they are and "lead them out" to the knowledge we want them to have.

Electronic keyboards or synthesizers offer an abundance of instructional applications, ranging from basic keyboard introduction to timbre design. Many synthesizers are now classified as music workstations since they include on-board sequencers (which record the note events making up a score), effects processors (which shape the sound), and disc storage capabilities (which save the students' work). Exciting lessons in composition and improvisation can be developed with such instruments. They can make elements of form graphically clear to students.

A synthesizer also allows you to prepare accompaniments for choral rehearsals or performances. For example, my concert choir was to prepare a touring operetta production of Gilbert and Sullivan's *Trial by Jury* to present at the elementary and middle schools in town. Considering what to do about accompaniment, I knew I did not have an orchestra available nor the services of a competent accompanist. Therefore, I decided to sequence the orchestration on a Roland D-20 synthesizer. Playing each part in separately from the full score proved to be a great deal of fun, although time-consuming. The final product was a very usable orchestration of the piece. While the synthesizer did not give me the timbral accuracy of an actual orchestra, it did prove to be a lot more convenient (not to mention more in tune), and it suited the comic character of the work perfectly.

Computers. The choice of a computer for a particular program is very much an individual matter, since there are now so many excellent programs for almost any computer; however, user friendliness is a priority for most music teachers, who have little time for learning advanced computer skills.

Students may use the computer for a variety of applications, ranging from theory tutorials to sophisticated sequencing and printing programs that allow students to capture their performance at the keyboard and translate it into a beautiful printed score.

Of course, the same programs the students use can turn out clear scores and parts for your own compositions, arrangements, and exercises for the classroom. You can also record accompaniments on the sequencer program for playback on any MIDI synthesizer or sound source you choose, with complete control of tempi, keys, and timbres.

Dedicated Hardware. There are a variety of instruments available that are dedicated to specific tasks and can be of great assistance to your program. I have found two such instruments invaluable: TAP Master and Pitch Master (both from Temporal Acuity Products).

The TAP Master is a rhythm practice tutor that allows a student to develop rhythmic reading skills as he or she taps written rhythms of graduated difficulty to a variety of styles of music. The TAP Master keeps score of the accuracy of the responses and gives immediate reinforcement of accurate responses. Similarly, the Pitch Master keeps track of the accuracy of pitch responses of a voice or an instrument directed toward a microphone. The exciting aspect of using the Pitch Master is the fact that you are able to create your own materials. For example, a choir director could provide a tape recording of a choral piece in which the student hears three parts being sung and is asked to sing his or her own part along with the tape.

Tape Recorder. It is easy to overlook the obvious when we search for applications of technology in the music classroom. Many wonderful musical examples are available on video tape for use in the classroom, and most schools have the means to record programs that might be of value to students. The audio tape recorder is also a versatile teaching tool. The imaginative teacher will use it in creative ways–its uses are numerous and the cost is relatively low.

If a teacher is purchasing an audio tape recorder for the classroom, he or she might want to consider one of the many multitrack cassette units available that include mixing capabilities, limited equalization, and effects send/return options. These can be wonderful tools for teaching students the basics of recording technology, balance, intonation, and general musicianship. It's amazing how excited a student becomes when he or she records a simple rhythm track and some chords from a synthesizer/drum machine, overdubs some guitar or flute notes on another track, sings along with some original lyrics on a third or fourth track, and then adds some reverb to the final mix.

Of course, this same recorder (or tape deck) can be used to play commercial recordings as music examples. I also use it to provide accompaniment to a vocal or choral selection. Many teachers shudder at the thought of taped accompaniments; however, there are strong arguments for their use, particularly in the classroom. Ask yourself, for example, which comes closer to the intentions of the composer: (a) the sound of a piano, probably in need of tuning, played by an accompanist more or less able to follow a conductor, depending on his or her abilities, or (b) an inflexible, but accurate tape of professional musicians playing the appropriate instruments in tune and with good balance? Your answer might be the taped accompaniment. Today, of course, you can also opt for a sequencer-driven sound module, which lets you have complete control of tempo and key and gives you the capability to prepare the music yourself.

Technology-Based Instruction

Due to advances in music and sound technology, we must reconsider our entire approach to music education. While these tools can make many of our tasks easier, quicker, and more effective, the real news is that they open up new ways of looking at the process of teaching music to students. I have tried approaches including:

- Teaching to the technology: Show the students the capabilities of the equipment. They will then find a "need to know" and ask pertinent musical questions. You will find that the students learn more than you would have been able to teach in a more traditional classroom.
- Teaching scientific concepts: Teach the students about sound wave generation, timbre, and envelope. Look for opportunities for interdisciplinary concepts (related to math or science). For example, to teach an understanding of synthesis it is essential to teach some basic physics of sound.
- Teaching composition via sequencers: Let the students create music from a hands-on or "sound before sign" approach.

Today's sequencer technology allows us to view the composition process from a more global approach, considering formal elements (form, progression, style, instrumentation) even before we delve heavily into notation. To quote Edwin Gordon, we can now put "sound before sign" even in the composition process.

- Teaching musicianship via the recording studio: Use the studio to provide students with a concrete approach to such abstract concepts as intonation, balance, stereophonics, equalization, effects processing, and timbre. The multitrack recorder provides a convenient platform for teaching aural skills. You don't need a professional-level recording studio or ultra-fancy equipment to do this.

Rethinking the Electronic Music Class

In the 1970s, when many of us first began teaching electronic music, it was usually an esoteric course in which we directed students in exploratory projects, which lead to the creation of avant-garde pieces by connecting a series of modular sound generators and wave shapers, or perhaps by splicing together tape loops of "found sounds."

Today, such classes have disappeared for the most part, being replaced, if at all, by courses representing a variety of uses of today's musical technology. Most of these newer classes seem to gravitate around the teaching of basic keyboard skills, using synthesizers instead of electronic piano labs, with the addition of computers used for tutorial purposes to help instruct the students.

While this may be a more realistic approach to music in the classroom, let's not overlook what might have been lost in letting these earlier programs die or be transformed. The lack of controllability of the earlier synthesizers led us to a more basic approach to sound and control of sound elements in the creation of a piece of music. Therefore, it might be argued that our students were being offered a unique opportunity to be creative in designing their "sound pieces." I am not suggesting a return to such course offerings, but I, for one, have found it useful to look at them to see what good we might have discarded with the less valuable.

Advances in sound technology offer us some unique opportunities to encourage creativity in the art of music and sound design. We must take advantage of these opportunities and design curricula that foster such creativity in our students.

Curriculum Development

Every program in music technology should be based on an understanding of the basic elements of sound and sound synthesis. Courses should be developed, therefore, not beginning with the elements of music (meter, rhythm, tonality, etc.) but rather with the elements of sound (frequency, amplitude and timbre). When our students can understand and control these, we can move onward to the elements of music.

Creativity-based courses are essential, not only for the complete development of our students but also for the future existence of our profession. As our society is forced to reevaluate its educational structures, only programs that meet definable student needs will survive. One of the essential ingredients of a complete education, most lacking in our present system, is creativity. Any program that cultivates this quality will be prized.

Creativity-based projects can range from simple units to entire courses of study. One that I have often used with young students includes preparing a "commercial" advertisement for the school's morning announcements. If the drama or music departments are advertising an upcoming play or concert production, we will offer to record a morning announcement to advertise it.

Ordinarily, the sponsoring organization or some of its students will provide the script, and our class will provide the music. While this can be a very simple project, I like to include research on the styles most appropriate and make the best tape possible, even if only twenty to thirty seconds worth of music. Students are first asked to listen to the music behind radio and television commercials. They are asked to make tape-recorded excerpts of some favorites to bring in to demonstrate different styles of music used for different products. Together, they determine a style of music most appropriate for the message being given. The music is prepared, usually composed by the students, performed on anything from a cappella vocals (even monophonic plainchant) to student rock bands. If drum machines and synthesizers are available, this can be the easiest approach. Once prepared and timed to meet the needs of the script, it is taped onto a multitrack cassette deck. The script is then taped onto an additional track and, in the final mix-down, is appropriately balanced with the music. At this mix-down stage, any desired reverberation or other effects are added to any or all tracks to "dress" the performance.

Another often used project that has even greater creative potential is the creation of sound effects for school plays. For a recent production of *South Pacific,* my class was asked to create sound bites, including the sound of World War II vintage propeller-driven airplanes taking off and the sound of such planes diving and shooting as heard through a static-filled radio. Using an old analog synthesizer (Electrocomp Music Laboratory 200), we patched together several combinations of tone and noise generators, signal switcher, filters, and reverberation until we had just the right sounds. These were recorded onto stereo tape for playback during the performances. The students were very proud when they heard these realistic sounding effects and saw their names in the program as "sound designers."

One additional advantage to projects such as these is their suitability for inclusion in portfolios of each student's work. For those teachers wishing to use the portfolio assessment model of Project Zero, in which a portfolio of each student's work is kept from year to year in a subject area to document the progress being made over an extended period, these projects would fit right in. A student's portfolio in music, as a matter of fact, could consist of several years' work on a cassette tape, as well as printed material.

Classroom Support

Technology can also be used as a tool for basic classroom support. The software and hardware that help with teaching and learning objectives can also support activities such as classroom and department management. You can create computerized data bases of music libraries, uniform and instrument inventories, student test scores, addresses, phone numbers, and schedules. You can use word processing programs to simplify communications with parents and colleagues, streamline test construction, and print programs. Spreadsheets will help you calculate test scores, grades, program funds, or any other numeric data.

Computer-based programs, such as *Band-in-a-Box* (produced by PG Music), can be used to create exercises for jazz-band students to practice improvisation with ever-changing backgrounds. Tapes can be prepared for students to take home for continued practice.

Testing can become much more manageable by using some of the new technology. As a choral director, I spent more than fifteen years searching for a reliable method of monitoring and grading the progress of singers in my choirs. My goal was to capture the performance of each student while singing within the choir in order to evaluate that performance on a series of criteria.

I can now achieve this testing goal. Using a multitrack recorder, I set up four microphones across the front of the rehearsal room. With an appropriate piece of music to measure the desired characteristics, the choir stands in its usual sections and sings through the music several times. Each time it is sung, the microphones are placed in front of a different singer in each section. Each of these singers is then recorded on an individual track of the recorder.

As the students begin to sing each repetition, it is important to list the students who are being recorded on each microphone (see figure 1). The singers announce their "quartet number" before beginning. This allows me, at the time of scoring, to score each singer relatively anonymously. When the taping is completed, it is possible to listen to all of the sopranos, one after the other on the same track, scoring them on each of the criteria selected for evaluation. When this section is completed, the altos, tenors, and basses can be likewise scored.

The most important element of such a procedure, of course, is developing the criteria and the scale to be used. In my case, seven criteria were selected, and the scale was from 1 to 5 (see figure 2). After scoring each singer on all seven criteria, I copy the names from the list to the score sheet (see figure 3) and give each student a printout of his or her scores, including a composite picture of strengths and weaknesses as a choral singer.

If a student, or parent, wishes to question the scores, an appointment is made and we listen to the taped performance together as we look at the test criteria. It usually has taken about thirty seconds for each student to agree that the scoring is quite accurate. Finally, I have the means to support my grades and my advice to students with concrete data, thanks to the use of a few microphones and a multitrack recorder.

New Curricular Trends

Many new directions in curriculum development are possible through technology. Some of the most exciting developments include two hardware-based, curriculum-oriented projects: Yamaha's Music in Education project, based on a network of keyboards attached to a computer, and a similar project of the Vivace corporation, which plans to load curricular material in the resident memory of a music workstation.

Other trends include using technological advances to make routine practicing of traditional instruments more palatable. Michael Katz, the author/composer of *Jump Start!* (Gracenote: West Simsbury, CT) instrumental materials, says that the goal of his project is to create materials that are "easy enough for anyone to play, yet interesting enough for everyone to enjoy." This is accomplished by providing taped accompaniments and examples of every exercise in the instrumental series at graduated tempi, starting with first-time playing and progressing to performance tempo. Words are also provided for each song.

Many curriculum-oriented programs, it should be pointed out, offer workshops to users. These programs provide new ways of approaching the age-old art of music education.

Summary

It is clear that today's technology is challenging the music educator to rethink his or her approach to the classroom. It is also clear that today's music educator has an opportunity to become a leader in the development of new applications of today's and tomorrow's technology.

Developments in music technology have always influenced the arts of music and music education. Not all changes are readily accepted. Just as Baroque church musicians were replaced by the great organs developed during that period, many musicians today feel that they must resist the advent of instruments that are replacing them. Yet, if we remember that the fundamentals of music and musicianship never change, we can deal more easily with innovations. Our task, as music educators, is to help our students develop their musicianship, using whatever available tools help in this process.

Simsbury High School Music Department

Quartet #	Soprano	Alto	Tenor	Bass
1	Angela	Amy B.	Todd	Jon K.
2	Bridget	Courtney	Dan C.	Josh
3	Alice	Amy L.	Graham	Chad
4	Lori T.	Carly	Billy	Andy
5	Erin	Jennifer	Steve	Art
6	Sharon	Shelley	Matt S.	Dan M.
7	Sandy	Bonnie	Jon S.	Matt P.
8	Karen	Anne		Don
9	Patti			Mike
10				
11				
12				
13				
14				
15				
16				
17				
18				
19				
20				
21				
22				
23				
24				
25				
26				

Figure 1. A choral testing chart

Simsbury High School Music Department

Choral Adjudication Form

Students will be evaluated according to the following categories on a taped performance of a selected choral work:

I. Tone Quality:
5—Tone is full, relaxed, open and well supported throughout the voice range
4—Tone is relaxed, open and supported throughout most of the voice range
3—Tone is moderately relaxed, with open throat but with some minor tension apparent
2—Tone is somewhat breathy or pinched with some tension and/or insufficient support
1—Tone is harsh or breathy with apparent tension and/or lack of support

II. Diction:
5—All consonants are clearly articulated
4—Unvoiced consonants are consistently distinct; voiced consonants are usually articulated
3—Unvoiced consonants are usually articulated; voiced consonants are sometimes muffled
2—Unvoiced consonants are sometimes articulated; voiced consonants are often muffled
1—All consonants are muffled or inaudible

III. Pronunciation:
5—All consonants and all vowels are properly pronounced with proper inflection
4—All consonants and all vowels are properly pronounced with some incorrect inflection
3—Some consonants are mispronounced, vowels are correct form with incorrect inflection
2—Some consonants and vowels are mispronounced
1—Consonants and vowels are consistently mispronounced

IV. Note Accuracy:
5—All notes are correct pitch and duration
4—Most notes are correct pitch and duration
3—Most notes are correct but some pitch and/or duration discrepancies occur
2—Many incorrect pitches, or some singing the wrong part
1—Mostly incorrect pitches, or often singing the wrong part

V. Intonation:
5—All notes are in tune
4—Most notes are in tune
3—Many notes are in tune
2—Some notes are in tune
1—Few notes are in tune

VI. Phrasing/Breath Control:
5—All phrases are properly shaped (dynamics) and breaths are taken quietly, and at appropriate times
4—Most phrases are properly shaped (dynamics) and breaths are taken at appropriate times
3—Some phrases are properly shaped (dynamics) but some breaths are taken at inappropriate times
2—Few phrases are properly shaped (dynamics) and many breaths are taken at inappropriate times
1—Phrases are not shaped and breathing is erratic

VII. Ensemble:
5—All attacks and cut-offs are accurate
4—Attacks are consistently accurate but some final consonants are slightly early or late
3—Attacks are consistently accurate but many final consonants are early or late
2—Many attacks are accurate but cut-offs are consistently early or late
1—Attacks and cut-offs are consistently inaccurate

Figure 2. Test criteria

Simsbury High School Music Department

Choral Adjudication Score Form

Date: *1/93* Group: *Concert Choir* Section: *Soprano*

Adjudication Piece: *Wondrous Cool* Composer: *Brahms*

Student #	Voice Range	Voice Part	I	II	III	IV	V	VI	VII	Total	Name
1	g-g"	Sop II	4	3	4	4	3	4	3	25	Angela
2	f-a"	Sop I	3	3	3	4	3	2	3	21	Bridget
3	g-b"	Sop I	3	2	3	3	4	3	3	21	Alice
4	g-a"	Sop I	5	4	5	4	4	3	4	29	Lori T.
5	e-c"	Sop I	4	4	5	4	4	3	4	28	Erin
6	g-a"+	Sop I	3	2	3	3	4	2	3	20	Sharon
7	f-g"	Sop II	4	2	2	3	3	2	3	19	Sandy
8	f-f"	Sop II	3	4	3	5	4	3	3	25	Karen
9	g-b"	Sop I	4	4	3	4	3	4	4	26	Patti

Figure 3. Score sheet for students' performances

TECHNOLOGY
A Hands-On, Creative, Interdisciplinary Approach to Teaching Music

Walter Mamlok

Newtown Middle School has more than nine hundred students from an affluent, suburban Connecticut community that is highly supportive of its music programs.

When seventh-grade students walk into the music lab, their mouths drop open. In the center of the room is a circle of keyboards, headsets, cables, and computers. On the walls are posters of their music heroes, rock stars, put together in a collage. In a cabinet is a small mixing board, amplifier, sound processor, and dual cassette deck. As the students enter, I'm playing a B. B. King song. Then I'll play a cassette recording of a student composition that used the same song as a guide. In both cases, I'm asking the students to write in their journals what they are hearing, what they like about each piece, and what concerns they might have about each piece. The students are surprised when I tell them that the second song they heard was composed by students the previous year.

The music lab is aimed at the nonperforming music student and is quite popular at my school. Yet, why are performance groups generally viewed as more successful than the average general music class? If you visit middle schools or junior high schools in Connecticut, both the music teacher and the school administrator are quick to point to the performance groups as the pride of the music department. Is the success of the band, orchestra, and chorus due to the type of students involved or to the way they learn their subject matter? What would happen if students could experience general music in a way that approximates the way band, orchestra, and chorus students experience music? Today's technology allows general music students to do just that.

The way I have applied this new technology to help me teach music in middle school is not a traditional conservatory approach. Music is an abstract concept. In order for students to understand the different concepts that make up music (e.g., the five elements of rhythm, timbre, harmony, melody, and form), they should be in the formal operation stage of reasoning. According to noted child psychologist Jean Piaget, the development of formal thought could start as early as age eleven and does not fully develop until the age of sixteen or seventeen (Woolfolk, 1990); therefore, the conservatory method of teaching is inappropriate. A more useful method is one that serves as a bridge between the different developmental stages of the adolescent child.

Today's technology helps take the abstract and make it concrete. The music lab at the Newtown Middle School has four Ensoniq Performance Sampler (EPS) work stations, two Apple IIgs computers, and one Macintosh SE computer. The EPS work station was chosen because of its on-board sequencing features, sampling capabilities, disk storage, excellent sound reproduction, and ease of use. The basic premise for the program is to provide a hands-on musical learning experience. It is my belief that by

Walter Mamlok is an instrumental and general music teacher for grades 6–8 at Newtown Middle School in Newtown, Connecticut.

teaching students to compose music, all of our goals for music can be reached. These goals include understanding the five elements of music, music history, and music appreciation.

Getting Started

Because there are four keyboards in the music lab, class size is restricted to no more than sixteen students. The first thing I must do is divide the class into four cooperative learning teams. The students are responsible for keeping individual writing journals. Each team member has specific tasks. The "manager" organizes the project according to the order of assignments. The "timekeeper" makes sure everyone has an equal amount of time on the keyboard and that the project is on schedule. The "encourager" is like a cheerleader and helps team members complete their tasks. The "foreman" makes sure that everyone does, in fact, complete the assignments.

The students' journals become their music books. The journal is divided into two sections, a glossary and a daily diary. When new terms are introduced in class, students add them to their glossaries with a definition in their own words. At the end of the period, they write down (in less than fifteen words) what they did in class that day.

Students also use the journal as a planning book for their assignments. They must have a specific style in mind for each composition or project, and they must identify a music group they can listen to that has recorded in that style. When they have a finished composition, part of the grade is based on whether or not they have a song in their chosen style that sounds like their chosen group.

For example, this past year I had a group of students who wanted to create a heavy metal rock song based on the music of Led Zeppelin. They brought in a cassette of the song they liked, listened to the song for the percussion pattern, notated it, and recorded it on the sequencer. From there they went back to the recording to listen to the bass line to get ideas for their own composition. Then they recorded a pattern that fit their drum part. While this was happening, another member in the group was busy using the Appleworks word processing program to create the lyrics for the song. (We have a computer lab in the Newtown Middle School where the students learn Appleworks.) All of this activity was recorded in the diary part of the journal.

When I teach certain musical concepts, such as rhythm, students take notes in the glossary section of their journals. This idea is not new, but the application of technology to make the process of music composition available to everyone is new. It is through the process of composition that the students learn about music. Remember, the students that take the music lab are not the band, orchestra, or chorus students. They are the nonperforming students in the school.

Teaching Rhythm

Rhythm, probably the most important element of music, can be a pattern of sounds within a beat or group of beats that can make up measures. The tempo controls the pattern. As the tempo quickens, the pattern gets faster and vice versa.

Middle school students begin their composition by creating a drum pattern. They can create a drum pattern by filling out a rhythm graph (see figure 1). Their next step is learning how to program the EPS sequencer so that they can hear their creation. Working in their four-member groups, each student is responsible for programming his or her own pattern. Each part is then entered separately. Listening to the click track set at sixteenth notes, at a tempo of one quarter note equals 25, the students help each other by counting aloud and playing the correct sound in the correct place. Then they must decide at which tempo their completed pattern sounds best.

As a pattern is completed, you, the teacher, are witnessing what is, from the student's point of view, the birth of one of the greatest drum beats ever. When the students play their patterns for their peers, it is always exciting. At the same time it is also tense for it is the first time that their musical composition, their own creation, is exposed and open for criticism. An interesting phenomenon happens. The students realize that there are other good patterns. Some are not better but simply more interesting than their own. It is only at this point, after they have created and critically listened to their own patterns

	1		3		5		7		9		11		13		15	
Closed HH	X		X		X		X		X		X		X			
Open HH															X	
Tom Tom														X		
Snare					X								X			
Bass Drum	X						X		X							X

Figure 1: A rhythm graph

and those of other students, that they are willing to accept and understand the abstract concept of the use of silence in music.

It becomes evident, after looking at the graph in figure 1, that the tie into math and fractions is a natural progression (no pun intended). By asking the question "What is the percentage of bass drum to the total pattern?" you have started to use an interdisciplinary approach in teaching music. The answer has to be "less than 20 percent." There are five sounds that make up the total pattern. Each sound becomes one-fifth of the total, or 20 percent. Each box of each part (made up of sixteen boxes) is then worth one-eightieth or 1.25 percent.

Teaching Form and Harmony

After each group member has created a pattern, the patterns are designated as A, B, C, and D. Then the groups play the patterns together as a rondo. This accomplishes two goals. The first is understanding another abstract concept of music, form, and the second is learning how to string together the different patterns, called sequences, in order to create a composition.

Understanding harmony can start with a bass line and the establishment of a home key. Students will begin to understand a bass line when it is explained to them as a pattern similar to the percussion pattern that they have already created except that it now involves pitch. (It is always fun to copy a student's drum pattern to a bass instrument track to help explain this concept.) I give the students a simple definition of pitch: high and low or up and down. As they listen to their drum pattern, they slowly start to create an ostinato. Using only the white keys, they decide on their home note. (Since their drum pattern is only one measure long, it might be necessary to extend this pattern to two measures.) I'll tell them to play their home note more often than any other note. They can visit their neighbors next door, but must always return home. They can go farther away (like to the mall) but not very often (too expensive). See figure 2 for an example.

If students are having trouble with this step, I send them back to the rhythm graph. This time, however,

Figure 2. A bass pattern with a home key

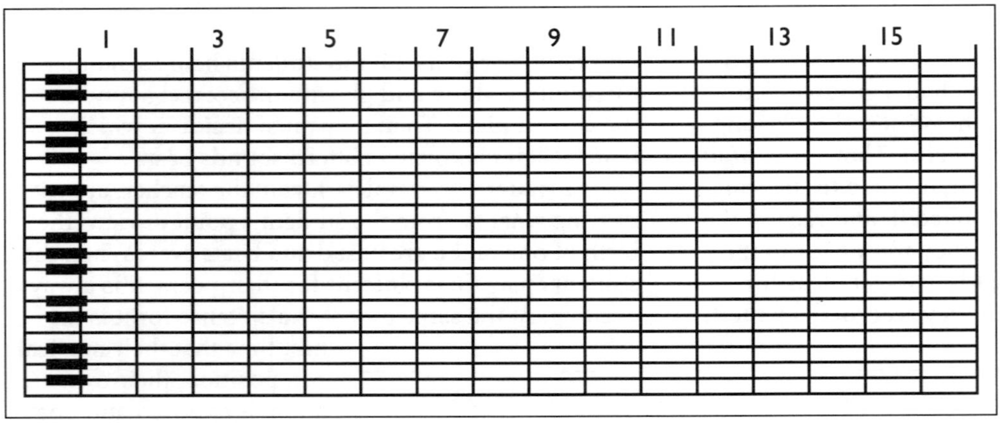

Figure 3. A rhythm graph with keyboard added

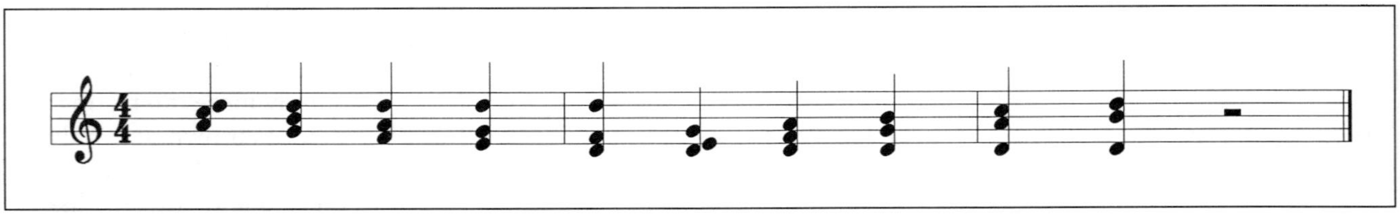

Figure 4. A pattern (in D) with chords added

the graph is modified to show white and black keys (see figure 3). They will fill in the boxes following the same rules as before. Then they will record that pattern in a fashion similar to the one they followed in recording their drum pattern.

Once they have recorded a bass line, it is time for chords. In a traditional approach, harmony is an outgrowth of melody. However, since the music lab students are nonperformers, having very little experience with traditional band, orchestra, or vocal training, I have found that treating melody as an outgrowth of harmony works best.

Using a two-measure sequence, each student will place one finger of either hand on the home note and will spread two fingers of the other hand to play any other white keys along with the anchor note. Figure 4 shows some possibilities using D as the home key. Some chords sound better, while others will create movement and will suggest resolutions to the tonic. The important thing is that the students are becoming aware of these subtleties. After playing different chords over their drum and bass parts and deciding on which ones to use, they are ready to record their harmonic pattern.

In each step, it is important to realize that the students are listening to each other's successes and failures and trying to figure out why one pattern sounds better than another. It is these discussions that make learning about music fun because together they are asking "why" and "what if," and the questions are being generated by their curiosity.

The most difficult job as a teacher is to refrain from using your value system in judging your students' work. You must learn to accept their work as the beginning of their journey toward understanding how music can touch the soul and make people laugh or cry. Only then will the students begin to understand the emotional and aesthetic value of music. By listening to the music they like (top forty, rap, rock, etc.) and comparing it to the music they create, each student begins to develop critical listening skills, a more refined value system, and an understanding of why some pieces are very good while other pieces will not last very long.

Teaching Melody

Melody is the most difficult concept of all to understand and create. When you set up rules and boundaries, however, and give students a scale to work with, the task becomes a little easier to complete. Using the twelve-bar blues form helps solve some of the students' musical problems. The blues form sets up boundaries that the students are already familiar with—American pop music's roots are based in the blues. The blues scale is easy to see at a keyboard (see figure 5), and when the students learn the harmonic progression I, IV, I, V, I, the home key or tonal center concept becomes very concrete.

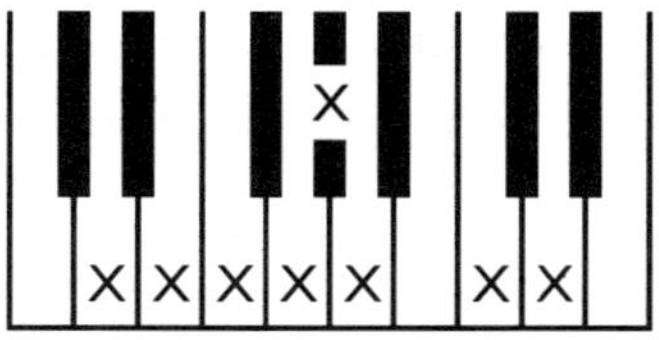

Figure 5. A blues scale

Expanding the two measures that the students have created to the necessary twelve measures is easily accomplished by using the copying functions of a sequencer. Talking about the dominant as seven half-steps above the tonic and the subdominant as seven half-steps below the tonic brings into focus why the tonic is the tonal center. When the students transpose the bass part and their harmony part to the subdominant at measures 5 and 6 and then play it back, they are thrilled. At this point, you have an opportunity to explain parallel and contrary motion. The dominant transposition happens at measures nine and ten. When the final transposition is completed, the students are ready for melody.

Understanding the basic blues scale is only important to you, the teacher. The students are not ready for the theory behind it. If you consider D as the tonic or first step of the scale, your scale notes would be D, F, G, G#, A, C, D. If you add "re" and "la" to the scale, you have all of the white keys between D and the octave higher, plus the student would be able to play the middle black key of the set of three black keys. For a student of limited keyboard skills, this is easy to play because it is easy to see.

Once the students have set up the form (twelve-bar blues) and created the scale, they are ready for some rules:

- Don't jump around a lot. Let your fingers walk to the higher or lower pitches.
- Vary your rhythm by playing some notes longer than others.
- Remember that silence is important. Listen to your different parts and play with them, not over them. Give your melody space and breathing room.

Assigning each student a different instrumental sound makes that student responsible for his or her own melody. Once a melody is completed, mute that track out so that the next student will hear only the bass, rhythm, and harmony parts. Once each student has completed a melody, everyone listens to each other's and tries to determine which melodies sound good together as a duet, trio, or quartet. Talk about counterpoint! Guess what we have been listening to at this point? Bach's two- and three-part inventions and the "Little Fugue in G Minor."

Connecting with Other Disciplines

After the students have created their blues compositions, they can move on to areas such as lyric writing (a natural activity for integrating the English curriculum into the music program), program music, writing commercials, sampling, and recording techniques. I was fortunate to have one group of seventh-grade students finish a song, complete with score, lead sheet, and accompaniment. I gave this to the choral teacher, who premiered the composition at one of the school concerts. I had another group write a story and set the narration of that story to music. These students received credit from me as well as from their English teacher for creative writing and from their computer teacher for word processing work. The literary magazine also published some of the students' scores and lead sheets.

Since music and the arts reflect our society, when we listen to American pop music and try to understand its history and development, the students are made aware of certain facts in American history. They learn, for example, what factors contributed to the development of the blues, Tin Pan Alley, and American musical theater. The history lessons become a natural outgrowth of the class because the students have been actively engaged in creating music.

Completing Assignments

The students' work is not considered complete until they have recorded it onto a cassette and made a hard copy (printed score) of it. I do not expect each group to perform its compositions for the recording session; however, I do expect the groups to make arrangements to have someone sing their song. This means finding students, giving them the lead sheet, rehearsing, and making all the final recording decisions, just like record producers. Having the hard copy piques the curiosity of some students to learn more about reading music. But more importantly, it also gives them something of which they can be very proud. Their accomplishments are now concrete.

Reference

Woolfolk, A. E. (1990). *Educational Psychology,* 4th ed. Englewood Cliffs, NJ: Prentice Hall.

INSTRUCTION AND EVALUATION

INSTRUCTIONAL PRACTICE OF PROCESS-ORIENTED INSTRUCTION

PROCESS OR PRODUCT IN MIDDLE SCHOOL MUSIC EDUCATION

Judy Bowers

The educational focus for middle school students in the United States has gradually evolved from being the bridge between elementary and high school training with a watered-down high school approach to being a more transitional approach that nurtures specific needs of early adolescence. These special needs have had an impact on both curriculum and teacher training programs, thus distinguishing middle school students from either an "advanced-elementary" or "pre-high school" philosophy. This change in educational thrust has influenced the role of the arts—specifically music—in middle school education.

Judy Bowers is assistant professor of choral music education at Florida State University in Tallahassee.

Before the middle school movement, American schools generally implemented a junior high school plan, primarily combining grades 7-9, although local needs occasionally dictated other grade-level groupings. The junior high school model was designed to bridge the gaps between elementary school instruction and the more rigorous expectations of high school academic work (Sanders, 1973). High school procedures and skills were frequently addressed in this model, and feeder programs for upcoming academic and activity demands were often present. Expanded activity, including curricular, extracurricular, and cocurricular events, was viewed as opportunity for self-discovery of talents and areas of interest—an important step in the maturing process. Thus, junior high schools organized skilled teams for athletic competition, selected performing groups for the arts, and developed competitive academic teams across varied subject areas and activities for academic scholars. These competitive student outcomes became a part of the educational product of the public schools. Competitive opportunities result in both success and failure for participants, but this win-lose reality often has been viewed positively as an additional opportunity for managing realistic lifetime experience.

Change came when the British model of middle school education was imported and reshaped to fit the American public school system. Organizational structure typically refers to grades 6–8, although various arrangements exist using grades 4–8 to accommodate local needs (Curtis & Bidwell, 1977). Implementation of the middle school concept somewhat diffused the educational product focus by structuring for student needs: academic and social needs, interest exploration, discrepancies in maturity level, and student goals and ambitions. This framework emphasizes individual needs and allows for learner variation in pace and competency expectation. It allows for personalized purposes, standards, and methods that nurture the growth and development of each student (Curtis & Bidwell, 1977). Alexander and Kealy (1973) suggested four criteria for middle school curriculum: Is the curriculum balanced (organized knowledge, personal development, and continued learning skills)? Is continuity provided? Is the curriculum plan flexible? And is curriculum individualization provided? In contrast to the junior high school philosophy of selecting the best for competition, the middle school approach seeks to offer participation opportunities for students of varying ability and training. The focus of instruction is on the learning process involved rather than the final product or student outcome.

When music issues are removed, differences between junior high schools and middle schools seem clearly defined. To quickly evaluate philosophical differences, one can examine these two school models using the example of girl's volleyball.

A junior high school approach might involve selecting the most highly skilled players to field a school team, which would travel across town (or out of town) to vie for the area junior high school volleyball championship. All area teams would reach a relatively high standard of performance in the quest for first place, regardless of the ultimate champion. The product involved here is the highly skilled play that wins the championship. High school volleyball programs likely would benefit from this structure—select teams playing other highly motivated select teams.

The middle school approach to volleyball would differ in several respects. First, all girls wanting to play would have some opportunity to learn the game and participate (regardless of natural ability or prior experience), so this would entail multiple teams rather than a selected best team. Second, students likely would not travel to other towns or schools to compete after school hours—intramural games would provide most playing opportunities. Third, strong and weak players might be spread evenly across all teams to provide a competitive climate for all games. The process allows all interested students to learn the game, and playing is the focus of this model, rather than the skill level of the final game. Although this process might not provide a small group of highly skilled players to augment high school programs, it ideally results in a large group of interested students who can determine their interest and ability through experience in middle school with the option to choose development of their competitive skills in a high school setting.

By using the volleyball example, two key questions are posed: First, does this one sport (volleyball) meet educational goals for physical education, and second, how much will student skill and performance levels be influenced by including all students in a less competitive setting?

Differences and parallels can be noted between junior high school and middle school when moving from the volleyball example into music settings. As did the volleyball team, junior high music performance groups traditionally have selected membership based on ability, training, experience, and often extramusical factors such as academic ability, self-discipline, and attitude. Enrollment, however, is not restricted to only a select few, but limited by ensemble balance needs, facility and equipment availability, schedule conflicts, and teacher preference. Generally, many students may participate in music ensembles, and this is supported by high school programs that need well-trained, experienced musicians in their feeder programs.

Middle school music groups ideally allow any student to participate, regardless of innate ability or prior music training, with curricular concentration on skill building for lifelong music enjoyment and music making. Critics of this system point to scheduling problems resulting from ensemble grouping demands, equipment shortages for instrumental programs, and a less satisfying musical experience for musically talented students. Ideally, high school programs should benefit from an increased pool of students who may choose to develop competitive music skills in a high school program.

Finding Common Ground

Perhaps another question to consider is "Can performance groups meet the music literacy standards of the music curriculum without sacrificing performance skill?"

Amidst the turmoil of school reorganization and differing philosophies, there may be more common ground for music instruction than is first observable. Performance groups that provide a base of comprehensive musicianship allow students to actively make music while learning lifetime skills. Conversely, Regelski (1981) called for "action learning" (active experience gained to reach a goal) in general music to provide relevance, practical application, and active music participation. If both performance and classroom instructional settings can allow students to enjoy making music while learning comprehensive musicianship skills, then perhaps individual student preference could determine the learning environment.

Although the performance product may be the ultimate goal in choir, band, and orchestra classes, many good teachers acknowledge the importance of reaching this performance goal through a logical learning experience that includes music concepts, music reading skills, historical background, and the use of a wide variety of instructional techniques in rehearsal. For several decades there has been a call within the performance group setting for comprehensive musicianship, which speaks to the music learning process (Garofalo, 1976; Miller, 1976). Siltman (1978, 1979) pointed out deficiencies resulting from the organization of students into highly select choral groups and detailed possible solutions (new groupings to alleviate selection based on balancing choirs, choral arrangements to provide success for voice change difficulties) in a series of articles. Recently, a creative method detailing eleven steps to a comprehensive choral curriculum was developed to serve as a model for building effective choral programs (Whitlock, 1991). There is continual and growing support for comprehensive musicianship in performance settings (Jones, 1990; Merrion, 1989).

If performance groups in middle school education allow all interested students to participate and learn lifetime music skills through a specific performance medium, however, the needs of all students still may not be met. Specifically, students who choose individual performance, in either public or personal enjoyment settings, and students who prefer to learn music in a nonperformance setting all need opportunities for musical experience and learning. A variety of course offerings can address these students. Guitar and keyboard classes can provide individual, active music experience while learning basic skills. In the general music class, creative methods for teaching music skills, multicultural aspects, music listening, use of technology (MIDI instruction), and keyboard techniques have been developed and can be used to enrich the students' experiences at secondary levels (Hughes, 1991).

Middle school education requires flexibility for students to develop skills at an individual pace, to discover abilities and interests, and to gain confidence and understanding of personal strengths and weaknesses through a broad range of experiences. Because the arts reside in the core curriculum, arts education should be available to all students. Thus, the specific role of music in middle school education should also be defined to meet the needs of all students, and an inclusive curriculum can provide the necessary flexibility. Student performance groups, for example, can learn comprehensive musicianship while developing individual talent and ensemble training. Guitar and keyboard instruction can provide comprehensive musicianship training and provide students with skills for a lifetime of personal enjoyment as well as personal strengths and weaknesses. General music classes can bring music to students who select broad-based musical investigation in a nonperformance setting.

All these music delivery methods can seemingly provide a comprehensive approach to music education. Student choice opportunities regarding the forum for music learning add a dimension of flexibility to the middle school music curriculum.

Advocates of the traditional product approach often express concern about the quality of performance groups when the teaching focus moves from the end (the product) to the means (the process). Quality performance enriches the learning experience and the aesthetic experience for the performers and the listeners, so it seems a valid goal for musicians young and old. No statement has been made about performance quality of groups composed of any interested students rather than selected students. Why must we assume that these groups cannot perform sensitively, whether in class, for parents, or in contests? This same issue is present at every school music contest, except the variance is between schools with lots of highly trained students and those with limited numbers of talented singers or players. Less able groups succeed grandly when the director or teacher tailors the technical demands of the music to the training level and ability of the group. Can this not occur in middle school performance settings?

Traditional methods of instruction may require modification to bring music to all students—the talented, the motivated, the well-trained, the novice, the at-risk—to every category of the American public school student. Let us not assume that middle school education cannot provide quality music making for all students, whether through performance groups, through personal performance activities, or through music making in classroom settings. Rather than debate organizational structure, the focus must shift to the development of effective instructional methods and innovative curricula.

Changes in public education imply changes for teaching practice and teacher training programs. If traditional methods and organizational structures are altered, careful planning is necessary to ensure successful experimentation with a new process. Teacher training or retraining is a critical factor in the successful implementation of school programs. Input into program design, substantive training in new skills *prior* to implementing change, and opportunity for revision throughout the process are factors important for teacher success.

In addition to training, appropriate materials and supplies must be accessible, and in-service and workshop presentations must update teachers on available teaching sources and instructional methods. Performance groups have often relied on selected literature for building the curriculum, with development of all other concepts dependent on the creativity and time constraints of the teacher. Currently, choral teachers have access to textbooks that include quality literature as well as guidelines for teaching music skills, music concepts, musical styles, and vocal production (Fowler, 1988; Heffley, Schott, & Land, 1982; Whitlock, 1982).

Investigation of comprehensive musicianship instruction for instrumental settings has provided evidence that suggests that comprehensive musicianship students are more musically literate than those receiving a traditional rehearsal focusing only on the performance goal. Gebhardt (1979) has developed an integrated plan specifically designed for junior high school band students. Various examinations of comprehensive musicianship cited by Merrion (1989) feature intact performance groups with altered *teaching* approaches rather than teaching comprehensive musicianship to altered groups.

The trend toward comprehensive musicianship for all students, regardless of the music setting, is continuing in American public schools. Offering music instruction to all students at the middle school level further supports a comprehensive music curriculum. Variety in delivering comprehensive music instruction through performance groups, classroom music, or class instruction for personal music making may actually provide the flexibility to meet the needs of all students with more talent or less, interested or not, successful, disadvantaged, or at-risk.

References

Alexander, W. M. & Kealy, R. P. (1973). From junior high school to middle school. In Romano, L. G., Georgiady, N. P., & Heald, J. E., Eds. *The middle school.* Chicago: Nelson-Hall Company.

Curtis, T. E. and Bidwell, W. W. (1977). *Curriculum and instruction for emerging adolescents.* Reading, MA: Addison-Wesley Publishing Company.

Fowler, C. (Ed.) (1988). *Sing!* Houston, TX: Hinshaw Music Textbook Division.

Garofalo, R. (1976). *Blueprint for band: A guide to teaching comprehensive musicianship through school band performance.* Portland, ME: J. Weston Walch.

Gebhardt, L. (1974). The development and evaluation of an integrated plan of study providing for increased musical perception and skills by students in the junior high band. *Dissertation Abstracts International,* 34, 4312A. (University Microfilms, No. 74-28259).

Heffley, R., Schott, S. & Land, L. B. (Eds.) (1982). *Something to sing about.* New York: G. Schirmer.

Hughes, W. (1991). State of Florida offers a model high school for general music workshop. *General Music Today,* 4 (2), 14-15.

Jones, T. (1990). Why I stopped being a band teacher and learned how to teach MUSIC! *The Middle School Journal,* 21 (3), 44.

Merrion, M. (Ed.) (1989). *What works: Instructional strategies for music education.* Reston, VA: Music Educators National Conference.

Miller, S. D. (1976). Comprehensive musicianship. *The Choral Journal,* XVII(1), 5-7.

Regelski, T. A. (1981). *Teaching general music.* New York: Schirmer Books.

Sanders, S. G. (1973). Challenge of the middle school. In Romano, L. G., Georgiady, N. P., & Heald, J. E., Eds. *The middle school.* Chicago: Nelson-Hall Company.

Siltman, B. (1978). Breaking the vicious circle: Music for the middle school boys choir. *The Choral Journal,* XVIV(3), 9-10.

Siltman, B. (1978). Arranging for the boys chorus—only half of the challenge. *The Choral Journal,* XVIV(4), 11-14.

Siltman, B. (1979). Literature for the junior high male chorus: More than singing. *The Choral Journal,* XVIV(5), 18-20.

Whitlock, R. (1982). *Choral insights,* Vols. 1-3. San Diego, CA: Neil A. Kjos Company.

Whitlock, R. H. S. (1991). Choral curriculum as it affects performance at the secondary level. *The Choral Journal,* XXXII(3), 39-45.

EXAMINING MUSICAL PRACTICES IN MIDDLE SCHOOL TEACHING

Regina Zakrajsek

There are four band directors at Valley Middle School, which is in the rural area of Apple Valley, Minnesota. The jazz ensemble at Valley Middle School has won several awards at jazz festivals in Minnesota and Wisconsin, and the instrumental music program holds the "Selection of Excellence" award for exemplary music education by the Minnesota Alliance for Arts Education.

Throughout the entire field of education, much discussion has been given to the issue of whether product or process should guide instructional philosophy and what types of practices are best suited for each emphasis. In many public school districts, outcome-based education is emerging as the prevalent philosophy. It attempts to focus on the student achieving the product, or outcome, with the implication that if the product is correct, then the process that leads to that product would also be correct. This approach works well in many disciplines such as math or science, but the essence of music making lies as much—and sometimes more—in the process of creating the music as it does in the resultant "product" of music performance. An examination of product and process in middle school music instruction can identify subtle issues of pedagogy, as well as some of the larger issues involving critical thinking skills.

In many world cultures, the unique social aspect of music making focuses on the process; villagers gather for festivals and times of celebration to spontaneously create music together. In addition music is not usually rehearsed apart from the celebration; rather the rehearsal is the performance—the process is the product. Children learn the structure and stylistic characteristics of their folk music through this process of spontaneous creativity rather than in a rehearsal setting far removed from the performance. This is not to say that music made in this way does not have a high level of performance energy and critical praise. The special place of artists and musicians within most cultures in the world gives credence to their authenticity and influence on the culture.

In my musical experiences with very young children, it is obvious that the emphasis in their minds is on the process of making music rather than the product. Preschoolers often incorporate spontaneous improvised music into their individual and group play, making up melodies and lyrics to fit the situation. As children grow, the joy of making music continues to be rooted in social camaraderie and process. Certainly, the concept of a stylized concert performance is one that is taught to them; it does not naturally flow from their spontaneous music making. In fact, the importance of the final performance is often held in higher regard by the adults involved (i.e., teachers, parents) than by many of the students. Indeed, some middle school students who have been actively involved in their band or choir rehearsals fail to attend the resultant concert for what seem to be comparatively unimportant reasons. For children who do perform, fear of failure is a common emotion that results in a focus on audience impact rather than the joy of making music. I often hear students

Regina Zakrajsek is the director of the honor band, two seventh-grade bands, the jazz orchestra, and various small ensembles at Valley Middle School in Apple Valley, Minnesota.

exclaim after a concert, "We were just terrible!" as well as other comments that focus on imagined mistakes rather than the positive emotions previously shared in rehearsals.

Our Western European tradition of process (rehearsals) existing completely separate from the product (stylized performance) is the exception rather than the norm for the musics of the world. This traditional approach focuses on the final performance as a monolithic product and often leads to a concentration on the soloist, or conductor at the expense of the collective capabilities of the ensemble. That emphasis on the "star system" is quite prevalent in the current programming of most American symphony orchestras, and the parallel in music education is becoming more and more product focused as demands for public performances of school ensembles increase at the expense of nourishing musical creativity. This heavy emphasis on a calendar/concert-based music curriculum needs to be balanced by additional factors that enhance and focus on process.

As an example, much of the music we perform is predicated on skill development through technical exercises such as scales and arpeggios. There exists a correspondence between Western music and technical development, and we need to find a similar correlation between repertoire that invites improvisation and creativity and exercises that develop techniques in the areas of listening, responding, and interacting. In other words, if we want to focus more on creativity, we will need to explore musics and processes that rely on creativity and improvisation as basic to their structure. The exchange of global information has advanced to the point where such examinations of world cultures and artforms are readily available to the ambitious educator if only an appropriate teaching context can be formulated.

One way I try to achieve this goal of focusing on process rather than product is through the practice of interdisciplinary teaching. The belief that children learn better, faster, and more completely when they can explore and experience the interconnections among individual disciplines is gaining much credibility with educators, and further research continues to examine the focus on interconnections. For music education this could be the key factor in moving away from the calendar/concert-based, music-as-entertainment curriculum toward a curriculum in which the arts are given equal emphasis within the school's overall curriculum and philosophy. Indeed, history shows us that from the time of the ancient Greeks through the Renaissance, the study of music was one that emphasized its connections with the other subject areas. Interdisciplinary teaching will also open up the repertoire to include musics from all cultures and societies. In addition, integrating the study of music into the total curriculum will involve *all* students in music making on a daily basis as opposed to our present practice of separating music students from those who do not study music. (Even within our music departments we further separate and categorize choir students, instrumental students, and general music students.) An interdisciplinary team of teachers with backgrounds in math, science, social studies, language, art, and music can act as consultants for groupings of students exploring the interconnections of these disciplines under the broad heading of a general topic area.

In addition, both my experience and current educational theories underline the fact that young people learn in a wide variety of styles, ranging from reading and writing to listening and participating. Any comprehensive educational system should address this variety of learning styles through a wide range of approaches. Here again a balance between product and process focus could address a much wider range of student learning styles, as long as one understands the taxonomy of critical thinking skills involved in each emphasis. As an example, when process is the focus, students will:

- participate more creatively;
- connect the past with the present;
- evoke a range of styles;
- embrace the abstract;
- question/examine the sequential.

When product is the focus, students will:

- participate more uniformly;
- dwell in a single timeframe;
- perfect a single style;
- embrace the concrete;
- reject the random.

The ability to objectively measure learning in discrete units becomes more difficult in the process domain than in product domain. Interpretation and other higher-level critical thinking skills are much more difficult to measure and often subjective in nature. Yet the accurate playing of scales, arpeggios, and other rudimentary exercises is often the basis for evaluating the basics of musical product in our present course of music study available to students. Much more attention should be given to ways in which the expressive and interpretative aspects of music can be introduced and reinforced as well as music's interconnection with other subject areas. Methods of evaluating this learning need to accompany this focus along with full attention to appropriate repertoire, creativity, and critical listening. Moreover, a greater process focus will be driven by the additional factors of musical style, instrumentation, venue, and of course the organizational and cultural focus of the music studied.

Short of this rather radical restructuring of our school music programs, what are some small steps in pursuit of process emphasis that can be realistically taken? Creative processes are very often an individual experience and therefore difficult to translate to a large ensemble. The importance of encouraging and developing process focus in the learning experiences of our students, however, dictates that methods should be found for their incorporation and my experience shows that these methods can be found.

Toward a Greater Balance: Some Steps for Process

Begin by deemphasizing the separation of rehearsal from performance and audience from performer. Invite parents to rehearsals or have open rehearsals in the evening or on Saturdays where parents can participate with their child, either on an instrument they played in high school or simply by sitting next to them during the rehearsal. Work on deformalizing the concert experience both on the part of the audience and the performers. List the specific goals and objectives worked on during the semester in the program notes for the concert and discuss with parents during the concert how process is used to achieve broader goals of critical thinking and creativity. Choose students or groups of students to demonstrate or talk about certain concepts and skills.

Work actively to incorporate music from other cultures into your repertoire. Begin a venture into interdisciplinary team teaching by incorporating music from a culture being studied in the geography and social studies classes. Give groups of interested students opportunities to further explore a culture's music through study or performance of indigenous folk music, performance practices, instruments, or composition in the style of that culture's music. Play recordings of music from the culture being studied. Bring the art teacher's expertise into play by asking them to provide opportunities for students to view and create art from that culture. Include the home-economics teachers in a study of foods from the culture. Work with your principal to provide a common prep time for the teachers involved in planning these interdisciplinary explorations.

Begin to incorporate creativity and improvisation into your large ensemble experiences. Here are some ideas that I have tried. Along with your own, these hints can be developed into full-length improvisatory pieces and incorporated into a concert program. Take care that the pieces do not become merely novelty pieces on a concert, but serious explorations in improvisation and creativity, and discuss the process involved in the development of the piece with the audience.

Question/Answer: The teacher sings or plays a simple four-beat rhythm to each student. Students answer with a unique four-beat rhythm. This exercise can be expanded to include four-beat melodies, and further expanded to eight beats and beyond, depending on the capabilities of each student.

Influence a Dancer: A group of musicians form a large circle around a dancer. Students improvise on their instruments or with vocal sounds to influence the dancer to dance to their own particular line of improvisation. As is usually the case, very soon after beginning this improvisation, loud cacophonous sounds begin to permeate the room. At this point it may be beneficial to discuss various ways of gaining someone's attention, i.e., a soft legato sound or a lyrical melodic line in the midst of a group of loud staccato sounds.

Clusters: Students are asked to play or sing any pitch at random in a soft, continuously sustained manner. The objective is to find the group tonal center. During the process, the students gradually and softly change their pitch until a tonal center begins to emerge. Students continue moving toward that center until a unison note is achieved–they should be encouraged to use the full range of their instruments. It also helps to stipulate that any notes can be used except concert B-flat (band) or concert A (orchestra). The undulating and shimmering effect should be discussed. It may also help to darken the room somewhat.

Less Is More: Students randomly choose five pitches (either as a section or individually). Each pitch is then performed only once by each person during a designated time frame of fifteen to twenty seconds. (First tries usually result in students using up their five notes in the first five to ten seconds of the piece.) Afterward, discussions and adjustments can take place concerning the thickness or thinness of texture, the style of the notes played, the volume, the phrasing, and judicious timing. This exercise can be expanded to include short rhythmic motives or short melodic phrases, and the time limits of the piece can be expanded.

Each of these exercises provides a framework for focusing on a greater emphasis of musical process and can help to establish a return to the balance between product and process in the educational goal of the music lesson. The Hopi Indians used the word *koyannisqaatsi* to refer to a life out of balance, hopelessly tilted toward destruction from excessive extremes. In our contemporary commercial-oriented culture, we have increased the tendency to worship the bottom line at the expense of quality and integrity of value. The practice of management by objective is one that emphasizes the achievement of the ultimate product, often at the expense of the process (and people) involved in reaching that objective.

Those of us committed to music education should not fall into such a narrow vision of a product prone system that fails to honor the traditions of musical process as a valuable educational tool in the total framework of musical learning. Both product and process are essential outcomes for quality music practice and education. Each contributes to the total knowledge and experience base of the learner, and neither should become overly emphasized at the expense of the other. When a healthy balance between these approaches is achieved and maintained, the student can benefit from both without losing the spirit and wonder of making music.

INTERDISCIPLINARY INSTRUCTION

MERGING THE EXPLORATORY AND BASIC SUBJECTS

James P. Garvin

Definitions are always important in clarifying what we mean. When I speak of exploratory teachers, I am referring to those people in our middle schools who teach subjects not identified as part of the central academic core. Generally, exploratory subjects are not taught five days a week and are seldom included in teaming organizations. Exploratory subjects include music, art, home economics, technical arts, health, computers, physical education, drama, business, languages, and so on.

In the team arrangement, the exploratory teachers generally teach across grade levels; they do not teach a common group of students. Core teachers generally teach one grade level and a common set of students. Exploratory teachers sometimes see themselves as baby-sitters, watching over students to provide teams of core teachers with common planning time, which is essential to team effectiveness. It is impossible to schedule unless students can be assigned to exploratory activities. Exploratory teachers do not have a common planning time, and they see this as discriminating against both their professional status and their specialty areas.

James P. Garvin, a former middle school teacher, is executive director emeritus of the New England League of Middle Schools, which he served as executive director from 1978 to 1993.

This problem is further aggravated when core teachers infer that although exploratory teachers work with their students, they are not important enough to participate in the team activities. In some instances, core teachers use the exploratory instructional class as a place to have students make up tests or receive special help. This creates dissension and fragmentation and destroys any possibility of building a common community of respect.

Basic to this problem is finding ways to change human attitudes. There are those who firmly believe that exploratory subjects are a waste of time and resources. They perceive that somehow these subjects do not represent "academic rigor" but rather a "service station" approach to education. There are those who will tolerate exploratory courses as long as they do not interfere with basic subject demands. Then there are some who actually believe that those who teach the exploratory areas are second-class citizens in the pecking order of professional importance. Unfortunately, there are school leaders who use the exploratory classes as opportunities to schedule special school activities or convenient places to send students who can't behave in other classes.

These are but a few of the prevailing attitudes that must be changed if schools are to function as communities committed to a common mission. Every subject should be important in an exemplary middle-level school—or it should not be offered. Schools wanting to build healthy communities must work at programs designed to bring the basic subject teachers together with the exploratory arts teachers through dialogue and planning for change.

Having visited more than nine hundred middle-level schools, I want to report that there are schools that have worked on this problem. The purpose of this article is to describe some of the practical activities I have seen that work. These are schools that once had many of the attitude problems I have described, but now work successfully because beneficial change was made a priority by leadership.

Team-Initiated Activities

Sharing Team Meeting Minutes. Good teams assign someone to record team meeting activities. These records should be passed on to all teachers who work with the same students. If exploratory teachers know of the activities, issues, and concerns of teams, they can be a valuable extension of the team. Exploratory teachers know these students differently because of the less restrictive climates within which they work. They can establish a different kind of rapport, similar to the adviser/advisee relationship. They generate high interest, producing positive student/teacher relationships. The relaxed tenor of these subjects leads to students revealing more about themselves than might be the case in the basic subject areas. This can be extremely effective for tracking the evolution of students' concepts and behavioral changes.

I remember a team that had difficulty understanding why one of their bright twelve-year-old girls decided to stop working in school. She attended every day, but she literally went through the motions and produced very little. The team was at a loss as to why this had occurred. They made it an agenda item at the planning session. As hard as they tried, they could not figure out why this bright little girl stopped working. It was a policy in this school to send all team meeting notes to the exploratory teachers. One of the art teachers knew the reason for the problem and made plans to attend the next team meeting. At the meeting, she proceeded to explain to the team why this young lady had this problem.

It so happened that this young girl had fallen in love for the first time! As the art teacher described this event, she paused and said, "Gosh, I hope we never become so old that we forget what it was like for us the first time we fell in love as an early adolescent." This little girl came to school every day only for the purpose of meeting her eighth-grade boyfriend. Everything else seemed unimportant.

The significant thing here is that it was the art teacher who knew the answer to the problem. Somehow, in the course of time, because of the relationship she was able to establish with this girl in the art room, she was able to obtain information that the core teachers needed, which ultimately solved the problem for both the team and the student.

Placing team minutes in the hands of the exploratory teachers can provide valuable assistance to team problems. Teams need to remember that students do not belong exclusively to them and that students are with other teachers throughout the day who see them differently and relate to them in ways often not possible in the academic areas. Teams need to take advantage of this difference. Communicating to exploratory teachers through distribution of team meeting minutes is one way to bring it about.

Sharing Curriculum Plans. Important handouts in curriculum areas could likewise be useful for exploratory teachers to receive. This might include short- or long-term assignments, introductions of new units, bibliographies, long-range projects, appointments, or anything else that might be helpful in describing student expectations to exploratory teachers.

If a history teacher is going to spend six weeks on Greece, the exploratory teachers might be able to reinforce that subject. The music teacher might teach Greek songs or Greek dancing. The home economics teacher might teach students to prepare Greek food, the English teacher might teach Greek literature, and so on.

Curriculum demands in the exploratory areas are less restrictive, providing opportunities for flexibility not possible in other areas. Once exploratory teachers know what teachers in other areas expect, they can shift direction to develop interdisciplinary possibilities.

Passing on information of this sort requires very little time and effort. It begins with the attitude that networking between teachers is important and that others respond positively when an effort is made to recognize them through sending information.

If students catch on that teachers know what other teachers are doing, it sends a message that teachers see cooperation and working together as important. There is no better way to teach cooperation skills to our students than to model it in our own work.

Visits to Unified Arts Areas during Common Planning Time. When core teachers are in common planning sessions, students are generally in the exploratory subjects. I suggest that at least once a week, one member of the team be assigned to visit students in these activities.

When teachers visit the exploratory classrooms, several nice things happen. First, they see their kids in a different climate, behaving differently than in the core classes. Students who are behavioral problems in the core areas might be actively involved in projects. They will take teachers by the hand and show off what they are doing. They will be anxious to show how they prepared for their projects and the steps they took to get their work where it is.

Students work together in cooperative ways in these areas. They are free to move around, ask questions, and make mistakes without embarrassment. Exploratory teachers are not hesitant to use "best instructional practices."

Teachers in exploratory areas are delighted to have other teachers visit the room. (I wish I could say this is true in the core areas. I've visited schools where it is a policy that visitors are not allowed in core classes unless preannounced.) In the exploratory areas, teachers are never threatened by visitors.

Core teachers who visit exploratory classes can use the time to become acquainted with the exploratory teachers and to discuss certain students they teach in common. They might strike on something they can do together in future projects.

The advantage goes beyond teachers becoming acquainted (as important as that is). It allows kids to see their teachers talking and working together. It produces a model we want all kids to emulate in our classrooms and hopefully throughout life.

Core teachers should report back to the team on all visits. Follow-up discussion should be scheduled in the common planning time agenda to discuss how to integrate team activities into these important exploratory programs.

Teacher Exchange. Core teachers should look for ways to free up exploratory teachers so they can attend an occasional team meeting. This can be arranged by finding a time when the exploratory teacher has planned an activity that can safely be monitored by a core teacher.

This exchange affords an opportunity for the other team members to use the team meeting to discuss students and activities with what I call "their extended team member." It gives the exploratory teacher a feeling of belonging to a team and a feeling of importance as a resource person to others teaching the same students.

When exploratory teachers are invited, it is important that team members not monopolize the discussion and intimidate their colleagues. Exploratory teachers should be accepted as equals and treated accordingly. They should be made to feel important members of the team.

Field Trips. Field trips that include exploratory teachers can be a natural way to develop professional harmony between teachers. People come to know each other best when working around a central task. When that task takes place outside of the school building, it provides an openness and freedom that sheds professional armor and opens opportunities to know one another as human beings.

I once visited a school where a seventh-grade team planned a community project that included five exploratory teachers. The students on the team wanted to raise money to combat hunger. They got citizens in the community to sponsor them for each mile they walked in a twenty-five mile event.

The day of the event was a Saturday (teachers had to agree to do this on their day off). Once they started the walk, it started to rain. After ten miles, it poured. After fifteen miles, students had blisters on their feet, but did not want to quit. After twenty miles, kids were helping kids, teachers were carrying kids, and no one wanted to quit. As they all crossed the finish line, they looked like drowned rats, exhausted and hurting but proud that together they helped each other finish.

After the walk, they sat in the cafeteria of the school so exhausted hardly anyone wanted to talk, but no one wanted to leave. They had developed such a bond among themselves that they didn't want it to end. The struggle together developed a sense of community. They experienced a group worthwhileness from caring for each other.

Think of how these students reacted to each other in school the next day, how the teachers reacted to each other, how the core teachers reacted to those exploratory teachers who had walked with them, and how the students reacted to the teachers.

Teachers working together through community events, camping trips, or day trips enhance opportunities to see each other differently. These activities provide the vehicle for human encounter where professional status or title means little. Teams, by virtue of working with a common group of students and having a common planning time, can arrange for these events in ways impossible in the traditional junior high. They can include exploratory teachers in the planning and implementation of such events.

If I were a principal, I think I would expect every team to do such an event at least once a year.

Out-of-School Socials. Believe it or not, I have seen team members so close that they socialize with each other outside of school hours. Some develop their best ideas for team activities in less formal, friendly environments. Some simply make it a point every Friday to gather at a local pub for rest and recreation. This type of activity provides another opportunity to become acquainted in a fashion not always possible in the school. Activities of this sort afford good, nonthreatening opportunities for inviting exploratory teachers who work with the same students. Activities designed for having fun outside of school often help to remove professional barriers that prohibit and restrict relationships in the school setting.

Some team members want their "space," making close personal relationships difficult. Some have such extremes in lifestyles that socializing could be counterproductive. It may be that, in these cases, a formal activity might better serve the purpose. A dinner party or a night at the theater might be less threatening.

Regardless of the personalities of a given team, they should spend time during a common planning session brainstorming the prospects of doing something outside of school together that would allow them to know each other and those who are not directly involved on the team but teach the same students. Exploratory teachers should not always wait for teams to initiate activities. They should take the initiative to plan activities to invite teachers from different teams.

Principal-Initiated Activities

Early-Release Days. Most schools have days scheduled throughout the year for in-service work. These are commonly done on half days after students are released. They provide good opportunities for leadership to allow teams to meet with exploratory teachers in extended common planning sessions. In-service time is an ideal time to plan an interdisciplinary unit involving the arts. Sustained interaction with exploratory teachers over three hours enhances dialogue and builds relationships.

Many staff development days are wasted by bringing in people from the outside to speak on issues that seldom make any difference in effecting classroom change. Change does not affect school behavior unless teachers value one another and are comfortable talking to each other about ways to bring it about. Using staff development days to foster this dialogue shapes a climate of trust and comradery basic to sustaining professional growth.

Using Substitute Teachers. Bringing in substitute teachers costs money. Principals who believe that dialogue between teachers is important find ways to bring in substitutes.

A substitute teacher could allow an exploratory teacher to be freed up for an entire day to visit as many team meetings as possible. Remember that these people are still teaching across grade levels and teach students from many teams. Therefore, they need to visit as many team meetings as possible. It can't be done unless they have the day free to do it.

When such a day can be arranged, it should be planned and organized in advance. Teams should know when to expect visits. Regular team agendas should be altered to take advantage of the invited resource person. Team teachers and exploratory teachers should develop a mutual agenda in advance of the meeting. Items for discussion should be agreed upon mutually and time allotted equally.

If money is not available for substitutes, I suggest principals work to free up their own time to replace exploratory teachers. Think of what an endorsement this would make to the importance of such a mission!

Team Assignments. I have been in schools where administrators have juggled schedules, arranging for exploratory teachers to be free when a team has common planning. This allows the exploratory teacher to be assigned as a direct member of a team. It gives him or her identity on a team and greater opportunity to plan and dialogue with team members on a regular schedule. Even if assignments can't be made on an everyday basis, administrators should continually work to free up schedules so it can happen periodically.

I have heard of schools where schedules were developed to bring teachers in before school started for team meetings. This allowed for all exploratory teachers to be freed up for team assignments. It allowed for teams to meet with other grade-level teams if necessary. It shortened the school day for the students but allowed time in the morning for teams to meet.

Another possibility is to extend the team block to provide a time during the regular school day when all students are with the team in an unscheduled pure time. This would create time for exploratory teachers to work with the team over that period. It would not be planning, but it would at least bring exposure of exploratory teachers into the team process.

Adviser/Advisee. In most adviser/advisee programs, all teachers are assigned to meet with a small group of students several times a week for the purpose of building better relationships and providing a support base.

It might be worthwhile to have teachers working in pairs as advisers. This would allow for a mix of core and exploratory teachers working together around a common cause.

Activity Programs. These are programs that allow students to choose one of many high-interest options that are offered two or three times a week. They are often regarded as minicourses or electives. In some cases, these activity programs involve multiple grade levels. Normally every teacher offers something, and on occasion parents and community leaders come into the school to present options.

Activity programs foster an ideal opportunity for pairing up teachers from the arts and core subjects to offer an activity of mutual interest. Getting kids together in an activity of high interest with teachers who have the same interest is a good match. Selecting teachers with similar interests representing different disciplines, with the same outside interests, is also a good match for building human relationships.

Interdisciplinary Team Week. Weeks ought to be designated throughout the school year to bring all disciplines together to focus on central themes. Themes can be suggested by teachers or students.

Throughout the week, all teachers are encouraged to find as many ways as possible to focus their instruction on the theme for that week. Students learn that problems are better resolved when subjects are not fragmented. They also learn a variety of ways that the theme fits into the entire school curriculum.

At the conclusion, leadership should find ways to have faculty members report to each other on how they used the theme in their curriculum. This could provide a forum for interaction to better appreciate each other and the different disciplines.

The Need for Leadership Support

The suggestions given in this article are merely an exercise in futility unless leadership is committed to building mutual respect between staff members. They must be committed to the elimination of "caste systems" that have been allowed to grow within our schools. This division not only exists between the core teachers, but it is magnified when it exists between core and exploratory teachers.

Leadership must develop a mind-set directed toward the elimination of this disease. It will not just go away. It will be much easier to ignore it because everyone expects it. After all, we have practiced it for 50 years or more!

Not too long ago, I stopped a seventh grader and asked him what he thought about his exploratory teachers. His comment was, "They are nice people, but they are not my real teachers." It was sad. Here a student had already gotten the message that the only real teachers in the school were those whose courses had to be passed to graduate. The message had been clearly communicated that those who work in the exploratory areas were second-class citizens.

Exploratory teachers need to be affirmed as important to the school mission. Leadership must affirm the vital role they play in keeping kids in school. Principals must affirm to all faculty that the arts are important in the curriculum and vital to the success of the total mission of the school.

More importantly, principals must do something about seeing that it becomes more than rhetoric. It must be converted into programs that allow core teachers to plan, think, dream, teach, and counsel together with those who teach other courses. Unless a concerted effort is put forth, the consequences will be fragmentation, division, and turf wars, all of which destroy community.

After a few years, much of the climate of a school represents the attitudes of the principal. After three years, principals should put a mirror in their office and look into it every morning. What they see is what they've got.

Productive schools have principals who are committed to principles. They insist that people work together to promote a central cause, regardless of which grade level they teach or which discipline they represent.

The mission of a middle school is to send a message to early adolescents that working together is essential to enhancing the quality of human life.

Note

This article is an edited reprint of James P. Garvin's *Merging the Exploratory and Basic Subjects in the Middle-level School: Practical Suggestions That Work* (Rowley, MA: Garvin Consultant Services, 1989). Reprinted by permission.

AN ARTS-BASED INTERDISCIPLINARY PROGRAM FOR MIDDLE SCHOOL STUDENTS

Aimée C. Timmins

Eastern Middle School, located in the urban area of Silver Spring, Maryland, has more than nine hundred students. Its student body represents more than fifty countries. The school is unique in that the arts lead the academic team.

The whole student—the student who values and demonstrates sensitivity, decision making, problem solving, intuition, and creativity—is a phenomenon whose time has come. Middle-level schools can, through arts-enhanced interdisciplinary experiences, help students become whole learners. Such guided arts experiences can be coordinated in a way that preserves the integrity of each subject.

Middle-level students are at a critical stage in their physical, emotional, and academic development. Arts instruction can have a positive effect on these students because it combines considerable higher order thinking processes with hands-on kinesthetic learning. Music and art activities also directly support student self-esteem, as they so often result in performance-based assessments. Such experiences give students a chance for immediate and authentic feedback.

Eastern Middle School in Silver Spring, Maryland, has found a nontypical approach to interdisciplinary teaming that integrates the aesthetic, creative, and academic development of the middle-level student. The staff has found an effective way to integrate fine arts instruction into the academic program. The A.R.T.S. (Arts to Reinforce Traditional Studies) Program is an interdisciplinary two-year sequence blending art, music, photography, computer technology, and dance with the regular academic program. Art and music classes retain their curricular integrity yet are expanded to include process and content connections with other disciplines. As the program evolves, natural bridges between social studies, art, English, science, and music are crossed.

Aimée C. Timmins is the arts coordinator and resource teacher for Eastern Middle School in Silver Spring, Maryland.

Building a Program

The interdisciplinary team of teachers experimented with several instructional approaches before deciding to focus on concept, process, and product-based interdisciplinary arts connections. The team chose culture-based units for the first year of the program. This approach gave the teachers time to simply practice making connections and become familiar with each other and each other's curriculum.

After the year of experimenting, the team began to design and schedule interdependent units around broad-based concepts—thinking skills and common products—rather than designing culture units. In the second year, units were designed around themes such as interdependence/independence, uniqueness/universality, or tension/growth, and processes such as classifying and transforming. Teachers developing the program sought to retain the integrity of their own curriculum while searching at the same time for an interdisciplinary approach.

The program was designed to integrate the student's day in a way that the traditional middle school does not. Rather than segregating the arts from the academic subjects, the arts served as the primary tool for facilitating connections. Traditional seven-period-day fragmentation was eliminated and replaced with an eight-period schedule that promoted flexibility.

The A.R.T.S. Program's success can be attributed in part to its staff, who are truly committed to educating the whole student and who are curious about and interested in each other's subjects and methods of teaching. In fact, the results of team planning sessions and conversations are often shared with A.R.T.S. students. Students are even invited to attend and contribute to the planning process. They share in the curriculum enhancement.

A visitor to the A.R.T.S. Program would see that materials and projects underway in the science class are revisited in English, music perspectives, and art and culture classes. In each class, the content may remain the same, but the students are asked to approach it in a variety of ways. Common key questions and vocabulary terms appear in each of the students' classrooms. As the day goes on, students are keenly aware that a "conspiracy" is at hand. Work and lessons are supervised by several of their teachers and are approached from the scientific, literary, musical, and artistic points of view. There is a sense of relevance in this type of instruction, as the quality of the performance in one class affects the quality of the work in another. This relevance is the key to engaging all middle-level students.

Examples of Units

For one unit, science class served as the starting point. Students studied a classification mechanism known as the dichotomous key, used to identify organisms through a series of choices between alternative characteristics. Then, upon entering the fine arts lab, the students were met with the day's objectives: (a) to become familiar with artifacts of an Indonesian sculpture exhibit (at the Sackler Gallery in Washington, D.C.) and (b) to sort sculpture cards according to a dichotomous key. Next, in the music perspectives class, the objectives outlined on the board revealed to students that they would be required to apply a dichotomous key to categorize an assortment of ethnic instruments. Some of the students' immediate comments about the music teacher and her class were "She knows!" "This is a conspiracy!" and "She's one of them."

Met with this type of instruction, students soon realize that what they learn in one class can be applied in another. They quickly catch on and begin to look for and expect connections. Their own thinking becomes playfully flexible and creative.

Because the A.R.T.S. teachers are deliberately scheduled to have planning time together, they are able to determine processes and products of writers, scientists, and artists that share common elements. For example, they summarized the similarities of the composing process and the scientific method (see figure 1).

Sometimes it is the common product that helps students integrate their day, as in the case of an interdisciplinary unit called the Fable Project. Within all of the A.R.T.S. team classes, this project has students engaged in the creation of original fables, which they are expected to present, using a variety of modes—musical, visual, oral, and textual.

In their music perspectives class, students listen to and study professional treatment of leitmotives or signature melody. Examples are presented such as the ring and sword motives from Wagner's operatic cycle *The Ring of the Nibelungs;* the duck motive from Prokofiev's *Peter and the Wolf;* and the Darth Vader, Princess Leia, and Jedi knight motives from John Williams's music for the *Star Wars* trilogy. Students, working in pairs, are then given the task of writing their own signature melody for the main character of their own original fable.

Students discuss, listen to, and then compose

Similarities of the Composing Process and the Scientific Method

Composing Process	Scientific Method
1. identify/play the theme to be transformed	1. identify the problem
2. identify plot points for theme	2. research known data
3. choose a possible transformation device	3. hypothesize
4. listen to usage examples	4. research
5. improvise possible transformations	5. experiment
6. notate/sketch/record attempts	6. collect data
7. listen to and analyze the results	7. analyze the data
8. draw a conclusion	8. draw a conclusion
9. identify alternative transformation	9. identify a new problem/question
10. cycle back and try the process again	10. research

Figure 1. The composing process and the scientific method

music, using techniques such as sequence, fragmentation, retrograde, inversion, augmentation, diminution, modal shift, metric shift, and change of timbre. As determined by the plot, the students experiment and transform their leitmotiv according to one of these devices. They can transform the leitmotiv by using a computer (Macintosh), MIDI keyboard, composing software (Deluxe Music Construction Set), and other instruments. The transformation ought to represent the character's psychological state at a given point in the plot. In English class, the students are asked to justify their reason for each transformation.

Although the fable is written in English class, the character's traits are identified and supported through the science class. Finally, the art course supports the preparation of the final product through training in design, drawing, pen and ink, and watercolor techniques, both in traditional media and on computers. In the final stage, students present their fables orally, musically, and visually. During their telling of the fable, they play their motive (from a school-supplied synthesizer, MIDI keyboard station, xylophone, or on their own chosen instrument), and their character's clay figurine portrait is on display. The portrait even becomes a component of a video or Hypercard presentation of the fable.

Excerpts from teacher discussions during the process of developing the fable unit reveal some of the philosophical consensus-building of the interdisciplinary team:

Science teacher:
If students are asked to master not just performing a piece or an experiment, but also the process of creating, developing precision, they will be more able to transfer that skill to other situations and other classes. Let's be more deliberate about the processes we expect them to learn...We need an activity that allows them to focus on their observation skills and apply their knowledge of classifying living things.

Art and culture teacher:
Students need to build skills in contour-line drawing and pen and ink, but it ought to allow them to work toward a meaningful goal...something which goes beyond the art room walls.

English teacher:
Mid-level students are trying to figure out who they are. Activities that challenge students to express themselves in a variety of ways give them a chance to discover their own gifts and strengths.

Music perspectives teacher:
Students need the chance to compose for a variety of media, such as a literary or film project. Doing so forces them to consider plot points, environmental and atmospheric influences, and even a character's psychological journey. A multimedia literary project may challenge them to make decisions regarding tone, setting, suspense, character traits, and the elements of a good story and good composition.

Use of Technology

The A.R.T.S. Program has over time acquired technology to support its vision and day-to-day student activities. The A.R.T.S. Lab currently uses 22 MIDI keyboards, connected with a cluster of 8 Macintosh LC, Macintosh LCII, and Macintosh Classic computer stations. This provides the arts classes with technology tools for writing, data base, drawing, music composition, budgeting, and Hypercard integration.

One of the more recent discoveries was the ease with which students integrate their research through Hypermedia. Students working in teams of four recently researched the history and use of musical instruments from the Far Eastern, Middle Eastern, Baltic, and European regions. This research, while supporting their work in world studies classes, combined research skills, writing, editing, graphics, and computer scanning with listening and musical decision making. The students created their own Hypercard stacks to share the sound, shape and construction, history, and contemporary music of their instrument. They have plans to distribute these stacks to elementary schools and local libraries so that elementary students and the community will learn about musical instruments from middle school students.

It is now common to hear students ask each other:

- "Do you think we should web, chart, write, or draw our answers and ideas today?"
- "I need to add music to our story. Do you think we have time to start composing today?"
- "This piece needs a better structure. We need a unifier. I think I'll go back to the main theme and shorten it. Why don't you draw the overall plan on the computer while I do this?"

Students will commonly ask the music or art teacher:

- "We don't want to lose the idea our team is working on. Are we going to have time for journaling our thoughts in class today?"
- "Can we check the lab to see if any other students left suggestions on our screen about our Hyper-music today?"

In yet another unit, students create *Operatoons!* Listening to chosen operas, students create multimedia cartoons that depict the key components of an opera, such as recitative, a climactic aria, orchestral atmospheric foreshadowing, visual backdrops, and caricatures of the key protagonists and antagonists. The team is quickly moving toward having students compose their own opera from the basic structures they learned through the *Operatoons* unit.

Scheduling of Classes

The A.R.T.S. Program involves a two-year sequence in which blocking of classes is the norm. Teachers in the program directly influence the school's scheduling. The A.R.T.S. team leader, who summarizes the teachers' key scheduling needs, and the master scheduler, working as part of the administrative team, draw up the school schedule. The team asks for (a) a three-period block scheduled in the beginning or end of the day, (b) common students scheduled into the program, (c) heterogenous grouping, and (d) common planning time for art, English, music, science, and world studies team teachers.

The teachers may use the block to schedule flexible configurations of students. This type of schedule allows groups within a team to move freely, with no interruption to the rest of the school. Individuals, small groups, and whole classes can mix and mingle as planned for particular learning goals.

For example, in the first semester of the program, the science and music teachers blocked two groups back to back, designating them as Groups A and B. This enabled both the science teacher and music teacher to keep one group for 2, 3, or even 4 consecutive class days to work with students for extended labs. On Monday, then, both Group A and Group B might double Period 1, and Period 2 would be dropped. On Tuesday, both Group A and Group B might double Period 2, and Period 1 would be shortened or dropped.

Because all of the students in the program met during Periods 1, 2, and 3, it was possible to have any combination of sharing of students, doubling up of teachers (to team teach), assembling together to prepare for large-group experiences or field trips, and moving individual students into different sections.

Observations and Results

A.R.T.S. students are not necessarily interested in the arts as a vocation or avocation. Rather they select the program with the intent of seeing the world or a given challenge from a variety of viewpoints: from the artist's, the composer's, the writer's, the scientist's, and the student's.

Multicultural arts-enhanced instruction also helps students explore their own cultural identity and develop self-esteem. Multicultural art and music experiences allow students to find identity within their own heritage as well as understand commonalities among people.

During the first year of the A.R.T.S. Program, when the teachers designed an interdisciplinary unit around a geographic region's culture (based on the social studies curriculum), the teachers found that the culture unit did not naturally encourage students to make conceptual connections on their own or formulate insightful questions about the human experience. As a result, the team decided that it would be more meaningful for the students to explore a variety of cultural and artistic practices within a given concept-based unit. In the second year of the program, interdisciplinary units were developed and presented around conceptual and process connections. The major concepts chosen were creativity; unique/universal; change-evolution/revolution; and dependence/independence/interdependence.

Clearer comprehension and more in-depth discussions were immediate results of the new approach. Students drew inferences with regard to such matters as the universal nature of tone production, modes of expression, performing practices, roles of the creator, and ritual occasions for art and music. The A.R.T.S. team came to realize that by participating in multiregional units, students were truly engaged in learning and were willing to analyze and go beyond differences to examine the similarities among peoples. This approach also encouraged a sense of belonging for those students who were newly arrived in the United States.

The A.R.T.S. team found that technology, tools, and interdisciplinary activities that allow students to discuss, challenge viewpoints, collaborate, play specific roles, and operate as partners, trios, or small groups are inherently motivating. Peer-evaluation experiences gave students a chance to formulate and articulate thoughts, viewpoints, and preferences in a structured way. These processes, inherent in music and art criticism, became a staple in other classes as well.

The scheduling of teacher meetings is a critical factor in the design of a team-based program. Within the traditional middle-level school, someone or some discipline normally gets left out of the teaming process. If a team of teachers is going to meet, students must be attending classes other than their own. Typically this translates to excluding the arts educators from the teaming process so that they can teach the students while the "academic" educators and counselors meet.

Team and counseling discussions often focus on strategies for supporting a particular student. Although the arts classes may be the single arena in which an at-risk student is tapping into his or her area of giftedness and finding success, the arts educators are usually left out of the crucial collaboration process. With no one there to speak for the area of giftedness and substantive successes of the student within an arts environment, this critical portion of the child's multiple intelligence development is missing in the strategy session. Better articulation among these two groups of teachers brings about better success for the integration of the academic, creative, and aesthetic intelligence of the child.

In the A.R.T.S. team design, combining fine arts and academic arts is mutually supportive, and team meetings involve teachers from both areas. Eastern Middle School's nontypical approach to interdisciplinary teaming more fully integrates the aesthetic, creative, and academic development of all middle-level students. Breaking the mold of the traditional middle-level team has netted results that are refreshing, substantial, and vital to many students and their parents.

Notes

The author acknowledges the assistance of Eastern Middle School educators. Contributions were made by Katherine Bender, science teacher; Patricia Broda, art teacher; Becky Flores, art teacher; Kathryn Shuey, English teacher; and John P. Goodloe, principal. Editing assistance was received from Marlene Hartman, principal; Carol Starr Nelson, social studies resource teacher; and Phyllis Kaplan, supervisor of aesthetic education for Montgomery County Public Schools.

The following resources provided background information: Richard Paul Janero and Thelma C. Altshuler, *The Art of Being Human: The Humanities as a Technique for Living* (New York: Harper & Row, 1989); Francis R. Link, ed., *Essays on the Intellect* (Alexandria, VA: Association for Supervision and Curriculum Development, 1985); Eunice Boardman, *Dimensions of Musical Thinking* (Reston, VA: Music Educators National Conference, 1989); and Heidi Hayes Jacobs, *Interdisciplinary Curriculum: Design and Implementation* (Alexandria, VA: Association for Supervision and Curriculum Development, 1989).

MULTICULTURAL EDUCATION

Keith Hampton

The University of Chicago Laboratory Schools have approximately fifteen hundred students from an urban, multicultural neighborhood–Hyde Park. Hyde Park is a transient community because of the residents' connection with the University of Chicago; it is also a richly diverse community.

Being an educator in America means having to work within a rapidly changing and ethnically diverse society. As a result, we are constantly in contact with students from a variety of different religious beliefs, socioeconomic backgrounds, and ethnic groups. The process of teaching these students becomes compromised unless we are provided with, and provide a basis for, the understanding of the language, values, and customs that characterize the students' individual ethnic identity.

The best way to learn about another culture is to become immersed in it by visiting the country and learning the language. Another approach is through participation in the cultural offerings of a people. Learning to perform authentic ethnic music helps with the understanding of a particular group's customs and values.

The challenge for educators has been focused on how to provide the opportunity for cultural immersion within the narrow confines of the classroom environment. This becomes important as we strive to provide an opportunity for students to have a positive learning environment free from negatively biased cultural stereotypes. A school and classroom environment that supports an appreciation of, and a respect for, people who may be different from ourselves should be the goal of every educator. A multicultural educational focus provides just such an opportunity to get to know other Americans better. The flexibility inherent in the middle school approach is well adapted to providing such a focus.

Keith Hampton is a choral and general music instructor at the University of Chicago Laboratory Schools in Chicago.

Multicultural education focuses on more than just the racial identity of a group. It encompasses gender identification, religious beliefs, mores, values, family structure, and socioeconomic background. It enables students to witness for themselves the positive qualities of their fellow classmates by erasing misconceptions and negative stereotypes that are fostered by ignorance and lack of understanding. It assists students in maintaining and strengthening their own identity while learning about the similarities and differences within their group and other groups.

In an attempt to provide a meaningful curriculum, schools often attempt to relate to everyone in the same way. Schools would be better served, however, if the diversity of their population was celebrated and shared. With this approach, the contributions of each group combined with that of other groups will make for a stronger sense of community, which will, in turn, enrich the curriculum.

An example of how a school can celebrate diversity is my approach to the winter holiday season. I had observed that this season is often a very tense time in most schools. The reason for this is that often the parents of Jewish students speak out against Christmas celebrations that pronounce Christ as being the Messiah. As a result, schools often try to compromise this celebration by leaving out songs or symbols that accurately tell the story of Christmas. In other words, there is an attempt to take Christ out of Christmas. The Christian parents often feel put off by this attempt and refuse to take part in any holiday programs or songfests.

In an effort to lessen tensions and show the similarities of several ethnic groups, I presented a Festival of Lights program with my middle school general music classes. This program featured Duwali, which is celebrated by families from India; Chanukah, which is celebrated by Jewish families; Christmas, which is celebrated by Christian families; and Kwanzaa, which is a nonreligious celebration observed by some African American families. The link between all of these celebrations is their use of candle lighting ceremonies. Each group presented its own nonwatered-down ceremony with Bible readings, Hebrew prayers, Hindu prayers, or proclamations of Kwanzaa's seven principles. All the candles were placed on a common table that represented our shared similarities while at the same time showing our diversity. The program was very well-received by parents, faculty, and students. Those present felt enriched by the knowledge gained from this program of sharing.

Parents are, of course, excellent resources for educators and students because they can provide answers to questions about cultural customs and rituals. Each family unit personifies the important role of multicultural education and fosters the development of the student's identity within the family group.

Music is a universal language. It reflects the culture in which it is found and offers the student an instant insight into the things of value found in that culture. Venturing into the music of different cultures presents the educator with exciting and often easily understandable avenues for teaching about different groups of people.

Getting Started

When choosing repertoire and music materials, the music educator often wonders if his or her students can recreate the aesthetic intent of the composer. Many times a composition that has its origins in a non-Western ethnic tradition is overlooked or not considered because of the teacher's insecurity about achieving an authentic interpretation. The following ideas and questions provide some concrete suggestions and guidelines for facilitating the performance of this richly diverse music at the middle level:

Language/Dialect

- Whenever possible, find a native speaker who can teach the correct pronunciation of the text as well as provide a translation of the text. For example, I always try to choose songs that are representative of my school's student population. One of my Polish students shared a carol with his fellow sixth graders. He not only provided the music and an English translation, but also taught us how to pronounce the Polish text.
- If there is no native speaker available, try to locate a transliteration (phonetically spelled out version) of the text.

Vocal Production

- What are the chief characteristics of vocal sound? (Is the sound reedy, chesty, nasal, breathy, or some other quality?)
- How can the sound be approximated in an approachable, appropriate, and healthy manner?

Style (Performance Practice)

- What is the most appropriate instrumental accompaniment? (Will a guitar, piano, or some other instrument work?)
- What are some of the most commonly used vocal embellishments?
- What is the role of the soloist in relation to the choir?
- Is the use of improvisation both appropriate and "in style"?

Music Scores

- Where is the music available? Publishers that offer multicultural music include Lawson-Gould (distributed by Alfred Publishing Co., P.O. Box 10003, 16380 Roscoe Blvd., Suite 200, Van Nuys, CA 91410-0003; 818-891-5999) and West Music Co. (P.O. Box 5521, 1208 Fifth St., Coralville, Iowa 52241; 800-397-9378).
- Is the music authentic? Is there any information about the piece given on the front cover or in notes?

Recordings

- Are there any recordings available? Possible sources include Smithsonian/Folkway Records (distributed by One World Records, 1350 Avenue of the Americas, New York, NY 10019; 212-975-0575) and publishers such as West Music Co. that offer recordings as an accompaniment to some of their sheet music.
- Is the performing group or artist of ethnic origin?
- If the performers are not of ethnic origin, is the performance authentic?

Performing Groups

- Are there any ethnic musicians or choral groups located locally who would allow visitors in their rehearsals? For example, I had an opportunity to hear ethnic performing groups when I served as guest conductor of a multicultural choir festival. I heard several Mexican choirs, a Filipino choir, and a Polish choir. I asked the choirs if I could have a copy of their music and if I could attend their rehearsals. By doing this, I have been able to hear firsthand how they rehearse and vocally approach their music.
- Where can a listing of ethnic artists be obtained in your area?

Arts Councils

Arts councils are often a good place to begin the search. Teachers can check their local telephone listings for arts councils, commissions, or agencies. Another source of information is the National Assembly of Local Arts Agencies (NALAA), 927 15th St., N.W., 12th floor, Washington, DC 20005 (202-371-2830).

COLLABORATION BETWEEN MIDDLE SCHOOLS AND HIGH SCHOOLS

William Erlendson

The San Jose (California) Unified School District enrolls nearly thirty thousand students of quite diverse backgrounds. Five K-12 magnet schools offer enhanced learning opportunities in music and other arts. These schools practice collaboration between the middle and high school levels, employ interdisciplinary strategies, and have developed alternative sources of funding.

The city of San Jose, fifty miles south of San Francisco, is a unique and ethnically diverse community of 780,000 residents, representing over seventy different nationalities. As one of thirty-seven school districts in Santa Clara County and one of eight in the city of San Jose, the San Jose Unified School District is the largest in the county. Embracing the major portion of the city, the boundaries of San Jose Unified encompass more than fifty square miles. The district's unique geographical characteristics–it is twenty-four miles long from north to south, but only four miles wide at its widest point–contribute heavily to its problems of ethnic imbalance. San Jose Unified enrolls 29,800 students and has twenty-seven elementary schools, seven middle schools, and seven high schools. The student population is 40.8 percent Anglo, 41.3 percent Hispanic, 11.1 percent Asian, 3.3 percent Black, and 3.5 percent other racial or ethnic backgrounds.

The desire to reduce, prevent, or eliminate minority group isolation, as well as to enhance the achievement of all students, has created the need for resources to expand and design relevant and meaningful educational programs in the arts that go beyond the boundaries of the classroom walls. Accommodating a 1986 court order to desegregate all district schools, San Jose Unified School District established five K-12 magnet schools in the academics, visual, and performing arts. The educational opportunities in music and the arts for students who attend these magnet schools today contrast dramatically with the opportunities available to students who attend other schools in the district. A magnet school has a defined curricular theme that, ideally, permeates all subject areas. The San Jose Unified magnet schools in the visual and performing arts have additional staff, an expanded curriculum, and extended school days to offer students enhanced learning opportunities in the arts.

William Erlendson oversees desegregation and the fine arts program as assistant to the superintendent of San Jose Unified School District.

Many of the music education programs in these schools address the unprecedented influx of students from diverse cultures and the need for heightened career awareness in the arts for both middle and high school programs. They use program strategies for both middle and high school that are collaborative, offer new or enhanced approaches to curriculum, have developed alternative sources of funding, and have defined new methods to deal with shortfalls in existing funding.

Learning English and Learning the Arts

San Jose Unified School District has about six thousand students, out of a total population of about thirty thousand, who are limited in their English proficiency. This number has increased by 50 percent within the last five years. They are ill-equipped to cope with the rigors of either a monolingual or bilingual program. Many of the newly arrived immigrant students have been psychologically traumatized by war, the immigration journey, little formal schooling, and poverty. Reeling from culture shock, they fall behind and drop out. An estimated fifty to seventy percent leave school before graduation. Responding to research over the past ten years that demonstrates that combining movement, visual images, music, and dramatization with the process of language acquisition greatly accelerates the ease and depth of learning (see the California State Department of Education publications and Broudy, Gardner, and Ogletree on the "For Further Reading" list at the end of this chapter), Lincoln High School and Hoover Middle School submitted a Title VII grant request, Creative English and Arts Acquisition through Education (Project C.R.E.A.T.E.), to the United States Department of Education. The grant of $200,000 per year for three years emphasizes English acquisition and social development at the middle and high school levels by infusing multicultural music and arts experiences into the physical education and social studies curricula.

Artists in Schools

To provide additional multicultural arts opportunities for students and to offer in-depth instruction in music, visual arts, dance, and drama, San Jose Unified works closely with the California State Department of Education and the California Arts Council to sponsor a model Artists-in-Schools program in the fine arts magnet schools. Artists apply for funding to the Arts Council. When an artist is accepted, the district and the State of California share the expenses of the program. The artists are paid to work twenty hours a week for nine months under the supervision of credentialed teachers. In both the middle and high school settings, artists offer small group and individual lessons during the classroom music instruction periods. Small groups of students are pulled out of the regular fine arts classroom for additional instruction in specialized arts programs. Specialized programs in music include instruction in a variety of multiethnic, classical, and jazz performance styles. Artist/student groups rehearse during lunch, after school, and on weekends in African, Brazilian, and Cuban percussion; electronic music; and small wind ensembles. These groups incorporate a variety of improvisational styles. Both the artists and students arrange music for the groups.

The advantages of the program are many. It helps satisfy a need in middle and high school music programs for expanded avenues of expression that are multiculturally oriented; it accommodates a variety of musical backgrounds and talent; and it offers diversity in instrumental performance options. In addition to these educational benefits, the California Artists-in-Schools program brings a heightened community awareness of outstanding school programs and the cultural needs of the ethnically diverse student populations. As part of the professional performing community, the artists bring their knowledge of the community and community needs to the programs they serve.

Implementing Multimedia Programs with Grants

Electronic keyboarding and MIDI (Musical Instrument Digital Interface) music programs allow students with diverse backgrounds and language abilities to develop musical skills and talents from a variety of creative perspectives. A 1987 grant from Casio, Inc., provided 720 electronic keyboards for the elementary and middle school classroom music programs throughout San Jose Unified. Prior to the grant, classroom music was nonexistent in the elementary schools, and resources for middle school music exploratories were sparse. The prospect of receiving a set of keyboards stimulated school principals to carefully scrutinize their staff for teachers with musical background, and to begin to assess strategies for regular classroom music instruction. Middle school teachers found the keyboards invaluable for hands-on music activities. If we hadn't received the grant, the estimated cost per school to implement the program without the grant would have been approximately nine hundred dollars.

The MIDI programs developed in 1984 at San Jose High Academy were motivated by a need to instruct an ethnically diverse classroom of students with limited English skills and a wide range of talents and abilities. Additionally, the program was intended to develop new career paths in music for students who did not have the traditional background and training in music education but had an interest in music. Adding electronic keyboards and MIDI to the instructional process provided these students with compositional, improvisational, reading, and listening skills, and a learning pace that reflected their abilities and interests. Unhampered by limited English language skills, students had the additional opportunity to develop abilities in music technologies that were practical and meaningful to future careers.

In the middle and high school magnet programs in San Jose Unified, grants from Apple Computer, the David and Lucille Packard Foundation, Casio Inc., and the Yamaha Corporation of America have provided musical instruments and other funding for more than seventy-five MIDI stations. The MIDI stations are in classroom configurations of twenty-four beginning student stations (each with an Apple IIe computer and a Casio CZ1 keyboard) with one teacher station. Advanced stations (with Macintosh SE computers and

Yamaha V-50 keyboards) are located in a separate room to accommodate several peripherals and to offer students additional opportunities in music composition, ear training, arranging, and music history. The software used in the programs includes Passport *Master Tracks* and *Master Tracks Pro,* and programs from Electronic Courseware Systems and Temporal Acuity Products.

In the 1990–91 school year, the Lincoln Academic, Creative, and Performing Arts magnet program began to look at the broader curricular implications of technology in the middle and high school music and visual arts programs. The leadership at Lincoln recognized that most careers in the arts are influenced by technology. So, with the support of business partners, local universities, and community arts groups, the school embarked on an aggressive campaign to introduce interdisciplinary and cross-curricular arts education using technology and multimedia as learning catalysts. Middle and high school students collaborate with the teacher in the use of interactive sound, imaging, video, and presentation hardware and software to create cross-curricular projects that integrate music and the arts with other subjects. By focusing on music and the arts as learning catalysts, multimedia education frees students with limited English skills in grades 6–12 from the constraints of textbooks and chalkboards. The students have ways to express ideas other than writing and speaking.

"Greek and Roman Technology" was a student project created for a world cultures class. The first part of this series of materials was a videotaped comparison of two construction methods: post and lintel, and arch. The world cultures teacher, the physics teacher, and the student collaborated on the script and storyboard. Animation, scanning of slides, and freehand art were used. The computer art and illustration teacher guided the assembly of the project, and the artist-in-residence for advanced electronic music helped with background music from the time period. The music was produced on a MIDI keyboard with voice-over added. Finally, the production was converted from the Macintosh computer to standard video signal and then recorded on videotape. The world cultures teacher now uses the tape in all of her classes to expose students to interdisciplinary learning concepts.

For the multimedia program, twenty-four student Apple IIcx workstations and one teacher workstation were purchased for Lincoln High School, and a room was remodeled to accommodate the equipment. Lincoln applied for a "Computing in the Arts" Specialized Secondary Program grant from the California State Department of Education, and was one of two schools in the state to be approved for model program curriculum planning and staff development for the 1990–91 school year.

Currently (1993) in the third year of the grant, total funding for the multimedia program has approached $500,000. In addition to California Department of Education funding, in 1993 both Lincoln High School and Hoover Middle School received a Federal Magnet School Assistance program grant to expand and upgrade the multimedia arts technology programs and provide additional resources in arts education. First-year funding of approximately $800,000 has allowed both schools to further curriculum development and create additional outreach opportunities incorporating the use of video and multimedia. With the funding, the San Jose State University Improvisation Studies program now offers Lincoln students performance classes designed to explore ethnic music and related improvisational styles. San Jose Civic Light Opera utilizes professional dance artists to offer multicultural dance in place of regular physical education for students identified as "at-risk." Students attending nearby Hoover Middle School participate in the Lincoln High School Computing in the Arts and other visual and performing arts programs in a nongraded 6–12 environment that promotes students on the basis of talent and ability.

There are three goals of the interdisciplinary arts technology program. The first is to implement a preprofessional integrated arts program that infuses technology and computer-assisted instruction in beginning through advanced courses in music, visual arts, theater, creative writing, and dance. An integrated center for Computing in the Arts program provides students in both the middle and high school the opportunity to create collaborative art projects that draw from each of the five artistic disciplines through the use of video, audio, and laser technology. The second goal is to restructure the total school with a focus on the arts and computing in the arts across the curriculum. The third goal is to develop an audio and video production lab that can be integrated with the Computing in the Arts program and offer students preprofessional training in video and audio arts. A long-term objective of the multimedia program is to provide enhanced opportunities for students in grades 3–12 in the uses of technology in music and arts education through career awareness and exploration, and career definition and choice for students who demonstrate a talent, interest, or ability in the arts. The 1993–1994 school year is providing the staff and students of Lincoln High School and Hoover Middle School a number of exciting challenges that include identification and use of alternative student assessment models, exploration of extended school day options, flexible scheduling, nongraded environments, new instructional delivery systems, and a myriad of new programs designed to increase student participation and interest in the arts. Although some of the technology in programs described here may be too expensive for many schools to duplicate, the curriculum provides successful models in arts education that can be replicated for little cost.

A synchronized bell schedule at Hoover Middle School and Lincoln High School, which share a campus, was implemented in 1991 to enable the schools to share resources. For example, small groups of students from the middle school will be able to use a MIDI station at the high school; they will work on a variety of projects based on collaborative learning models.

The Castillero Academic, Creative, and Performing Arts Magnet Middle School in San Jose Unified implemented a successful strategy for procuring outside funding in music and the arts for traditional program enhancement. Their need statement, the most crucial part of applying for a grant, was clear: *String programs in California public education are dying. The exchange program will encourage students to continue their education in string instruction, provide additional community support for music education, and set a precedent for other school districts to interact and share resources.* Their string orchestra received funding from the California Initiatives Fund grant program to develop a student exchange program with another string orchestra in the state. Other ideas that received grants at the middle and high school level have included instructional partnerships between community and school music groups, community artists-in-schools programs, development of multicultural music ensembles, and creation of technology-assisted music education programs that offer creative instructional options for at-risk youth. The funder usually wants to see a unique educational approach that targets specific student populations, has community support, and presents opportunities for continued funding after project completion.

Maintaining Music Instruction with Limited Funds

When music instruction in grades 4–8 was threatened, San Jose Unified established the Saturday Academy instrumental music program. Instruction by credentialed teachers and artists is offered at school sites each week from 9:00 to 11:00 A.M. Parental participation is encouraged. Students receive a school district instrument and district-purchased instructional materials, and the small classes facilitate in-depth instruction. The principal of the Saturday Academy envisions the program expanding in both curricular offerings and increased student (and parent) enrollment. An advantage of the Saturday Academy elementary and middle school program is the parent participation. Parents volunteer to supervise the students, take attendance, and serve as instructional assistants. A number of the parents have opted to learn to play musical instruments along with students in the class.

The question has been asked repeatedly: Did students learn as much in the Saturday program as they would have in the regular day, twice-a-week pull-out program? As far as could be ascertained, student progress was on a par with the traditional pull-out program. The explanation for a comparable progress rate may be attributed to the longer time (one hour) given to the lesson on Saturday, the involvement of the parent, less distractions to learning during the instructional time, and the strict attendance policy (no more than one absence per semester). Obviously, students will learn more if they are given additional instructional time beyond the once-a-week program. However, fiscal realities in San Jose Unified School District demand creative approaches to education that will ensure that elective programs continue in spite of fiscal shortcomings.

The innovative Saturday program is a part of an overall district planning and restructuring effort to expand the traditional five-day instructional week. Other delivery models in the planning stage include flexible block scheduling, evening classes, and year-round school. Flexible block scheduling offers variety in the time and frequency of core and elective courses. Some of the options include offering classes in two-hour modules twice a week, ninety-minute blocks three times a week, or other configurations that may result in more or less than the weekly five-hour instructional time allotment. Flexible block scheduling, most often used at the middle level, is used at Lincoln High School and allows for more in-depth time for selected visual and performing arts, and lab science courses. Also, alternating the larger and smaller blocks allows high school students the opportunity to work as peer tutors in instrumental music, choir, electronic keyboarding, and the visual arts at the middle school.

In nearby Abbot Middle School, in the San Mateo City School District, all middle school students have the opportunity to take music instruction despite funding cutbacks. Sixth-grade students are required to take a music class: music appreciation, band, choir, or orchestra. They alternate music instruction with computer instruction during the week. In addition to the alternate day class, they are required to take three exploratories. Seventh-grade students alternate music instruction with required physical education. Eighth-grade students have a similar schedule. The choral instructor notes that the advantage of the program is that every student in the school receives music instruction. The disadvantage is that the alternate day schedule does not provide the breadth of exposure to music that a daily instructional program would.

One solution some have advocated is to provide a

full-year music elective for eighth-grade students. This would allow students previously exposed to music in the sixth and seventh grades the opportunity to make a serious choice to include music in their studies. The student participation figures are impressive. Out of a student body of 700 students, 280 participate in the choir, 120 in the band, and 35 in the orchestra. In a time where elective programs at the middle level are sparse, the Abbot Middle School program offers an intelligent alternative.

Alternatives in music education require that school staffs and district administrations look carefully at all facets of student learning, changing demographics, and financial constraints. Contemporary music education objectives and outcomes must define broad-based curricular directions that recognize multicultural values and ethnic diversity, current technologies in the arts and related career paths, increased community support, and parent participation. The successful alternatives to middle and high school music education must value tradition in combination with what students from a variety of socioeconomic and cultural backgrounds require today to develop emotionally and intellectually. By proactively responding to change and student interests and exploring viable collaborative alternatives to traditional middle school and high school music education models, today's music educators are in a better position to create culturally responsible citizens that possess an understanding of the past and a vision for the future.

For Further Reading

Academic preparation in the arts. (1985). New York: The College Board.

Broudy, H. S. (1987). *The role of imagery in learning.* Los Angeles: The Getty Center for Education in the Arts.

Eisner, E. (1978). *Reading the arts and the creation of meaning.* Reston, VA: National Art Education Association.

Gardner, H. (1983). *Frames of mind: The theory of multiple intelligences.* New York: Basic Books.

Ogletree, E. J. Curriculum for two modes of consciousness. *Contemporary Education 49* (Summer 1978), 205.

Ostrander, S., and Schroder, L. (1979). *Superlearning.* New York: Delacorte.

Technology in the curriculum: Visual and performing arts. (1987). Sacramento, CA: California State Department of Education.

Visual and performing arts framework for California public schools: Kindergarten through grade twelve. (1989). Sacramento, CA: California State Department of Education.

ASSESSMENT

MIDDLE SCHOOL MUSIC ASSESSMENT STRATEGIES

Christopher Doane

The issue of assessment stands as a cornerstone in the educational enterprise. While there are many areas of the education program that may legitimately be examined as part of the assessment process, one of the most important of these areas is the evaluation of student achievement. While media coverage of this issue emphasizes student achievement in the areas of reading, writing, and computational skills in the high schools, the focus of attention on evaluation is, in fact, much broader and more comprehensive.

Observers familiar with traditions might suggest that the education profession is undergoing revolutionary changes in its view of assessment. Traditional assessment practices, often numerically based and using standardized or teacher-generated tests, have recently been joined by more qualitative models designed to evaluate learning from a broader, more context-sensitive perspective. The ways in which these two contrasting approaches to assessment are integrated into future evaluation practices in education constitute one of the most important shifts in thinking about educational evaluation in recent years. The changes being instituted in programs around the country are not limited in their application; the changes are broadly based in curricular areas, and they are occurring in elementary schools, high schools, and middle schools.

Christopher Doane is professor and coordinator of music education at The University of South Florida in Tampa.

While one of the areas of the public school curriculum that has largely escaped the current spotlight of public scrutiny has been evaluation in the arts and, in particular, music education, the dramatic changes in educational assessment have many of their origins in arts education (Eisner, 1985). The lack of attention may be partly due to the public and school administration preoccupation with standardized academic test scores and the perception that the current ills of our society are coincident with the drop in those scores. In such a climate, the measurement of achievement in music class may be perceived as being relatively insignificant in the face of broader issues and problems that challenge all elements of the education program.

Certainly it is true that the music education profession, in middle schools or otherwise, has not uniformly embraced the kinds of formal evaluation structures so prevalent in more traditional academic subjects. More widely found in music programs are the informal means of evaluation that have served the profession since its inception: the audition for placement in an ensemble, the selection of music for a particular group of voices or instruments, performances at public concerts, or student appearances at music festivals and contests. These informal measures are useful in providing valuable information to evaluate certain aspects of a music program; however, they cannot provide the kinds of comprehensive data that can be used to make an informed judgment about the broad spectrum of learning that occurs in a balanced music education program. Further, these sources of information are not often regarded as the equivalent of the achievement criteria that are employed in other subject areas of the school curriculum.

Perhaps in an effort to be perceived as a legitimate subject area of equal standing with reading or mathematics, music education programs have sometimes adopted the practice of evaluating student achievement using the same models as those subjects whose content is fundamentally different, but whose prestige and standing in the public and education community is admired and coveted. To this issue, Thomas Tunks provides the following perspective:

> *In our efforts to gain and retain acceptance in university and public school curricula we have adopted the "rules of the academy" and tried to show that the arts, specifically music, can be like other academic subjects.... Important risks, however, are associated with an inadequate perspective of measurement and evaluation in music. We could confuse the two, and fail in attempts to measure the unmeasurable. Or we could limit evaluation to an extension of measurement, and ignore the qualitative dimension that makes music unique and important in the first place. Still another possibility is that music educators, not having adequate evaluation tools, could simply abandon attempts at evaluation and lose the esteem of educational decision makers. (1987, p. 53-54)*

Looking specifically at the role of assessment in middle school music programs, the issues become even more problematic. In some school settings there are questions that deal with the examination of the validity of the music class as a core subject, as contrasted with the view of the music class as a source of enrichment or exploratory experiences. Issues concerning the commitment of the general public and the school administration to the educational validity of music study and the provision of the resources of time, space, equipment, and teachers may undermine the music teacher's efforts to undertake and maintain an effective instructional and assessment program. Music teachers in the middle school, however, cannot afford a degree of philosophical uncertainty if music is to maintain any of its justified centrality in the education of the preadolescent.

One of the needs that must be met in many middle school music education programs is the creation and adoption of a varied student assessment program that will provide appropriate and reliable information concerning the full range of personal growth that occurs in the music experience for students at this enormously important stage of development. Boyle and Radocy summarize the value of effective assessment in this way:

> *The quality of educational endeavors, whether for individuals or groups or at the preschool, elementary, secondary, or collegiate and adult levels, partly depends on the quality of the evaluation decision relative to these endeavors. It is therefore imperative that evaluation decisions in music education be the best possible.... Evaluation decisions in music education will approach their best when decision makers (a) have a strong, relevant information base, including both subjective and objective information, (b) consider affective and, where appropriate, aesthetic reactions of (or to) the individual, group, or endeavor being evaluated, and (c) [make decisions] with the primary goal of improving the quality of the learner's educational experiences. (1987, p. 8)*

By one estimate, teachers may spend from a third to a half of their professional time in student assessment activities (Stiggins, 1991). It would probably be fair to assume that music teachers spend similar amounts of time in various facets of the evaluation process in rehearsals and classes. Given the importance of the task and the time involved to design an assessment strategy, it is essential to consider the reason or use for which the assessment will be made, the specific performance that will be evaluated, the types of information that will be collected to support the evaluation, and the ways that the data or information will be used to produce a final determination of performance (Stiggins, 1987).

For example, individual or group diagnostic functions, the assignment of grades, the selection of individuals for extra coaching, or placement in an ensemble might be included among the reasons for student assessment. In clarifying the behavior that is to be evaluated the teacher must first decide on the content or skill that is to be assessed and the specific indicators or criteria that will be used to determine the level of student achievement. It is often useful to think of this area in terms of defining the criteria to be used to indicate mastery of a particular area and determining a range or continuum of behaviors, both positive and negative, that might be observed in making the assessment of student progress. Tools used to collect student data might include performance on a standardized test in music, teacher-made paper-and-pencil tests, music performance assessments, informal in-class observations, creative projects, and responses to student interviews or questionnaires. The information developed from those types of measurement tools might be used to assign achievement grades, to create rating scales, to create a portfolio of student projects that might be used as part of a long-term assessment plan, or for a wide range of other purposes.

In considering the various ways in which assessment issues impact teachers in the classroom, Stiggins (1991) has identified six areas of competency that teachers must master if they are to comprehensively assess the full range of student learning potentials and manage the classroom assessment environment effectively. These competencies are outlined in the sidebar at right.

The remainder of this discussion will focus on issues that concern the assessment of music learning among middle school music students and the consideration of some of the important elements in the formulation of effective assessment strategies. In examining these topics, one of the first problems encountered concerns the terms used to describe different aspects of the assessment process. Before developing the discussion in any greater depth, it may be useful to clarify the meaning of some of the more frequently used terms in this area: *testing, measurement, evaluation,* and *assessment.* For some educators these terms may be used interchangeably, but there are some important distinctions.

Testing is a systematic procedure for obtaining information about individual performance, generally through the assignment of a number or category to represent that performance. While tests are often regarded as very objective instruments, a degree of subjectivity may be introduced into the creation of tests through the selection of items for the test instrument and in the definition of the information or behaviors that represent acceptable versus unacceptable performance.

The process of *measurement,* on the other hand, establishes a basis of comparison between performance test results through the assignment of numerals to data representing objects, individuals, or events according to specific and systematic rules that accurately represent the level of performance indicated through the testing procedure (Boyle and Radocy, 1987). While the testing process allows for the systematic collection of relevant data concerning performance, it is through the transformation process of measurement that the data begin to take on meaning as a basis for the evaluation of performance.

Evaluation as a process is a broader concept than either testing or measurement, although effective evaluation is often based on relevant information supplied through testing and measurement programs. Through the process of evaluation individuals consider relevant information, gathered through both formal and informal means, with a particular goal of determining the meaning of this information from a broader perspective, introducing an element of qualitative judgment about the meaning of the data. Evaluation occurs with a specific purpose in mind. In schools, this purpose may be quite varied, ranging from determining student aptitude, achievement, and attitude, to program effectiveness and the evaluation of teacher behaviors and practices. What is essential to understand is that the evaluation process involves personal judgment that is balanced and informed by a consideration of all relevant and available information.

As a cautionary note, however, there has been a strong tendency in our society to invest a high degree of confidence in the power of numbers or scores to represent complex behaviors and levels of development. It is a dangerous practice to make important decisions about students, teachers, or programs without considering possible limitations of the measurement system in use. That is especially so when inferences about performance are generalized from scores or numbers whose source may be extremely restrictive or where conclusions cannot be justified by the context and breadth of information used to make those decisions.

Assessment Competencies for Teachers

1. *Determining classroom uses of assessment;* including making decisions about student progress as a teaching tool and as a classroom management tool.
2. *Defining achievement targets;* including understanding the behaviors, knowledge, and skills that represent the targets, and determining the most appropriate means of assessing those targets.
3. *Understanding the qualities of a sound assessment;* including determining learning goals, controlling for various sources of assessment interference, measuring the appropriate behaviors consistent with the nature of the subject area, and communicating the results of the student evaluation in a manner that is useful and understandable.
4. *Developing knowledge of appropriate assessment instruments;* including paper-and-pencil test instruments, observations of student performance, and direct personal communication with students.
5. *Understanding the interpersonal dimensions of assessment practices;* including the ways in which students interact with other students and teachers interact with students in the assessment environment.
6. *Delivering assessment feedback to students;* including expectations, the timing of the feedback, the manner in which the feedback is given, and the evaluation of whether the feedback has been understood.

The term *assessment* has been used several times earlier in this discussion and, for many educators, the term is often used interchangeably with testing or measurement. More recently, however, there has been a growing tendency to equate the term with the broader concept of evaluation (Popham, 1988).

In creating an effective assessment program in the middle school, it is useful to have some notion of the purpose for which the measurement data will be used. If the focus is on individual student performance, assessment efforts may vary from determining the level of student potential (aptitude function), the current strengths or weaknesses in a student's development (diagnostic function), the level to which the students have mastered particular skills or knowledge after instructional efforts (achievement function), or collecting information concerning the student's attitude about the learning experience (affective function) (Boyle and Radocy, 1987). While there are certainly specific expectations about the kinds of questions or tasks that may typically be found in an assessment program in any of these areas, it is important to observe that data generated for the evaluation of aptitude, achievement, or diagnostic purposes may be appropriate to assess conditions of student development in other areas as well.

Unquestionably, in order to assess student achievement, one must first understand the goals and priorities of the program in use. While the use of broadly stated and somewhat generalized goal statements have been a part of instructional programs for many years, the use of behaviorally stated objectives as a basis for evaluation has been more recent. There have been benefits in the adoption of this way of framing educational goals in this very specific manner. Educators have had the obligation to analyze and consider more deeply the specific components that make up the music education experience.

In considering the musical experience in what may become microscopic detail, there is a danger in emphasizing the attainment of goals that are clearly articulated and measurable, but may serve to trivialize the music education experience when compared to less specific goals that emphasize the potential richness of the musical art form. When taken to an extreme, it is possible to generate an overwhelming number of learning objectives, the pursuit and measurement of which may take an enormous expenditure of resources and energy, but do little to further the students' deeper understanding of the musical experience. In part, it may be this implicit realization that has contributed to a less than enthusiastic adoption of traditional measurement-based evaluation approaches by the typical music teacher.

There has, however, been a wide range of both general and specific objectives identified for middle school music education programs in states and school systems throughout the country. These objectives help to identify learning goals for general music, band, orchestra, and choral music programs. Another source now exists for teachers and curriculum planners: the National Standards for Music Education, approved in January 1994 by the National Committee on Standards for the Arts and published in the MENC publication, *The School Music Program: A New Vision* (1994).

These standards spell out what students need to know and be able to do in music at three target levels—fourth, eighth, and twelfth grades. The achievement standards, which spell out levels of mastery expected on the part of students, are listed under nine content standards: Singing, alone and with others, a varied repertoire of music; performing on instruments, alone and with others, a varied repertoire of music; improvising melodies, variations, and accompaniments; composing and arranging music within specified guidelines; reading and notating music; listening to, analyzing, and describing music; evaluating music and music performances; understanding relationships between music, the other arts, and disciplines outside the arts, and understanding music in relation to history and culture. Students who participate in vocal, instrumental, or other types of performance ensembles are expected to achieve in all of these areas, as well as in more specialized types of learning more specific to the performance medium studied.

The School Music Program: A New Vision identifies seven ways that curricula based on these standards will be different from those followed in the past. First, they will follow skills and knowledge as objectives. Second, they will involve diverse genres and styles of music. Third, they will develop students' creative skills to a new level (note the content standards for improvisation and composition). *A New Vision* notes that, "many students gain considerable information about music and acquire rudimentary performing skills, but too few have ample opportunities to improvise and compose music.... These experiences will require greater emphasis in the future because of their fundamental importance in learning music."

A fourth change in the curriculum called for by the standards is an emphasis on problem-solving and higher-order thinking skills. *A New Vision* states that, "Beginning in the middle school, students are capable of exercising considerable independence in learning, both as individuals and as members of groups. The learning tasks they are given should be challenging, thought-provoking, and related to the real world of music as it is experienced outside the school. Cooperative learning should be stressed. Students should be encouraged to take initiatives and to accept a share of responsibility for their own learning." A fifth point is the inclusion of interdisciplinary relationships—another point especially important for the middle level.

The final two changes identified in *A New Vision* have to do with expanded use of technology and the development of "reliable, valid, and appropriate techniques for assessing student learning in music" as "an integral part of music instruction."

Often, the broad goals suggested by the standards (which were prepared by the national organization of music education professionals on the basis of an exhaustive national consensus process) can serve as starting points for the more specific objectives that are part of curriculum guides generated on the state, county, city/town, or school levels. Such clearly stated goals and objectives form the basis for an array of educational processes as well as assessment possibilities.

Consider, for example, the potential value of categorizing artistic learning in terms of specific aesthetic behaviors. Bennett Reimer (1971) provided an outline of such a model in his work, "Aesthetic Behaviors in Music." In identifying seven major categories of behaviors through which people may interact with artistic and nonartistic forms, Reimer provides a tool for organizing experiences with the arts from a number of entry points and varying levels of sophistication. A summary of these behaviors includes the broad areas identified by Reimer in the sidebar at right. In this model, the behaviors of perceiving and reacting—what Reimer labels the "ends" behaviors—may be attained through the process or "means" behaviors of producing, conceptualizing, analyzing, and evaluating. Taken together, the experience of these six types of behaviors has the potential for expanding individual potentials for valuing the aesthetic experience—the "outcome" behavior (Reimer, 1971, pp. 76–77). Extending this line of reasoning somewhat further into the classroom setting, these categories of aesthetic behaviors suggest specific processes that may form the basis for musical activities through which learning may be assessed.

Teachers may select from a broad range of measurement activities that may yield important information about student achievement in a number of important areas. Figure 1 describes some of the major elements to consider in the selection of types of assessment strategies to use. An evaluation of the most appropriate use for the assessment instrument, the typical kinds of exercises employed, advantages of the instrument, potential sources of inaccuracies, and how the instrument may influence student learning is included in the description. Teachers should consider a broad range of assessment activities to incorporate into their classroom assessment programs, keeping in mind that one approach to assessment is seldom adequate to sample the diverse kinds of learning inherent in the music class and the wide variety of characteristics of middle school learners.

Aesthetic Interaction Behaviors

GOALS BEHAVIORS

Ends Behaviors

Perceiving	Discriminating, discerning, apprehending, noticing, grasping, discovering, observing, recalling, relating, comparing, anticipating, distinguishing
Reacting	Feeling, undergoing, responding, going through, being absorbed, being moved, being affected, being touched, being caught up, sensing, empathizing

Outcome Behavior

Valuing	Admiring, approving, liking, choosing, favoring, cherishing, respecting, treasuring, identifying with

PROCESS (MEANS) BEHAVIORS

Producing	Creating, recreating, composing, improvising, singing, playing, conducting
Conceptualizing	Naming, verbalizing, identifying, writing, stating, defining, discussing, studying, reasoning, generalizing, theorizing
Analyzing	Comparing, classifying, locating, examining, contrasting, differentiating, systematizing, grouping
Evaluating	Judging, assessing, appraising, estimating, rating, justifying, deciding

At this point in the discussion it may be useful to review two important fundamental concepts in the use of measurement tools and strategies. First, the appropriateness of a measurement tool is known as its *validity,* the consideration of whether the measurement instrument or strategy really is measuring the skills, information, or attitudes that it purports to measure. If the measurement tool is not valid for a specific use, any conclusions reached through the use of that tool would be suspect. Critics of testing programs in the schools often base their objections to these programs on validity concerns, specifically that the measures employed are not appropriate to measure the content or learning in question.

One of the most important concerns in evaluation is making certain that the process or instrument chosen to gather data on student learning is valid for the type of information being sought, and that conclusions drawn from measurement efforts are appropriate given the particular nature of the information on hand. To reinforce this point, consider this commentary:

> *To use a test because it is well-known or is "generally recognized as a good test" without thorough examination of its appropriateness for one's particular purpose constitutes gross professional negligence on the part of the user. Although there are many considerations in test selection or development, the primary responsibility of any test user is to ensure that the test is appropriate for obtaining the desired information. (Boyle and Radocy, 1987, p. 26)*

The different types of validity discussed in the measurement literature may be conveniently divided into three types: *content validity, criterion-based validity,* and *construct validity*. Content validity is often established through a systematic comparison of the test instrument or data-gathering process with the skills, objectives, or content that the instrument is supposed to measure. For example, if students in a middle school orchestra were to be evaluated in their knowledge of musical terms, and the terms were selected from music literature being studied in class, then the items selected for the examination would possess content validity.

Criterion validity is developed by comparing performance on a measurement instrument in question with current (concurrent validity) or future (predictive validity) performance on a measure whose appropriateness is already established. If students, for example, took a countywide music achievement test in the sixth grade and there were some question of the test's appropriateness, the validity might be established by arranging the student scores in rank order and statistically comparing this order to a ranking of the students based on the music teacher's evaluations of student achievement. Depending on the relationship, a form of criterion-based validity would be established for the county test.

The establishment of construct validity, on the other hand, is somewhat different from the other two types of validity because construct validity is developed over a sustained period of time, often with multiple sources of supporting data that are considered in the determination of validity. Construct validity is determined by the extent to which a measurement instrument yields results that may be predicted on the basis of a specific theoretical construct or theory. This type of validity is often associated with concepts like music aptitude, intelligence, or the evaluation of attitudes.

A second major consideration in the selection of an assessment strategy or instrument is *reliability*. Reliability in this sense refers to the stability or consistency of the process or instrument. Unlike validity estimates, which are often expressed within a qualitative dimension, reliability estimates are expressed within a quantitative, or numerical, dimension. Additionally, a test may be reliable but not valid for certain purposes, but a test that is not reliable can never be valid.

There are several ways of establishing the reliability of a test instrument. Measures may be repeated over a period of time, there may be two or more identical forms of a test, or there may be an estimate of the reliability based on a statistical procedure that compares internal relationships between responses to items. The reliability of the test is reported as either a correlation coefficient (in the case of repeated measures or parallel forms estimates) or reliability coefficients. If correlations are reported, the range is .00 to (+ or –) 1.00. If reliability coefficients are reported, the range is .00 to 1.00. In either case, the closer the correlation is to (+ or –) 1.00, the more stable is the test. When making judgments about the achievement or aptitude of individual students, the reliability of the test instrument should be significantly higher than for those situations where groups of students are being evaluated. Standard measurement texts elaborate further on other considerations related to both validity and reliability, and the interested reader should consult texts by Popham (1988), Boyle and Radocy (1987), Borg and Gall (1983), Kerlinger (1979), or other authoritative sources for additional information.

In the selection or development of measurement tools it is important to consider several other practical questions in addition to those ideas related to reliability and validity. For example, how efficient is the measurement instrument in being administered within the time frame of the class and to the number of students that must be assessed? Are the materials in the assessment instrument intrinsically interesting to students or will motivation to perform be a problem? How long will the measurement process take? Are the results easy to score, evaluate, and communicate to students? Are there forms of bias imbedded in the process that will render the results invalid? Issues such as these are crucial to consider since even the most elegant of measurement tools may be impractical when faced with a diverse student population and the sometimes severe limitations of the classroom environment.

In most schools, traditional means of evaluation have focused on the use of paper-and-pencil types of measurement tools. While the use of these types of tools tends to predominate in many middle schools as well, there are additional sources of data with which to evaluate student learning in the middle schools. Among these additional sources are conferences about students, diaries and logs, interviews with students, informal observations, inventories of interests and activities, rating scales, audio and video recordings, and performance tests (Alexander and George, 1981). In music education programs, particularly in the sec-

Comparison of Various Types of Assessment

	Objective Test	Essay Test	Oral Question	Performance Assessment
Purpose	Sample knowledge with maximum efficiency and reliability	Assess thinking skills and or mastery of a structure of knowledge	Assess knowledge during instruction	Assess ability to translate knowledge and understanding into action
Typical exercise	Test items: Multiple-choice True/False Fill-in	Writing task	Open-ended question	Written prompt or natural event framing the kind of performance required
Student's response	Read, evaluate, select	Organize, compose	Oral answer	Plan, construct, and deliver original response
Scoring	Count correct answers	Judge understanding	Determine correctness of answer	Check attributes present, rate proficiency demonstrated, or describe performance via anecdote
Major advantage	Efficiency—can administer many items per unit of testing	Can measure complex cognitive outcomes	Joins assessment and instruction	Provides rich evidence of performance skills
Potential sources of inaccurate assessment	Poorly written items, overemphasis on recall of facts, poor test-taking skills, failure to sample content	Poorly written exercises, writing skill confounded with knowledge of content, poor scoring procedures	Poor questions, students' lack of willingness to respond, too few questions	Poor exercises, too few samples of performance, vague criteria, poor rating procedures, poor test conditions
Influence on learning	Overemphasis on recall encourages memorization; can encourage thinking skills if properly constructed	Encourages thinking and development of writing skills	Stimulates participation in instruction, provides teacher immediate feedback on effectiveness of teaching	Emphasizes use of available skill and knowledge in relevant problem contexts
Keys to success	Clear test blueprint or specifications that match instruction, skill in item writing, time to write items	Carefully prepared writing exercises, preparation of model answers, time to read and score	Clear questions, representative sample of questions to each student, adequate time provided for student response	Carefully prepared performance exercises; clear performance expectations; careful, thoughtful rating; time to rate performance

Figure 1. Assessment comparisons

Note. From "Design and Development of Performance Assessments" by R. J. Stiggins, 1987, TEMS—Instructional Topics in Educational Measurement, *Fall, 1987, p. 35.*

ondary schools, there has been additional use of performance tests, auditions, pass-offs, practice sheets, worksheets, estimates of student cooperation in class, and a host of other techniques designed to measure students' progress. In many of these efforts, teachers have transformed what has essentially been qualitative information about students' musical growth into a form of description that has its roots established in a quantitative or numerical model. Stated in another way, teachers often make qualitative judgments on student achievement based on widely diverse kinds of information, integrating and balancing that information to arrive at a single descriptor (an "A," a "satisfactory" conduct mark, or assigning a student to a position in a music ensemble) to capture and describe a specific level of development.

Teachers may create a learning environment that overemphasizes the measurement process and where a testing ambiance pervades the classroom. This approach to evaluation is increasingly being criticized within the larger education community for the artificiality that is brought to the assessment process and the inability of the process to accurately describe the range of student learning that may be occurring. The effectiveness of evaluation based only on quantitative models is currently being reconsidered from the point of view that there may be instances in which the best assessment of student learning may be made through the use of professional judgment and criticism, unencumbered by the artificiality of testing situations and more sensitive to the importance of learning context.

The importance of these alternative assessment strategies has come into clearer focus through the writings of people such as Elliot Eisner of Stanford University, Howard Gardner of Harvard University, Richard Stiggins of the Northwest Regional Educational Laboratory, and their colleagues and associates. Prototypes of assessment programs have been instituted through projects such as the innovative Pittsburgh Public Schools Arts PROPEL program established in cooperation with the Educational Testing Service (ETS) and Harvard University's Project Zero. New ways of thinking about the nature of intelligence and learning, the importance of the arts in a balanced education, and the usefulness of assessment practices in contributing to more effective ways of teaching have challenged the education profession to reconsider the usefulness and desirability of traditional testing programs and to develop new models of assessment practices, often based on contextually based judgment and observation. These innovative assessment systems have been variously labeled *alternative assessment, performance assessment* (Stiggins, 1987), or *authentic assessment* (Zessoules and Gardner, 1990).

In the Pittsburgh Arts PROPEL project, for example, assessment is guided by three important concepts central to the arts: *production, perception, and reflection*. In the production process in music, the emphases are on performing, composing and creating, and active listening with the focus of creating written commentary on what is heard. By developing the student perception process, teachers are able to focus on the developing powers of discrimination. By emphasizing personal reflection, the student develops a sense of self-knowledge, a greater awareness of personal goals, and an understanding of the means necessary to achieve those goals (Davidson, 1991). In creating evaluation tools to be incorporated into this approach to learning, the designers of Arts PROPEL made the assessment process an integral part of the learning environment. From this perspective, assessment becomes a learning tool woven into the fabric of the classroom for both teachers and students.

The primary means of evaluation in Arts PROPEL are two major types of projects, Domain Projects and Process Portfolios:

> *Domain Projects are rich sets of exercises involving production, perception, and reflection skills. Domain projects are sustained pieces of work, taking place over many class sessions focused on issues and questions that remain central to a particular domain. For example, one domain project in imaginative writing enhances students' skills in writing dramatic dialogues and scenes; another, in music, focuses on critical analysis of several rehearsals of a piece.... Domain projects encourage students to assume different roles and responsibilities as maker, critic, and judge. This focus on process allows multiple opportunities for assessment over time. In addition, these projects are designed to be compatible with diverse curricula and to be modified and revised as needed by teachers.*
>
> PROPEL process-folios *are designed to document the evolution of new understandings over time, allowing teachers and students to gather new insights about their development as learners. PROPEL process-folios are complete process-tracing records of the various attempts made by students in realizing a work or a series of works... For example, students may include initial sketches or drafts, self-criticism and criticism by others, successive drafts and reflections, a series of domain projects, ... or a plan for a possible succeeding project. (Project Zero: The Development Group, 1991, p. 7)*

Zessoules and Gardner (1990) point out that these types of projects emphasize the evaluation of a student's abilities to deal with complex understandings and allow the student to be evaluated as he or she works through authentic projects in the arts. Further, students begin to develop their own understandings of the arts through developing reflective thinking skills that emphasize independent judgment and personal investment in the artistic process. This growth in understanding and judgment may be documented over an extended period of time and may help to clarify the development process through which the student proceeds.

A description of how process portfolios are used in an ensemble environment is provided by Linda Ross-Broadus (1991). In a description of the ensemble portfolio program, she explains that the components of the portfolio are made up of Domain Projects (including rehearsal critiques and comparisons), Error Detection Scores, Student Questionnaires, Peer Interviews, Performance Exams, and Student Journals. One part of this program, the Rehearsal Critique, is described as follows:

> *The Ensemble Rehearsal Critique is based on the Arts PROPEL Production-Perception-Reflection model. An excerpt of a song, often sixteen bars in length, is performed by the students and tape recorded three different times during a grading period. This is the production component. Perception and reflection follow immediately. After each taping the students critique their individual performances or their section's performance specifying location*

Name ____________________ **ENSEMBLE REHEARSAL CRITIQUE** Date ____________________

Period ____________________ Piece ____________________

Instrument ____________________ 3/23/89 VERSION

Write down your critique of the ensemble performance specifying **Location** (where you performed particularly well or need to improve) and **Musical Dimensions** (such as rhythm, intonation, tone, balance, articulation, phrasing, interpretation, etc., or any dimension specified by the teacher). Using words such as "because," be sure to mention any links between your own or your section's performance and the ensemble as a whole. Also include remarks concerning **Revisions or Practicing Strategies** for yourself or the ensemble. Be sure to include the main problem in terms of its dimension and location in the place you or the ensemble should practice on before or during the next rehearsal.

		Critical Comments	**Revisions or Practice Plans**
Location	Dimension	My (Section's) Performance	For Myself (My Section)
		(Filled out immediately after performance)	
Location	Dimension	Ensemble's Performance	For The Whole Ensemble
		(Filled out after listening to recorded performance)	

ARTS PROPEL assessment form Specifics ☐ Suggested Revisions ☐ Critical Perspective ☐

USE OTHER SIDE OF PAGE FOR ADDITIONAL COMMENTS

Figure 2. An ensemble rehearsal critique form

Note. Figure 2 (above) and Figure 3 (next page) were originally published in The Quarterly Journal of Music Teaching and Learning, Volume 1 & 2 *(1990) in "Tracing reflective thinking in the performance ensemble" by L. Davidson and L. Scripp. For more information, contact Doree N. Pitkin, Managing Editor,* The Quarterly, *School of Music, University of Northern Colorado, Greeley, CO 80639. Reprinted by permission of the publisher.*

DOMAIN PROJECT: ENSEMBLE REHEARSAL CRITIQUE

Ensemble or Class ______________________ June 23, 1989 Version

Teacher ______________________

Grade Level(s) ______________________

Student ______________________

(Score Highest Instances*)

TEACHER SCORING KEY

Ability to offer specific references to musical elements while making critical comments and/or suggested revisions throughout the critique →

Identification of Musical Elements in Critical Judgements About Performances

NR = no response or not enough statements given

1 = **Does not refer to musical elements in performance** (e.g., 'bad'; 'great'; 'much better'; 'keep together')

2 = **Refers to isolated musical elements** and/or **makes overly broad, sometimes inappropriate or irrelevant references to the performance** (e.g., 'out of tune'; 'sloppy rhythm'; 'trumpets too soft')

3 = **Refers to musical elements with increased specificity, coherence and relevance to musical dimensions** (e.g., 'the flutes played the eight notes like quarter notes [rhythm]'; 'the accents in the trombones need more punch [dynamics]')

4 = **Makes many specific and appropriate references to musical elements in the performance** (e.g., 'the trumpets came in late and too loudly on measure 16 and never caught up until the end'; 'I forgot to give the half notes two beats on measure 3 but I held the quarter notes longer to make up for it')

Ability to suggest **revisions** or **practice plans** linked with critical comments →

Ability to Suggest Revisions or Practice Strategies for Improving Performances

NR = no response or not enough statements given

1 = **Does not refer to specific musical elements while suggesting how to improve the performance** (e.g., 'practice'; 'take your instrument home'; or 'listen to Mr. Dailar')

2 = **Offers overly broad, superficial or unconstructive suggestions** (e.g., 'play more in tune'; 'find the bad spots and practice them'; 'don't play sloppy')

3 = **Suggests more specific and constructive revisions or practice plans sometimes linked to critical comments on the form** (e.g., 'the flutes should use a hard and crisp tone'; 'the drums should tap their feet for better rhythm'; 'violins should practice with separate bowings')

4 = **Suggests highly articulated practice strategies and revisions clearly linked with specific critical comments on the form** (e.g., 'the flutes should play staccato like the trumpets do in the first version'; 'the percussion should practice the hard parts 3 times slowly, then at the tempo marked for more precision')

Critical perspective developed through musical elements or practice plans increasingly coordinated with critical comments →

Critical Perspective(s) Assumed by Students While Discussing the Individual and Ensemble Performance(s)

NR = no response or not enough statements given

1 = **Response insufficient for determining critical perspective** (e.g., 'very bad'; 'good'; or 'practice')

2 = **Description of one or more single points of view not coordinated with musical dimensions** (e.g., 'I was too loud'; 'we were out of tune'; 'the drums dragged')

3 = **Evidence for single coordination of musical dimensions between two points of view** (e.g., 'trumpets were too loud'; 'I couldn't be heard'; or 'sopranos missed their entrance, we didn't')

4 = **Evidence for more complex coordination of two or more points of view and causal relations across one or more musical dimensions** (e.g., 'after the sopranos came in the tenors got louder and I started singing flat'; 'the second time I sang softer and it was much better in tune')

(*highest instance = score the highest level of achievement demonstrated by the student)

ARTS PROPEL ASSESSMENT FORM

Figure 3. Teacher guide for evaluating student rehearsal critiques and using music vocabulary to describe their perceptions. Lastly, they reflect on what they have performed and heard; they then suggest revisions. (Ross-Broadus, 1991, p.5)

Projects such as Ensemble Rehearsal Critique can be instituted in middle school music performance programs without completely revising the curriculum. Teachers may still select literature and objectives or concepts to present to the ensemble while the music rehearsal process stays intact, with the same musical priorities of intonation, balance, expression, and so forth that the teacher may choose to emphasize. What may become markedly different in the classroom and rehearsal environment is the emphasis and time spent on discussing and writing critical reviews of the personal and ensemble musical preparation process and the student investment and identification with the musical process (Davidson and Scripp, 1990). An example of the form used to record these periodic student critiques is given in figure 2 and a suggested teacher guide for evaluating the student rehearsal critiques follows in figure 3.

In using the evaluation guidelines, teachers become more sensitive to student perceptions and ideas about the development of the student's personal musicality and that of the ensemble, while the students strengthen their own reflective thinking skills. Further, teachers remain flexible to guide and refine students' evaluative powers by whatever means seem appropriate. The relative strength of the student critiques and decisions of how the critiques fit into an overall classroom assessment program remains at the option of the teacher.

A description of other domain projects in the middle school music classroom is provided by James Charlton (1991), also a participant in the Pittsburgh Arts PROPEL project. Citing the program emphasis on the Production-Perception-Reflection process in music, he points out that the middle school general music program provides the foundations for needed skills and experiences that students require for successful participation in the more sophisticated musical settings of high school programs. Descriptions of the types of projects that might be used in a middle school general music program include invented notation projects, listening for form, rhythmic composition, melodic composition, and songwriting projects. Remarking on the flexibility and value of domain projects such as these, he states:

Since Domain Projects are designed to tap central skills in music and provide a window on students' development, it is possible to look at a student's accuracy, expansiveness, recovery time, degree and breadth of transfer, as well as the student's grasp of a particular musical element. The Domain Project represents ... a juncture of skills and concepts. Consequently, the general music classroom takes on a structure more similar to production classes, since by its structure the Domain Project repeatedly provides activities that support a climate for learning much like that of the rehearsal studio or workshop. (1991, p. 8)

Within the context of projects such as the performance portfolios and domain projects there is a close connection between instruction and assessment. Moreover, assessment occurs in a way that is fundamentally different from more traditional programs. In evaluation programs with a traditional orientation, assessment occurs primarily between the teacher and the student. In performance assessment programs such as those described here, however, evaluation occurs as a natural outgrowth of instruction and flows continuously between the subject area, the teacher, and the student. Speaking on behalf of the participating teachers in the Arts PROPEL project, Linda Ross-Broadus shares her perceptions of the ways in which instruction and assessment are fundamentally different from that of more traditional programs:

"1. With Arts PROPEL, students strive toward intrinsic goals of excellence instead of being primarily interested in better grades.

2. Students are challenged to think and solve problems instead of waiting to be told what to do by the teacher.

3. Arts PROPEL promotes a powerful way of thinking—students are more aware of what's going on around them.

4. Last, Arts Propel helps the teacher create a classroom atmosphere conducive to feedback. Students are more verbal. They critique and question the teacher, but not in an undermining way. They show that they understand the concepts and have internalized the elements of Production-Perception-Reflection (1991, p. 8)."

Assessment is an important part of the educational process. Perhaps in today's fiscal and social environment, which calls for educational accountability, it is one of the most important aspects of the school program. While music programs have often been slow to embrace many of the basic principles of traditional assessment practices that have long been a part of most of the other programs in the school curriculum, there are alternative assessment possibilities in music that show the promise of more closely infusing the process of assessment with the process of education. In middle school programs, the adoption of effective assessment strategies may help the music teacher in a number of ways: by helping motivate students to achieve in music, by providing information to the public and school officials concerning the contribution of music education to a balanced educational experience, by guiding student learning more effectively through providing timely feedback and direction, by providing assistance in the development of curricula and objectives in music education, and perhaps most important, by developing valid information for the profession concerning the ways in which musical skills and insights develop in students participating in school music programs.

References

Alexander, W. M., & George, P. S. (1981). *The exemplary middle school.* New York, NY: Holt, Rinehart and Winston.

Borg, W. R., & Gall, M. D. (1983). *Educational research, an introduction* (4th ed.). New York, NY: Loughman.

Boyle, J. D., & Radocy, R. E. (1987). *Measurement and evaluation of musical experiences.* New York, NY: Schirmer Books.

Charlton, J. (1991). Arts Propel domain projects in middle school music classes. *Special Research Interest Group in Measurement and Evaluation Newsletter, 11,* 8-12.

Davidson, L. (1991). Too often we test too little, too narrowly or we don't test at all. *Special Research Interest Group in Measurement and Evaluation Newsletter, 11,* 1-4.

Davidson, L., & Scripp, L. (1990). Tracing reflective thinking in the performance ensemble. *The Quarterly, 1* (1 & 2), 49–62.

Eisner, E. W. (1985). *The art of educational evaluation.* Philadelphia, PA: The Falmor Press.

Kerlinger, F. N. (1979). *Behavioral research: A conceptual approach.* New York, NY: Holt, Rinehart and Winston.

Popham, W. J. (1988). *Educational measurement* (2nd ed.). Englewood Cliffs, NJ: Prentice Hall.

Project Zero: The Development Group (1991). Unpublished manuscript (available from Harvard Project Zero, 323 Longfellow Hall, 13 Appian Way, Cambridge, MA 02138).

Reimer, B. (1971). Aesthetic behaviors in music. In M. Brace & K. Winter (eds.) *Toward an Aesthetic Education.* Washington, DC: Music Educators National Conference.

Ross-Broadus, L. (1991). Profiling individual learning through Arts Propel high school ensemble portfolios. *Special Research Interest Group in Measurement and Evaluation Newsletter, 11,* 4-8.

The School Music Program: A New Vision (1994). Reston, VA: Music Educators National Conference.

Stiggins, R. J. (1987). Design and development of performance assessments. *ITEMS - Institutional Topics in Educational Measurement,* Fall, 33-41.

Stiggins, R. J. (1991). Relevant classroom assessment training for teachers. *Educational Measurement: Issues and Practice, 10*(1), 7-12.

Tunks, T. W. (1987). The value of measurement/the measurement of value. *Bulletin of the Council for Research in Music Education,* no. 90, 53-59.

Zessoules, R., & Gardner, H. (1990). Authentic assessment: Beyond the buzzword and into the classroom. Submitted for publication in *Assessment in Schools,* V. Perrone, Ed.

ASSESSING MUSICAL GROWTH ACCORDING TO YOUR GOALS

Louise Frakes

The Mid-Prairie School District is in the conservative, rural community of Wellman, Iowa, where most people make a living by farming. The junior high school was built in the 1960s and has very outdated music equipment. Seventh-grade students are required to take general music, which meets every other day for one semester. Other than that, students in grades 5-12 may take band and students in grades 7-12 may take chorus.

Before I can begin to tell you how I assess students' musical growth, I must tell you a little about my philosophy and my program. I believe that general music class should prepare each student to become as musically independent as possible and to become adequate amateur musicians who will enjoy using and listening to music the rest of their lives.

To support this philosophy I teach six skills as my main goals for my students: singing tunefully; moving rhythmically; playing instruments; reading music; listening intelligently; and creating music. Along with these skills, I expect my students to develop a music vocabulary that will enable them to discuss music intelligently, to understand musical concepts, and to enjoy music making. I follow a spiral curriculum so that what students learn each year builds on what they learned the previous year.

Louise Frakes teaches at Mid-Prairie Junior High School in the Mid-Prairie School District, Wellman, Iowa.

Singing

Assessing students' singing abilities is best done by listening to them sing. I do not, however, require any student to sing a solo. By sixth grade, students usually know if they like singing alone in front of a group. For those who do, I try to provide plenty of opportunities; for those who do not, I listen as they sing in group singing. My goal is not to make all students into soloists, but to help each student feel comfortable and capable of singing in a group. My students generally sit in a circle, so it is easy for me to move around the circle as they sing and listen to each one. We also have a choral line-up where students stand in two or three rows when we are singing parts. For this arrangement I simply move up, down, and between the rows to see how well each student is doing and whether each can hold his or her part. While moving among the students, I often carry my grade book and jot down what I hear.

To make assessment quick, but understandable, I use this method:

- **+** good strong singer, accurate, with a well-produced and pleasing tone
- **S+** accurate, but not as confident
- **S** satisfactory
- **S-** tends to be a little off pitch
- **N** not on pitch
- **L** low singer
- **H** high singer

I try to make these notations at least once a month for each student. It's quick, simple, easy to use, and gives me a record of how each student is doing and who's improving, as well as some idea of what I need to do to help students improve (i.e., whether to focus on tone production, pitch matching, and so on). When students are not able to sing adequately in group singing, I try to arrange some time outside of class to work with these students individually (usually this is not too frequent by fifth or sixth grade).

Much of the vocal technique that I teach in group singing is based on the work of Ken Phillips from a workshop at The University of Iowa. These techniques are found in the book *Teaching Kids to Sing,* by Ken Phillips (Schirmer, 1992).

Moving Rhythmically

Moving rhythmically to music is also best assessed by observation. My students move to music in a variety of ways, including folk dancing, square dancing, choreographed movement, and free movement. Some students are better at one type of movement and some at others—often how well they do is a matter of motivation.

I make notes in my lesson plan book if a particular movement activity is well liked or rejected. This guides my planning for future years and also for particular groups of students. If I find that with one group of students I'm fighting a losing battle with a particular type of movement, I delete that activity and use a different one to teach that particular concept. Most students enjoy moving activities, so although I may delete one particular activity, I always replace it—there are many others to try. I also make notes in my grade book by names of students who are having difficulty or who are doing exceptionally well. Thus, at a glance I can tell who may need my assistance next time, and who would be capable of demonstrating for or helping others.

Playing Instruments

In order to tell how well students play instruments, the teacher has to hear them play. In a general music classroom this is no small feat since there are usually twenty to thirty students in class at one time. I want my students to be able to play many different kinds of instruments: percussion instruments, Autoharps, Orff instrumentarium, melody bells, baritone ukulele, and keyboard or piano.

When students accompany the class on the Autoharps, I use up to four so it's fairly easy to see who can play and who needs help or more practice. I have a column in my grade book headed "Autoharps," in which I record how well each student does using a simple code: **+**—good job; **S**—satisfactory; **N**—not yet able to do it. This also helps me keep track of who has had a turn and who needs a turn.

When we add Orff accompaniments to pieces, there are only six to eight instruments available, so it is fairly easy to determine who can do what. It is also relatively easy to design a part appropriate for the ability of each student, and again, a simple marking code in the grade book helps keep track of which students have had turns and how well they did.

When we play melody bells or baritone ukulele, I pair students up so that one watches while the other plays, and then they rotate. With ten to fifteen instruments going all at once it is much more difficult to tell who needs help. Students are usually pretty good about asking for help, though, and also at helping their partners.

I am fortunate enough to have the Yamaha Music in Education (MIE) keyboard lab in each of my schools. MIE is a lab of fifteen keyboards, complete with curriculum, that has been especially designed for the general music classroom. Each keyboard has five octaves and is assigned to two students. The keyboards can be set in a mode that blocks out the center octave and causes the remaining two octaves at each end of the keyboard to be the exact same pitch. Thus, every student has a two-octave keyboard that is exactly like everyone else's and that allows all students to play at the same pitch. If more than two octaves are needed, the keyboard can be changed back into normal mode, which means the full five octaves are available.

The curriculum that has been designed for these keyboards teaches basic music concepts by having students learn various accompaniment parts for songs that are played through the Macintosh computer. The parts are of varying difficulty, and the computer system allows you to set a tempo at which students can be successful. Also, a quiz on the main concept accompanies each lesson. All the keyboards are connected to the computer so that by playing their answers on their keyboards, each student's answer is recorded automatically on that student's computer card. The computer keeps track of the percentage correct each student has on each quiz as well as averaging the total percentage.

I have found that students are greatly motivated by these keyboards. They really work hard to learn to read music so they can play them correctly. The system keeps track of how well the students understand the concepts being presented, but in order to tell how well each student plays, the teacher needs to listen to each one (keeping track in the grade book with +, S, N). Taking time for this individual evaluation, allows the other students to turn off their speakers and practice using their headsets. This time to practice is often what is missing since we have so little available time, yet it is so needed.

Projects

At least once a year I have what I call "projects." To do projects, I put up a chart with all the students' names along one side and the list of projects across the top. The list of projects for sixth grade would be Autoharp, melody bells, baritone ukulele, keyboard, ensemble, sight sing, and create. Students are then given twenty minutes of each thirty-minute class for three or four weeks to work on their projects. The goal is for them to complete as many as possible within that time frame. They may pick any piece of music in their music book and learn to play it on whichever instrument they choose. They must complete two of the first four before attempting the last three. They must stay with the chosen instrument and piece of music until they can play it.

Once they have practiced it well enough to play it, they play it for me. If it is accurate, I check that one for them and they move to a different project of their choice and a different piece of music. Students get much-needed practice time and I get the opportunity to tell not only how well they play the instrument, but also how well they read music. "Sight sing" means just that: they pick a song they do not know and study the notation until they can sing it. They can get only the beginning note from the piano. "Ensemble" means they work in small groups to perform a piece in harmony, either vocally or instrumentally. "Create" means they create a piece of music that they can reproduce.

I usually do projects near the end of the year, as students need a good-size repertoire from which to choose. The teacher needs to keep in mind that this will be very noisy and frustrating because everyone is practicing at once and invariably everyone will want your attention at the same time. For me, however, the independence that I see develop during this time is worth the strain on the nerves that this much noise produces.

Music Reading

I use a basic Kodály approach to teach students to read music; however, I use note names as well as syllables and occasionally I also have students sing numbers for pitches. More recently I have moved into having students simply learn patterns such as *"do re mi"* repeated with "up by steps," *"do mi sol"* repeated with "up by leaps," and so on. I use the Kodály counting system but also teach traditional counting. I simply tell kids to use whatever makes sense to them—to just get the right sound.

When I say I want kids to read music, I mean I want them to be able to change the notation on the page into musical sound vocally as well as instrumentally. I emphasize reading intervals, although I expect them to know note names as well. It is easy to check to see if they know note names and note value names: simply give them a paper-and-pencil test. I do not spent a lot of time, however, on paper-and-pencil testing as I feel making music is more important. I have my students attempt to read every piece of music we sing. I do not have them sing with syllables; they study the notation and sing with the words, the way most adults do. If they have trouble with an isolated spot, then we might go over that place with syllables. As students grow in their ability to sight sing, it soon becomes obvious who the leaders are. I jot down this information in my grade book. I do not pretend that all of my students are great sight-readers all on their own, but rather that, as a group, they can and do read music. Some are leaders and very capable. The others know enough about following the notation that they can sing along even though they may not have been able to figure out the entire piece by themselves (especially the more difficult leaps or rhythms).

Another way that I check students' sight-reading ability is to use mystery tunes. I place a tune that the students know on the board before the students enter the room. Students then silently study the tune trying to hear it inside their heads. When they think they know what the song is, they come whisper the name to me and I mark it in the grade book. This gives me a fairly accurate assessment of how well they can read music and hear it internally.

Listening

I assess students' listening to music by how well they can discuss what they have heard or by how well they can interpret the music through movement. I also assess students listening by whether they can detect errors in the music they are making. A type of judgment about students' listening skills would be for them to determine the tonality, meter, instruments, form, and style of a piece of music they are listening to.

Creating

I try to encourage students to be creative with music in many ways. For example, I encourage them to move creatively to music they are listening to, to try to create or improvise a harmony to a song they are singing, or to create a piece of music or a small segment on the keyboard. It is important to be supportive of students' attempts to create and to remember that their creation is theirs. I point out the places that I especially like and tell them why I like it, but the piece is theirs and they can have it any way they think it sounds best.

Music Vocabulary and Tests

As students develop these various skills, I try to help them develop a music vocabulary that will enable them to talk about music and to help them develop music concepts that will further their understanding of music. Much of the knowledge level and vocabulary can be tested with paper and pencil. My written test for the end of sixth grade includes letter names of both treble- and bass-clef notes, explaining time signatures, identifying the major and minor keys from the key signatures, naming the various kinds of notes and rests, building chords, and sometimes matching the composer with the names of well-known pieces that we've studied. I also use the Cowell Music Achievement Test 2 at this level. (This test can be ordered from Richard Cowell, 12 Peacock Road, Lexington, MA 02173). I feel this test tells me a lot about how well my students have mastered many important concepts and also gives me the opportunity to compare how well they are doing based on standardized norms. These kinds of assessments tell you how much students know about music, but they do not tell you how well students can make music.

Creative Assessment

One fun way, using creative dramatics, to measure how well students know music facts is to divide the class into three groups and quietly assign each group a particular note value. Each group then has to work together to decide how to physically become that note using each member of their group. After giving them a few minutes to decide how they will become their assigned note, the groups take turns showing the rest of the class their note. The rest of the class then decides which note the group is and why. With my class, it was especially fun to watch them become a dotted sixteenth note or three eighth notes. In order for them to do the assignment the students had to know what each note looked like. This was much more fun way than the traditional paper-and-pencil drill.

Summary

What I have tried to show you is that there are many ways to assess students' musical growth. Sometimes the best and most efficient way is the traditional paper-and-pencil method, sometimes it's listening and observing. The type of assessment you choose will depend upon what your goal is at that time.

Assessing where students are in their musical growth is essential if we are to provide appropriate instruction. It makes no sense to keep teaching the things students already understand and have facility with, and it leaves both teacher and students frustrated if the teacher is presenting material that is way too advanced. Thus, by assessing where students are in their understanding of music concepts, in their development of musical skills, and in their use of music vocabulary, we as teachers will be better able to prepare lessons that will meet the needs of our students and that will excite them to learn more, use more, and make more music.

NATIONAL OVERVIEW
PAST, PRESENT, AND FUTURE TRENDS

Jeffrey Kimpton
Director of Education, Band and Orchestral Division
Yamaha Corporation of America

It is an interesting point in the history of music education that we are just now producing a book on the role of music in middle-level education. After nearly thirty years of experience, controversy, and frustration in trying to integrate music into the middle school, music educators now possess a sufficient level of experience, process information, and instructional practice that can be delineated. The fact that there has been nothing published previously is not so much an act of omission or tardiness as it is a sign that middle school music programs have reached a level of maturity through age and experience. It has taken a long time.

Attempting to share a national overview is always difficult, for each region of the country has distinct traditions about the place and role of music in the schools. Yet, after visiting countless middle school programs, sitting in music classrooms of every kind, observing rehearsals, labs, and class discussions, conducting surveys, and talking extensively with teachers and administrators from across the country, I can see a developing set of common problems and national criteria for success in middle school music programs that transcends regional differences or local practices. In spite of a love/hate relationship with the middle school concept in this country, years of personal and professional frustration, and great philosophical wandering, music educators have developed, without leadership, guidance, or a prevailing pedagogical model, an instructional practice for middle school music that is often moderately successful, sometimes inadequate, and sometimes linked with programs that could be considered "models of excellence."

A national overview of middle school music education presents far more questions than answers. What is the history of interaction between music educators and the middle school movement? What is the current state of middle-level education in this country, and what are the major characteristics of the music programs within it? What are the major characteristics of successful middle-level music programs, and what implications do they have for other aspects of music education? And finally, how can middle-level music programs adapt to the major trends determining the direction of middle-level education in the next century?

A History of Conflict, Compromise, and Experimentation

The rise of middle schools in the 1960s presented music educators with their first real national challenge in school program reorganization. Attempting to integrate music into the middle school meant that significant changes in philosophy about the role of schools, teachers, subject interrelationships, and student activities were necessary for everyone. These philosophical shifts provided great challenges, and conflicts, for music educators. In large part, those same challenges still exist today.

When confronted with middle schools, music educators were asked to fundamentally change an instructional practice and process that had been in place for decades. The prevailing concept of performance-based music education was deeply rooted in the junior high system. Herein lay grave problems, since the major philosophical premise of middle schools is that they exist as unique and distinct school entities, designed to nurture the growth of the adolescent child. Middle schools are inherently not interested in mirroring high schools, which is what junior highs tend to do. The hallmarks of middle school organization—greater ranges of student opportunity and experience, increased staff access, a decentralized form of program development and decision making, cross-curricular integration, use of new technologies, flexible scheduling, differentiated staffing, special programs for special kinds of learners, and unusual class/school scheduling and building organization—are the foundation of a philosophy diametrically opposed to that of centralized, performance-based, large-group junior high music programs.

Many administrators changing from a junior high to a middle school organization initially tried to totally reorient programs by means of a different focus, emphasis, or instructional plan so that they in no way resembled those of a junior high school. All programs were destined for some kind of change, especially music, because the primary method of instruction would have to change. Across the country there have been two basic reasons why music programs have been experiencing a difficult time adapting to middle-level education.

First of all, most music programs are parts of a large "pyramid" of skills and experiences, instrumental or vocal, leading to the top of the pyramid, which is the performance-based program in the high school. Changing to a middle school concept means possibly interrupting the organizational pyramid, which ultimately has an impact on more parts of the music program than just the middle school level.

Secondly, music in middle schools is typically categorized as an experiential class apart from the core curricular subjects of math, science, language arts, and social studies. Because it is grouped with subjects considered experiential (industrial arts, home economics, physical education, art, and, in many schools, foreign languages), it is perceived as a secondary subject that is often placed in a tertiary position of importance, after many special programs considered critical to adolescent social development take precedence.

Many music faculties actively campaign against middle schools in their districts, an action in which they usually do not succeed, and one that rarely endears them to school administrators and boards of education. In many cases, this campaign against the middle school concept has actually prevented the music faculty from participating in the planning process involved in changing to middle schools, further isolating music from the curricular and experiential core of the middle school instructional program. This act of opposition has led many music departments to self-imposed isolation, to what could be termed a form of curricular suicide, making music an anachronism rather than an integral component in the school instructional program. This may be why it has taken so long in this country to develop an instructional model in music for middle schools.

But the issue of music in middle schools involves more than just these two factors. It has long-term generational implications for our profession, and has led many music educators to adopt an inherently adversarial philosophical position with the middle school from the beginning. The issue, still being waged in many districts even after middle-level education has been in place a decade or more, is not one of art vs. entertainment, music for a few vs. music for all, or even performance vs. experience. Rather, the conflict is between the role of all subjects in schooling and the common practices of music programs. It is a conflict between consumer musical values and the experience, preparation, and musical values of music educators—a conflict between musical generations. It is also an internal conflict between music educators and their philosophies and teaching pedagogies. The issue centers around two questions: What is the role of performance? vs. What do we do about general music?

A Look at Current Practice

The current state of music in the majority of American middle schools is a mixture of compromise and tolerance, with an increasing amount of frustration and self-evaluation. Some programs are stagnating from little change while others are shining stars of innovative ideas and curricular vision. Here are some general characteristics and statistics about middle-level music education that may help put the typical program in perspective. This information has been drawn from research conducted by Yamaha on middle-level music programs (1986–1988), from research conducted in the development of Yamaha's Music in Education program (1987–1991), and from my personal observations in nearly 200 middle school music programs.

Typical Middle School Characteristics

- Organization usually includes grades 6, 7, and 8; fewer have grades 7 and 8, with a very small percentage having grades 5, 6, 7, and 8.
- The number of middle schools is growing to ease overcrowding in elementary schools.
- Middle schools tend to be found in urban or suburban areas rather than in very small or rural communities.

- The middle school organization is rare in private or parochial schools.

Organizational Format of Music Programs

- Band, choir, and, to a lesser degree, orchestra are offered as an elective to all grades (usually grades 6, 7, and 8).
- The large-ensemble performance program constitutes the largest portion of the music program.
- A small percentage of schools offer jazz ensemble, small-ensemble programs, or individual or small-group lessons.
- General music is almost always part of a sixth-grade rotational wheel.

Performance Groups

- The groups exhibit a high level of performance practice, provided students have started their training in the elementary grades.
- Lack of mature tone and repertoire difficulty are cited by teachers as the biggest deficiencies.
- Groups meet every other day in grade 6, and daily in grade 7-8 elective classes.
- Groups typically perform three concerts per year.

Beginning Instrumental

- About 50 percent of middle schools offer beginning instrumental instruction in grade 6; this percentage is increasing.
- Middle school beginning instrumental programs are usually not part of the rotational wheel; typically these classes meet all year, every other day, rotating with physical education.
- More schools are moving beginning programs for elementary students to the middle school as part of a budget-reduction plan.

General Music

- Programs are primarily vocally based, and are viewed by teachers as the primary tool for recruiting students into elective vocal ensembles in later grades.
- Few, if any, instrumental experiences, such as recorder or guitar, are provided.
- Average length of general music courses is nine weeks, with a substantial number extending over eighteen weeks and held every other day.
- Key learning outcomes include development of music-reading skills, vocal-technique development, knowledge of major musical periods/types and composers, and knowledge of major instrument groups; key activities include listening, singing, work sheets, quizzes, reports, and tests.
- Primary dependence for instructional materials is on basal music textbook series, filmstrips, and videos.
- A decreasing number of teachers require general music students to perform in evening concerts, citing student apathy and parental disinterest as major reasons.

Technology

- Student possession and use of technology in the home continues to increase at a rapid pace, with over 50 percent of the students indicating that they have a computer, keyboard, or both at home.
- Use of technology is growing at a measured but increasing pace in middle schools.
- Equipment used includes computers, keyboard labs, and workstations.
- Competition with other departments for technology funding is a critical problem for music departments trying to obtain technology.
- Teachers lack knowledge of the use and application of technology; many view the use of technology as a threat to performance programs.
- After-school use of technology by a small cadre of students is reported to be very high.

Staffing

- At least 50 percent of instrumental music teachers are full-time, with the remainder filling their schedule with elementary teaching duties.
- Most vocal/general teachers are full-time in one building, and teach all general music courses.
- An increasing number of instrumental music teachers are being asked to teach general music.
- Most music teachers regard sixth-grade general music as the weakest part of their instructional program.

Teacher Preparation

- Few universities or colleges offer specific music course content in teaching the middle school adolescent child.
- Most classes/programs in general music methods are taught by someone with primarily elementary experience.

Typical Concerns of Middle-level Music Educators

- the small number (only 5 to 8 percent) of incoming students having functional music reading skills
- insufficient time to teach basic musicianship in general music courses
- insufficient time to teach vocal performance skills in general music
- difficulty in dealing with students with highly developed and biased attitudes toward school music and school music activities
- concern regarding a lack of knowledge of contemporary consumer musical trends

- growing concern about dealing with diverse learning styles and multicultural applications
- lack of knowledge of technology, and concern about the threat it brings to school music
- difficulty in obtaining funds to update instruments, pianos, stereos, and technology
- strong concerns that music is on the way out of the school curriculum, yet little expressed interest in cross-curricular contact or teaching within the school building
- perception that instrumental music enrollments and program quality decline when beginning programs are removed from the elementary grades.

Indicators of Success in Middle School Programs

Typically in education we find an emerging theme of "indicators of excellence" stemming from a larger national movement, often spearheaded by research findings from a large national research base developed over a period of time and involving a group of individuals, university consortia, or schools of education. This has not happened in music education. In spite of a national preoccupation with identifying "excellence" in education during the past decade, little research has been done in the fine arts about what constitutes a good or effective music program. Although certain programs are often recognized for their excellence, there has been no development of criteria—even intuitive or subjective criteria—that would allow serious study of the characteristics of an effective music program. Certainly this could be very useful to the profession.

Success in middle school music programs has not come about through writings, readings, or discussions of many learned music educators. It has not come about through advanced research, espoused pedagogies, or crusades of any one individual, group, institution, or company. The successful programs are not the result of any new kind of technology, textbook, or pedagogy.

Looking nationally, we can characterize successful music education programs at the middle school level with several key statements. These statements could apply to effective music programs anywhere. Successful middle school programs are invariably the result of effective individual teachers or music departments, working alone and often in isolation, without the benefit of extensive resources, prior knowledge, a research base, or university assistance.

Successful practices and the environment that has nurtured them have come from a desperate need to find ways to motivate and stimulate children, to reach the adolescent learner in music, and to make a middle school format work for music. Indicators of effective programs most often demonstrate an individual teacher's common sense and practicality, a keen sensitivity to music and children, and a strong vision of program development and activity. Effective teachers use a process of validation that involves a trial-and-error method of developing and experimenting with new ways of teaching and learning, in-service work, conferences, journal readings, and a lasting desire to make music an integral part of the total school program. The following characteristics or indicators typify successful music programs:

1. *Successful middle school music programs are most often the product of key individuals with vision rather than part of broader local, regional, or national movements.*

In countless situations, success in the formulation of a middle school music program came from a music teacher working alone. Lacking in many cases the strong mandates often enjoyed by math, language arts, or science programs, and usually without the knowledge or approval of administrators, the teacher designed effective curricula and shaped course experiences. The teacher developed a different attitude about general music, performance programs, and the role of students and teachers in these programs. All this was done out of a necessity to survive in the middle school framework, rather than in response to a district mandate, national movement, or predetermined curriculum.

The majority of the teachers in these successful programs are not specifically trained in middle-level education. They have learned by experience, by a continuing quest for new ideas and materials, by attending workshops, seeking mentors, and requesting visits to neighboring schools, by questioning others about their programs and collecting an odd assortment of new ideas and materials, and by blending all of this into a highly defined and carefully structured curriculum. Above all, these teachers have an unquestioned faith in, and enjoyment of, middle school children.

2. *Successful middle school music programs are born of experimentation and flexibility rather than rigid organizational structures. They follow no strict philosophy or particular pedagogy.*

A majority of middle school programs follow no set district or school curriculum, yet have a highly defined and usually carefully annotated written curriculum that is constantly modified and improved. There is no strict adherence to any particular tradition or pedagogy. In fact, very few teachers in successful middle schools espouse a particular method, other than using what is educationally viable and what works for the teacher and the students. Even in larger districts with multiple middle schools sharing a common districtwide curriculum, there are totally different applications that clearly separate some schools from others.

Successful instructional sequences have been refined over the years with the continual addition and deletion of materials to fit the changing needs, interests, and motivational quirks of the students. There is a strong willingness to share curricula, materials, and suggestions with colleagues and anyone who asks. The task of developing these programs has been difficult for these teachers, so they have great empathy for those seeking success by borrowing.

3. *Successful middle school programs offer an eclectic range of opportunities for serious study, casual participation or consumption, personal and group musical achievement, individual creativity and improvisation, and personal exploration. Successful middle school programs offer a broad variety of options to every grade level and to all students, not just a few.*

In short, successful middle school music programs fulfill the MENC statement, "music for every child, and every child for music." From required "wheel" or experience courses to elective performing ensembles, elective ensembles, elective sequences of nonperforming courses, after-school and in-school lessons, and special activities, students may get involved in countless ways and in varying degrees of intensity.

There is a correspondingly high interchange of students between courses, activities, and experiences. Those who get involved with music in a consumer format may choose to extend participation in a performance format. Those who have had a strong performance background may get involved in composition or creative/improvisational activities, or choose to play a second or third instrument.

4. *Successful middle school music programs are fully supported by the music faculty and teachers in other disciplines, are integrated within the total school curriculum, and are supported by the administration through collaborative efforts.*

While many music programs exist in a form of curricular and physical isolation from the rest of the school, successful middle school programs have made consistent attempts to integrate music into the total academic experience of the child. Bearing out the truth in the statement "music is basic," successful music programs initiate and find many collaborative ways to integrate music into art, science, language arts, social studies, theater presentations, and before- and after-school activities for all students. There is a definite correlation between this interrelationship with the entire school curriculum and the support and interest of school administrators and fellow faculty members.

5. *The music staff actively and willingly participates as an integral part of school improvement efforts.*

The teachers of successful middle school music programs do not isolate themselves in their own departmental activities. They are active participants in cross-curricular and whole school improvement efforts. This is an important function, for other faculty colleagues become allies of the music program and support the role of music for the total education of the student.

6. *Successful middle school programs have clearly adopted the middle school philosophy and consider music an integrated part of the total learning experience of the child. Successful middle school programs are not tied to high school programs for their strength or guidance.*

Successful music programs for the middle school specifically exist to help the child at that level. While all music teachers fundamentally believe in a program that develops lifetime skills, perceptions, and consumer interests for later music participation, the effective middle school program does not purport to exist solely for the purpose of the high school program; nor is it meant to be controlled or influenced by the high school program. It is the quality of experience in the middle school that is most important to the music faculty and middle school administration.

A successful middle school program, however, does have a high degree of interchange between elementary and high school music programs and faculties in the area of concept development, skill acquisition, and student experience. The successful middle school music program is an integral and contributing part of the overall district music program and does not exist in isolation from that music program.

7. *Successful middle school programs offer all children both group achievement and individual creative and exploratory experiences. The programs have not compromised the role of performance, and students show quality work in performances, both formal and informal.*

The act of "doing" music in the middle school is important, and thus the sharing of music–performing, listening, making, and creating–is an important by-product of the middle school music program. This musical product is shared schoolwide and in a variety of ways, rather than through a few concerts and infrequent assembly programs. Successful music programs have long bridged the gap between performance and general music. These programs typically provide a wide range of activities and experiences that stimulate student interest and participation, whether through performance or study. There are usually many options for the display of musical achievement, including large-group, small-group, or individual performance; creative, exploratory, or improvisational activities; demonstrations; recitals; exhibitions; and informal concerts. It is the *breadth* of activities that blurs the lines between traditional kinds of experiences and causes a frequent interchange of both students and experiences.

8. *The quality of a good program is highly personalized–to teacher, students, principal, and parents.* The personal involvement of many individuals is the key to music-program ownership. Because of this, the ownership of the music program in successful middle schools tends to be shared with many, rather than claimed by a few. This has proven particularly important when curricular, financial, or scheduling prob-

lems threaten the health of the music department. It provides a powerful level of support.

9. Successful middle school programs have faculty who are dedicated to the age-group with which they work. Faculty members show an unusually high level of energy, humor, innovation, and spirit. They are collegial and tend to work well together on collaborative ventures.

There should be no mistake that successful middle school music teachers have strong egos. They have succeeded in wrestling a difficult animal. While egos and self-confidence tend to be high, there is an unusual spirit of cooperation, appearing stronger than that in other curricular areas.

10. Successful middle school music programs are, for the most part, strongly supported by school administrators. Principals are aware of the achievements of both groups and individuals, and frequently speak of the music program as "mine."

A surprising number of administrators in successful middle school music programs are current or former musicians and/or music lovers. They have supported their music program as a personal challenge, and are fiercely loyal to it in regard to budgeting, scheduling, staffing, and other areas of need. In many cases, these principals can speak more eloquently than music educators about the role that music can play in the total education of the child and can often provide vivid supporting examples.

Future Challenges

Thirty years ago, the middle school movement contained the microcosm of issues and challenges that music educators are now learning to integrate into the entire profession. The megatrends of current school reform—multicultural education, diverse student populations, program and school accountability, special opportunities for unique learners, multiage populations, differentiated staffing, school reorganization, cross-curricular and interdisciplinary instructional programs, skill-based education, year-round and magnet schools, and new technology and multimedia—represent many opportunities and challenges for music educators. Five of these, in particular, will seriously challenge music programs in the future:

- integrating technology and media into the school music classroom
- coping with school decentralization and the reorganization of students while continuing to meet the needs of diverse learner types
- providing new roles for the individual within the context of large-group and performing-group instruction to stimulate student and school achievement
- integrating subjects across the curriculum to draw important conceptual parallels between all disciplines, subjects, and thinking processes
- dealing with education as an ongoing political and social issue, reacting to the increasing needs and demands of the changing society of the twenty-first century.

These five issues will present some formidable challenges to all educators, and certainly to school music teachers. As government and the private sector continue to challenge traditional educational structures, music educators will need to learn to cope in a school environment where their educational destiny is literally out of their hands and, perhaps, even out of the hands of boards of education and school administrators.

The key to fostering greater success in middle school music programs lies in our ability to integrate performance, general music, and nonperforming elective activities into a cohesive program, in which instructional activities and experiences typically found in one area become an important by-product of the other. Just as the technologies of music making—electronic and acoustic—are merging, so too are instructional and process pedagogies, which have generally been at odds with one another in the middle school debate. It will be these integrations that nurture new visions and instructional innovations, helping maintain the health and vitality of music education in the middle schools of the future.